D1378273

WHERE HAS LAST JULY GONE?

WHERE HAS LAST JULY GONE?

MEMOIRS

DREW MIDDLETON

Quadrangle/The New York Times Book Co.

Library of Congress Catalog Card Number: 73-79922

International Standard Book Number: 0-8129-0392-7

Interior design by June Negrycz
Production by Planned Production

For
Absent Friends

CONTENTS

PREFACE

Since I began these memoirs five years ago some of my friends, a plain-spoken lot, have taken me to task. It was far too early, they said; better wait until my newspaper days are done. I decided to press on. I have not lived the sort of life that ensures a long and tranquil old age nor, I think now, would I wish it. "We owe God a death," and the moment of payment is chosen arbitrarily. So, had I postponed the writing, the book might never have been done.

My diaries, notes, and stories provided the factual sources for the book. Writing it has reminded me of the wonderful opportunity a reporter's job offers him: a front-row seat at the unending drama of man.

I count myself fortunate. I have worked in the, to me, most fascinating of all worlds: the huge, changing, kaleidoscopic world of international affairs. I have met, in all stages of sobriety and sanity, presidents and prime ministers, monarchs and mountebanks, heroes and rogues, generals and parsons, financiers and prostitutes. I watched at first-hand the greatest military drama of this century, the defeat at grievous cost of Hitler and Nazi Germany. I saw the rise and fall and revival of great nations. I was present when politicians and diplomats tried to shape the future or escape the unremitting past.

These memoirs cover the period from the spring of 1939, when I went to work in London as a correspondent for the Associated Press, until late in 1971.

The war took me to France and Belgium in 1939 and 1940, to Iceland in 1941, to Algeria, Morocco, Tunisia, and Sicily in 1942 and 1943. In 1944 and 1945 I divided my time, until Germany's surrender, between the United States First Army and Supreme Headquarters Allied Forces Europe.

I spent the first twelve months after the war in Germany: Berlin, Frankfurt, and Nürnberg. Early in 1946 I set out for the Soviet Union. Thereafter I was Chief of Bureau for *The New York Times* in Germany, Britain, and France and at the United

Nations. I believe I am the only correspondent in *Times* history to have held all four jobs, which include the three major European bureaus. My last job abroad was that of European Affairs Correspondent, which I held until my appointment as Military Correspondent in 1970.

This, then, is a personal history of a man as a reporter. My generation was trained to pay more attention to the situations in which it found itself than to personal adventures. Indeed, my own adventures, such as they are, would strike the reader, titillated by modern novelists, as very small beer.

Although I have tried to tell how correspondents work in the field, I have not bothered to recount what I know of the endless struggles and intrigue within *The New York Times*. This game of journalistic kiss-and-tell strikes me as a dirty one. To work closely with men and women, to accept favors and advancement, and then to retail the occasional meannesses and irritations of life inside a great institution is ignoble. As Bedell Smith used to say, you have to face yourself in the mirror every morning when you shave.

I've done a good deal of which I'm not particularly proud. I've drunk too much, played too much, stepped on too many sensitive toes. But I did my best to tell my countrymen what was happening.

Drew Middleton

CHAPTER 1

THE EVE OF ARMAGEDDON

1939

In London we may suffer, but no one has
any excuse for being dull.

John Lubbock

I

That April evening the air had the peculiar softness you get only
in London in the spring. The tulips nodded in their beds along
the Mall. The grass in St. James's park was startlingly green.
Out of the government offices came the politicians, the civil servants, and the secretaries. The men, swinging their rolled umbrel-
las, marched toward the clubs and their drinks. The women
gossiped as they waited for buses or sought the underground for
Barnes or Balham or Kensington. Serenity and confidence ruled.
Neville Chamberlain was at No. 10 Downing Street. On the Mall
the royal standard flapped lazily over Buckingham Palace;
George VI, King, and Emperor of India, was in residence. God
was in His Heaven, and God, as the Germans say, is an Englishman, and all was right with the world.

It wasn't, of course. All was wrong, horribly wrong, in April
of 1939. But the sprawling, noisy, somehow majestic capital of
the British Empire breathed indifference. One was told often
enough that the British had been frightened into their proper
place at Munich, that they were decadent, finished. Students of
international affairs even then were writing thoughtful volumes
on Britain's decline. There would be, they said, no war, because
neither the British nor the French would dare stand up to
Hitler. As far as the British were concerned, few predictions had
seemed safer.

In youth instinct often compensates for inexperience. I had

felt ever since Munich that war was coming. What shook me in those first days in England was the acceptance that, Mr. Chamberlain to the contrary, the conflict with Germany was inevitable.

In the train from Southampton a young man remarked casually, "Oh, there'll be a war all right. Hitler will start shoving troops about again, and then we'll be in. We'll never trust him again."

He was not impressed by Germany's strength. He conceded it was there—"They're stronger than we are"—but he assumed that Britain would win. He took it for granted that he and most of his generation would fight and that only a few would return. To an American, young in years and experience, his cheerful fatalism was startling.

My generation, I suppose, was the last to grow up in an America where the professional soldier or sailor was something of a rarity and the army and navy infinitely remote from ordinary life. My father's generation, indeed, regarded the graduates of West Point and Annapolis as misfits who had failed to make a place in a business society. To be sure, there were veterans of World War I about; but the few I knew were determined to forget the army, if not the war, and in the prevailing absorption with business they found this easy to do.

In retrospect I count myself fortunate that I came to Europe without deep political commitments. I had read history in a desultory fashion, and I knew, from the pages of *The New York Times,* something about international events.

But I had not been stirred, as had many of my more politically developed friends, by events in Spain. I had never demonstrated for or against anything; nor have I to this day. I thought fascism evil and that the world would be better off without Hitler, Mussolini, and Franco. What I knew of Communism repelled me. Man, as the comrades saw him, was quite different from man as I had found him. I was not, as they say today, committed.

Part of this was due to my previous job. I had been a sports writer on the New York staff of the Associated Press. Now, sports writing is a beguiling occupation. You travel more than the ordinary reporter. You encounter characters outside normal experience, although from what I hear the boxing world is slightly more decorous now than it was in the 'thirties. Above all, it is a glittering, exciting world that dulls the senses to all but its attractions. You are there; it takes a great effort to get away. In my case chance played a part.

An experienced Associated Press reporter, headed for Europe, suddenly became ill. I had put my name down for foreign service and within a week was headed for Europe. I was elated, as young men are, by the prospect of change. But I had no overwhelming psychological commitment to my new job. Nor was my academic background adequate. Perhaps I was fortunate. My ideas on international politics have been formed largely on the basis of my own experiences with men and events. Steady reading provided the background.

Events forced me to read. War is a long bore broken by moments of action and fear. In that first year in London and later in France with the British Expeditionary Force I read steadily: *Das Kapital, Mein Kampf,* books on contemporary politics, collections of speeches, studies of countries and situations, and military history and strategy.

I soon found that I had only a cursory acquaintance with the great writers to whom new friends referred. A five-month stay in Iceland was memorable, because in that highly literate land I could buy Tolstoy, Balzac, Cervantes, Sterne—and could read uninterruptedly. Literate friends helped, opening doors on a wider life, in which thought and action were fused and great issues were dissected, pondered, and occasionally explained.

I had one virtue as a reporter that is not uncommon: a ceaseless curiosity. But, perhaps, by the standards of the bosses then and now it was an unbalanced curiosity. I wanted to find out "why." I still do. Who, when, where, and what interest me as keys to the illusive why. So in London, that first night, I left my hotel to find out why the British were acting as they were.

War, remember, was only five months away. It had been building for at least five years. Yet in a pub off Oxford Street I found the company arguing, as Britons do on all but the most urgent occasions, about racing and football. It was a pub of a type now disappearing. There was none of the aseptic modernity of neon, chromium, and plastic. Dishes of sandwiches and that delicacy relished only by the English, called Scotch eggs, stood behind the bar. The mirror bore an advertisement for gin. The place smelled powerfully of beer. A coal fire burned in the grate.

Like most Americans I had been brought up on the myth that

all Englishmen are aloof, monosyllabic, cold to strangers. In ten minutes in that pub the myth was banished. Far from being taciturn, the English are a talkative lot, given, under the influence of no more than a couple of beers, to intimate confidences and long-winded argument about such arcane matters as the breeding of the last Derby winner or the identity of England's scrum half in the Calcutta Cup Match of 1938.

The rigid propriety of Queen Victoria and of that tiresome prig, Prince Albert, and a sprinkling of verbose puritans, preachers, and pedants have nourished the image of a cold, dull, moral people. In fact the English are highly frivolous, a mystery to their enemies, and the despair of their friends. They have drunk, gambled, and wenched their way through history.

I marvel at young reporters who think there is something unusual in the racy London of today; London has been swinging for centuries. The English of George III and the Regent displayed an almost lunatic indifference when Napoleon was assembling the Grand Army at Boulogne for the conquest of England. The English of Charles II scarcely interrupted that riotous and enjoyable reign to notice that the Dutch fleet was sweeping the seas. A Pitt or a Churchill may convince the English that the time has come to turn from the race course, the playing fields, the bed, and the bar. But it is uphill work.

That night I found it difficult to turn the men's talk to Britain's position. When they finally noticed my efforts, they agreed that there would indeed be a war. They did not like the prospect. But there was no need to become alarmed, to "get the wind up."

Naturally there were no protestations of patriotic loyalty. No one sang a few staves of "Rule Britannia," and I heard none of the witty remarks about Hitler so widely reported from other pubs a year or so later. One or two thought that Chamberlain might find a way out but this would only postpone the inevitable. "It" was coming.

There was then—it developed to heroic proportions later—a sense of defiant, isolated independence. As the crowd thinned, the barman, a huge man with an enormous moustache, told me that "the Yanks" had the idea that war was a thing of speeches and parades and "one big push at the right time."

"It ain't, it's a bloody, miserable business, which you'd 'a learned if you'd come in the last one when you should 'a done, which is when we did."

But he thought that "if we 'ave to fight, we 'ave to fight. That lot you was talkin' to, three of them's in the Territorials and two is in the Navy reserve. They're for it. They'll be all right, though. Not wot we was, of course."

I asked politely where he had served.

"In Belgium and France and for a bit in Italy, holding up the bleeding Italians. Make a cat laugh, that Mussolini would. Cor, wot I seen of the Eyeties we don't 'ave to worry. They'll run from us like they run from the Germans."

A little earlier Winston Churchill had said very much the same thing to Ribbentrop, then the Third Reich's Ambassador to the Court of St. James. The two men had been brought together at dinner in the house of one of the leading appeasers. Ribbentrop, guided by the host, had sought to convince Churchill of the folly of his policy of standing up to the Axis. The Ambassador went down the catalog of German strengths: the Luftwaffe, the panzer divisions, the industrial mobilization. At the end he said, "And don't forget, Mr. Churchill, this time we have the Italians with us."

"That's only fair," grunted Churchill, "we had them last time."

I left the pub and strolled down Regent Street to Piccadilly Circus. They called it the Hub of the Empire then. Outside the theaters long rows of taxis and private cars decanted elegantly dressed men and women. There had been a return to the formality of the prewar years since the coronation of George VI. The London I was watching then was the last to feel really sure of itself; the upper class could still touch, across a quarter of a century, the grace, the ease, the assurance that vanished in the terrible summer and autumn of 1914. They were bitterly criticized in 1939 for refusing to face the facts. But, in their way, they did face them. In the English a strain of harsh realism runs beside the streak of frivolity, and nowhere is it stronger than in this class. Seeing the worst approaching, its members are likely to play at bowls on Plymouth Hoe or to dance at the 400 Club. The men in their tailcoats and the women in their evening gowns and jewels knew better than most that in six months their bright, gay world could lie in dust and ashes.

My course led from the lights of the Circus and Leicester Square toward Trafalgar Square. Trafalgar Square is only a few hundred yards from the theaters and restaurants. But there you feel history. And for no tangible reason for, unlike the Place Vendôme or the Red Square, Trafalgar Square never has been the scene of a historic event. The sense of history arises from the presence on the tall column of that odd, baffling, brilliant figure, Admiral, the Viscount Nelson.

The Square's surroundings are London middle-class, except for the National Gallery. Advertisements for gin and cheap jewelry flash above the shops at the top of Whitehall. But the memory of Nelson's passionate, angry patriotism dominates the Square. It exists because of the greatest of sea fights and the greatest of admirals.

Over the years Trafalgar Square has become my homing point. Early in the war it was festooned with banners declaring "England Still Expects." At night the column often was lit by the flicker of fires from burning, bombed buildings. During the Campaign for Nuclear Disarmament in the 'fifties the leaders of that campaign spoke from the plinth. One wondered what Nelson with his fiery patriotism would have thought of them.

Down Whitehall the government buildings were dark and silent but curiously impressive. This was Great Britain of the late 'thirties preparing to measure her mature strength against the Germans and the Italians. These buildings were the headquarters of that political and diplomatic experience and expertise that had preserved and expanded an empire won by traders and explorers and the "poor bloody infantry."

A policemen stood in front of No. 10 in Downing Street. A light shone from an upstairs window, but Mr. Chamberlain, the bobby said, was in the country. Across the street the Foreign Office was almost completely dark. There were a few lighted windows in the upstairs floors. These were the rooms of the duty clerks. The Office seemed enormous, a citadel of diplomatic power. The Home Office, the War Office, the Admiralty, and the Treasury combined with it to make a Gibraltar of government, embodying a tradition of order and law.

The Houses of Parliament were empty. My footsteps echoed in the empty square. Here at Westminster Pitt and Fox, Gladstone and Disraeli, Lloyd George and Asquith, had had their hours. The ideas that taught men to restrain and, if necessary, execute a king and to govern themselves were more important than these ornate buildings.

Past the statues of Cromwell and Richard Cœur de Lion. A strange pair, these two, to be guarding Parliament. But what they guarded, of course, was not so much the Commons and the Lords but an embedded tradition of order and stability, a tradition that has had quite as much to do with making our world as the revolutions that have shaken our century.

All my life as a correspondent I have watched the struggle between, on the one hand, order and progress and, on the other, violence and revolution. Thus far order and progress have triumphed, either by force of arms or by the gradual evolution of revolutionary movements into orderly societies.

Beneath Westminster Bridge the Thames rolled, oily and placid, to the sea. The whistle of a late train came from somewhere near Waterloo. A tug's hooter sounded from where the river sweeps toward the Tower. The city, the river, and the buildings seemed as though they had been there forever and would last forever. I turned, found a late cab, and went home.

II

Because much of these memoirs deal with Britain and the British, it is apposite that they refer to the British as they were then, when the last glow of imperial glory still bathed those islands. In retrospect those months are cloudless and warm. I know they were not, but that is how I remember them.

Nowadays it is an article of liberal faith that the British generally were ashamed of their Empire and slow to defend it before foreigners. This was true of some and, indeed, had always been true. The second British Empire that developed during and after the Napoleonic Wars had as many critics at home as it did abroad. But it also had its defenders and believers. When politicians described that empire as a great instrument for good, they got more applause than boos. Great sections of the public knew nothing at all about the empire. But they took a complacent pride in it. In an odd sense it was theirs, something the British had made.

Decolonized Africans and Asians now give the impression that the empire was of their making. So it was, in the sense that in most cases they provided the manual labor, the civil servants of the lower grades, and some of the police and troops. But the planning, the implementation of the plans, the establishment of law and order, and the defense of the empire itself were in the hands of the British. Those who had done the work believed they deserved well of their country and of civilization. To have brought law and order, railroads and the telegraph, harbors and highways, and the first public education and health measures to great sections of the world seemed to them far from ignoble.

If Britain had prospered as a result, the payment for this prosperity had not been cheap. Not all the colonies were profitable. Nor did the prosperity accrue to those who had done the job: they went abroad to India or "the colonies" and worked for years in sun-blistered lands, plagued by disease and oppressed by lonely visions of those green, rain-swept islands they called "home." They were sustained not by high salaries or by graft, which was the loot of the eighteenth-century nabobs, but by a sense of duty, a devotion to an ideal of service which they, members of a people notably inarticulate when speaking of ideas, could scarcely describe. They returned from India or Nigeria or some lonely island dyspeptic or shaken with recurrent bouts of malaria, or they lived out their lives in country villages where few knew that, say, old Mr. Foster, who served so cheerfully on the local council, had ruled the restless millions of an Indian district.

These were the survivors. For so many died—in wars their children have forgotten or in sudden epidemics of tropical disease that took them in deliriums in which they saw for the last time England's green and pleasant land.

Only a few were able to express the philosophy by which they lived and died. Kipling said it best, but perhaps John Buchan was the most explicit:

> Empire is not to be regarded as a mere possession, as the vulgar rich regard their bank accounts—a matter to boast of and not an added duty. . . . It is a spirit, an attitude of mind, an unconquerable hope. You can phrase it in a thousand ways without exhausting its content. It is a sense of the destiny of

England. . . . It is not England plus a number of poor relations but one organic whole whose center is to be determined
by the evidence of time. . . . It is the task of developing the
wilds, uniting the scattered settlements, bringing the whole
within the influence of England's tradition.

A dream, of course. But not ignoble, not sordid.

The British city folk, who had lived through, and were strug-
gling out of, the Great Depression still cheerfully endured an
existence whose sordidness and monotony have no counterpart
in modern Britain or, indeed, in contemporary Europe west of
the Elbe. To see grown men and women defecate in the side
streets of the East End, to be approached by scrawny thirteen-
year-old girls with offers of their bodies, and to see drunks by
the dozen falling out of pubs on a Saturday night were commonplace. As a New Yorker I was accustomed to the sights, sounds,
and smells of poverty. Perhaps it was the weather and the unre-
lieved drabness of the poorest quarters of London or Liverpool
or Manchester that made English poverty seem so much the
worse. I marvelled then, as I do now, that this bitter existence
failed to curb the energies or dull the sensibilities of the people.

In material wealth the middle class seemed almost a generation behind what I had known in America. The cars, the re-
frigerators, the trips abroad, which seemed to have come rather
easily to the young married people I knew at home, were out of
the ken of the English middle class. I do not mean that they did
not live full lives. In some ways their lives were more full than
those of my friends in America. Most of them were better educated. They did more for themselves—riding, cycling, playing
games—perhaps because less was done for them. I found them
more likely to question the verities handed them by an older
generation less satisfied· with what life, in the spiritual and emotional sense, had given them than their counterparts in the
United States.

I found myself in Dublin, walking the streets in the soft, wet
dawn, quoting Housman to a girl I never saw again. There were
nights in the Hibernian Buttery and a party at a lovely house
by the Liffey, and one morning we walked out of a country house
and saw the sun come up over the Irish sea. Then were the small,

neat, Georgian houses, the rain-splashed sunshine on the horses at the Curragh, the old bookshops, the lovely sweep of the fields toward the mountains . . . ah, then. Later I learned more of Dublin.

Dublin and all Ireland at that time were nearer to their struggle for independence. The Black and Tans and the Easter rebellion and the great men were closer, just around the corner of men's minds. Now Dublin and all Ireland have grown middle-class and staid, the old ardors are quiet; Yeats, O'Casey, and the others, where are their successors? It may be that alien rule inspired the great burst of creative genius that marked Ireland in the last years of the nineteenth century and the first years of this. Certainly there has been nothing of great note since the English departed and left the Irish to themselves and their involved, domestic politics.

One morning, in a sleeper, I awoke and looked out on the rough fields and knotty mountains of Scotland. I spent a week in the Lake Country. Hospitable folk asked me to dinner, to lunch, to tea. The days were golden. But even then people were beginning to feel a certain apprehension when night fell.

There was a Saturday night on the Thames when, coming out from a dance, I first saw the thin pencils of searchlight beams probing the sky. We fell silent, and the music of the band sounded out of place. It was an American tune, "Love Letters in the Sand," and I remember thinking that in America it would have sounded fine. But not there, not then.

Another night Scotty Reston and I sat in his garden at St. Mary Cray. Sally was away, and Richard, his first son, lay asleep upstairs. In the moonlight and the scented countryside—St. Mary Cray was country then, it is a London dormitory now—we heard a plane throbbing inland from the coast.

"Sometimes I wish the Wright brothers had never been born," said Scotty.

"Some of them say war won't be so bad when it comes," I said.

"I don't believe that, do you?"

"No."

Then in late August we heard that Hitler's Germany and Stalin's Russia had concluded a treaty. After that it was merely a question of time.

The "I was just finishing a chop when the radio said Hitler had marched into Poland" school of writing bores me. Possibly because I cannot remember anything significant about that last weekend. I had done a couple of pieces on the military forces and probable military plans of the British, French, and Poles, pieces no better and no worse, I expect, than many others, since I had paid assiduous attention to Liddell Hart and other pundits whose work I was beginning to read.

I had a quick drink that Saturday evening with Scotty at the Rose and Crown and then set off across London toward a party. The blackout was new and curiously exciting, though by later standards inefficient. I made my way home about two o'clock in the morning through a violent thunderstorm. When I reached my house in West Kensington the rain had stopped. I pulled open the windows of my sitting room and looked out: London glistened in the darkness, there was not a sound. I thought pleasantly about a girl named Deborah I had met at the party, smoked a pipe, and went to bed. The telephone woke me to a bright Sunday morning.

"You better get in here," Freddy Vanderschmidt said. "We have ourselves a war."

Down the sidewalk before me, as I made my way to the underground station, walked two elderly women, hatted, gloved, and starched. One thin, old voice said, "Lucy, I do not intend to allow Mr. Chamberlain *or* the Germans to prevent my going to church."

In 1914 the coming of war had excited great outbursts of national enthusiasm across Europe. Bands played, crowds cheered the marching columns, and the capitals were gay. London in 1939 was different. The Strand and Fleet Street were nearly empty. The barrage balloons, slowly ascending, were the only sign of war.

At the office we waited for Mr. Chamberlain. In tired tones he told us on the radio that no assurance had been received from the Germans and that, consequently, Britain was at war. His voice was that of a broken man; he was there waiting in the Admiralty for his rendezvous with history. That weekend the navy had been informed that "Winston is back."

Soon after Mr. Chamberlain had finished I heard for the first time in earnest the piercing ululation of the sirens warning of an air raid. Fred Vanderschmidt, Bill Henry, a visitor from the *Los Angeles Times,* and I climbed to the roof. We wore steel helmets and carried gas masks. This equipment was considered necessary, even vital. For everyone believed then that the war would begin with prolonged and devastating air raids on London, Paris, and other major cities, the bombings interspersed with gas attacks. When the sirens stopped, we stood in the sunlight listening for the approaching planes. It was singularly peaceful, and the sun by now was hot. We lounged on the roof, smoking and talking. Soon the "all clear" sounded, and we returned to the office. I felt I had been robbed of a great experience. It was not a feeling that continued long.

That afternoon I went out to see how London was taking the war. There was more activity, more men in uniform and columns of army trucks rumbling through the almost empty streets. In the grubby area where Pimlico merges with Chelsea I parked outside a shabby house. As I did, a soldier came out, complete with rifle, bayonet, tin hat, and pack. A woman, white-faced, with a baby in her arms, followed. He said something, patted the baby, and then bent to kiss the woman. The edge of his tin hat touched her head, she moved back, and they both laughed shyly. Then he marched off down the street, his boots ringing on the pavement. She stood watching him, rubbing her forehead with her free hand, until he reached the corner and turned out of sight. So they went to war.

The six weeks I spent in London between that day and my departure for France and the British Expeditionary Force seem curiously unreal. There was a great deal to see and report and write, there were a few sirens to set the pulse leaping, there was the new Ministry of Information to explore, and there was that feeling, so moving to the reporter, that he is watching great events. Yet, despite the sandbags, the tin hats, the anti-aircraft guns in the parks, and the barrage balloons, the unreality persisted. The restaurants were full of pretty women and men in uniform. The pubs, behind the blackout curtains, were as packed and raucous as ever. Rationing, what little there was, had not affected anyone seriously. It seemed an odd sort of war.

At first there was a sense of relief. "It" had come, and it wasn't so bad after all. But, as my circle of acquaintances widened, I noticed that a number of people wanted something to happen. The national psychology seemed to be saying, now that they had at last come to grips with Hitler, the thing to do was to beat him and get it over with. There were those, too (not so many then as next year), who saw the war, not as a burden and a danger, but as a crusade to rid their country and the world of a menace.

Meanwhile the Wehrmacht ground relentlessly through Poland, and the Germans and their Russian allies divided the spoils.

An absurd overconfidence reigned in London. Economists explained how the economic pressure exerted by Britain and her Empire and by France and her Empire would, in a way never very clear to me then or now, destroy the economic basis of Hitler's Reich. General officers reminded us of the strength of the French Army: "the finest standing army on the continent." Admirals spoke of the "fleet in being" and said confidently that the submarine blockade, so nearly decisive in World War I, could not threaten Britain again. The Germans, we were told, had no other course but to throw themselves against the Maginot Line, where they would be broken and thrown back.

The very weather conspired to stimulate the idea that victory might somehow be won without fighting, without sacrifice. There may have been rain, but I recall a succession of crisp, golden days. People were not yet calling it the phoney war—that came later—but they were beginning to wonder whether there had not been a lot of fuss about nothing, whether Hitler, faced with two mighty antagonists, might not back down.

Occasionally I heard comments that indicated otherwise. One night in a restaurant I met a thin, intense young man, who appeared to be connected with some branch of the government. "You're a Yank, are you," he said thickly; we were both slightly drunk. "You better go home and tell them that it'll be bloody awful when it starts. I'll tell you why, too. The bloody French won't fight. They'll collapse. They hate each other worse than the Germans. Ever hear about 'rather Hitler than Blum?' You hear it a lot in Paris. The reserve divisions are shot through with Communism. So's industry."

The Ministry of Information took care to see that American reporters were given glimpses (no more than glimpses) of "Britain's war industry." They were right, from their standpoint, to restrict us, for in September 1939 industry was moving at a leisurely pace toward increased production behind the militant slogan of "business as usual." Sometimes, though, we saw behind the mask.

"Certainly, we've got the best fighter aircraft in the world," a Royal Air Force officer said. He then added, in almost a whisper, "But not enough of 'em. This stuff about shadow factories is all balls. We're not getting a tenth, no, not a twentieth, of the production we need. We'll pay for it, by Christ, how we'll pay for it."

I have often heard and read that in the first autumn of the war the British began a devilishly subtle campaign intended to bring the United States into the war. This notion conflicts sharply with the then prevailing attitudes of government, parliament, and people. Many were aware that they might require munitions and supplies from the United States, and others, certainly the Foreign Office officials, hoped for American diplomatic support; but at that moment, with Hitler quiescent behind the Rhine, governmental and public confidence was so great that there was little thought of American intervention. The British for a few months really thought that, with the French as allies and with Italy, then grotesquely overrated as a military power, out of the war, Germany could be beaten. When Mr. Chamberlain announced that the government was preparing for a three-years' war, he was regarded by many as overpessimistic.

That was the last time, I suppose, the British nation generally was to enjoy such sublime, unalloyed self-confidence. But through the wishful thinking, through the gaiety, there ran a bitter reality. In those weeks, before the blackout became too onerous and the casualty lists high, the British were saying goodbye to the long weekend between the German wars.

In 1945 one heard British officers remark of some other officer that he'd "had a good war." They meant that he had survived without serious wounds and perhaps won a medal or two. In a sense, I suppose, I had a good war. It thrust me into the middle of great events and gave me chances to write about them. Because of the shortage of experienced men I skipped much of the dreary apprenticeship that is the lot of many young reporter's today.

One afternoon the American, British, and Commonwealth correspondents were summoned to a meeting at the War Office. There we were addressed by Leslie Hore-Belisha, a chubby, polished, forceful man, who was His Majesty's Secretary of State for War. The selection of him for that post had shaken the higher ranks of the military establishment. He was a Jew, they said. He was an ambitious, plotting politician, they said. I knew Hore-Belisha much better later in the war, and I might as well have my say about him. He was highly intelligent, glimpsing the changing nature of war better than some of his generals. He was energetic and imaginative. He was a patriot.

That afternoon he told us he had been moving heaven and earth to get us off to the British Expeditionary Force and that we would leave as soon as our accreditations had been issued. We were handed mimeographed pages outlining our needs. These included, I recall, at least two horses and, if necessary, a servant. I went off to buy uniforms and other equipment, spending about five hundred dollars of Associated Press money. But, I reflected, I would be gone for months. So I bought recklessly: breeches and boots, a Sam Browne belt, a greatcoat, shirts and socks and ties. The German got it all, except what I wore, the next spring at Amiens.

When the stuff was delivered, I tried it on. I liked myself enormously in my uniform. I tilted the cap. I also put the belt on wrong. I had an enormous dinner at Simpson's in the Strand.

To the more experienced correspondents the months of the cold war were a waste. We were quartered in Arras in the Pas de Calais, an unpicturesque, dour part of France. Apart from the initial stories about the British Expeditionary Force there was very little news. I was too green to care. My elation survived. The routine stories interested me. It was strange, intriguing: a war even if there was no fighting, a foreign country even if it was dull, and above all new friends.

This was my first real exposure to the great men of my profession, the Americans Bill Stoneman, Webb Miller, Bill Chaplin, and Ed Angly. They had been everywhere and seen everything. At night when we sat over drinks in the Hôtel de l'Universe or the Café du Commerce they told wondrous stories of Ethiopia when the Italians came or Vienna at the Anschluss or Berlin in the first days of the Third Reich. They were, as good newspapermen always are, helpful and kind to a youngster. I must have been an intolerable bore with my ignorance and enthusiasm. I was an eager pup among wise old hunting dogs.

The British made an impression: the correspondents included men of high professional distinction, such as Philip Jordan, Evelyn Montague, Kim Philby.

Thirty-odd years later Philby was unmasked as one of the most successful traitors in British history. We know now that he was, even in 1939, in the service of the Soviet Union's espionage organization. But then he was known as a brilliant young correspondent of *The Times* who had been wounded while reporting Franco's side of the Spanish Civil War.

Nothing is easier, in the newspaper business or elsewhere, than hindsight. I cannot claim ever to have had an inkling that Philby's loyalties lay anywhere but in Britain. What I do remember was that in a company not known for sobriety he was an outstanding drinker. I have since heard people say that even drunk —and he was good and drunk most days by four in the afternoon—his mind had a wonderful retentiveness. I never noticed this. He was a drunk, all right, simply a drunk. Not a quarrelsome drunk or a boring drunk. Since his treason has been disclosed, I have often asked myself why the Russians would entrust so many delicate enterprises to a man who, they must have known, drank too much. It is no excuse to say that the Russians drink a great deal. They do. But I have noticed in Russia and elsewhere that, when business is at hand, they conduct themselves with a propriety worthy of Y.M.C.A. secretaries.

Only once in my presence did Kim Philby ever say anything unbefitting a patriotic journalist with the proper background. It was in the autumn of 1940 during the German bombing of London. I had been invited to dinner by a woman who was interested in an air raid shelter in Spitalfields and wanted me to visit it. Kim was the other guest. That day the news had come that the Roosevelt Administration had pushed through Congress a bill expanding American rearmament. The woman asked me what it would mean. I answered that, if we really put our minds to it, we could produce more planes, more tanks, and more weapons than Britain, Germany, Italy, and Russia combined. I said there was nothing the United States could not do if its resolution matched its resources and its energies—something I still believe.

Kim turned to the woman and said, "You see, there's the real enemy."

I said this was a nasty remark, for the bulk of what we would produce would go to his country. Kim was taken aback. He mumbled that what he had meant was that America's economic strength was the real enemy of Britain's survival as a great power. I accepted this and went off to Spitalfields. What he meant, I believe in retrospect, was that the United States, not the warring states of Europe, were the real enemy of the government he served.

Again, in hindsight, it is easy to see how Kim fooled so many for so long. He was handsome in a bluff, English way. Even when he was drunk his manners were good. He was a man you could not conceive of as doing anything mean. He talked well of his experiences in Spain. Among many able correspondents he was outstanding. What moves such a man to treason?

The answer is that Kim was a product of a politically aware component of a generation maturing in a world that had become enfeebled by depression and was more and more menaced by the Axis. His loyalties to Britain were undermined by the flabby responses of the governments of Macdonald, Baldwin, and Chamberlain; he was enraged at his country's complacency. Communism seemed the only course. At that point someone from the Soviet Union exploited and perverted his idealism. Who it was we shall never know.

Late one evening I returned from a trip to the R.A.F. headquarters at Rheims. Entering my hotel I was invited by Philip Jordan to have a drink with Anthony Eden, who was then Secretary of State for the Dominions and in the process of shepherding a group of dominions cabinet ministers around the Expeditionary Force's front.

Eden was a name. Eden was a story. But in the next few hours I got no story. Instead I got my first impression of one of the most stimulating, able, and courteous men I have ever met. His life now seems tragic. A great number of his countrymen will never forgive him for Suez. After a long apprenticeship he reached the heights, only to fall because he pursued in power the objectives he had sought in opposition two decades before. Yet he has never wavered, in my recollections of a long friendship, in his detestation of authoritarianism of any kind and in his devotion to the democratic process.

I remember one comment from that night; in fact, I wrote it in my diary when I went to my room. It was bitterly cold, I recall, and I wore my greatcoat over my pajamas, as I worked at the table by the window overlooking the cobbled courtyard. What Anthony had said was:

"You may think that because the Germans have the men and the tanks and the planes and the revolutionary fervor, they will win. They won't. For what we have, the belief in democracy, is stronger than anything they have. There will be many defeats, many reverses. But in the end we will win, because we speak for the future and they for the past."

For me that time in France passed pleasantly. I travelled over northern France. I saw the French army and was unimpressed. But I was told by veterans of the first war that superficial judgments of the French were unwise. The French had been the same in 1914: slovenly, ill-disciplined, casual. But they had fought magnificently when the occasion arose, frequently under some of the worst generals in history. Gradually I accepted the idea that the French would play their part when the fighting started. But Americans, with their affinity for methodical preparation, in which we are not unlike the Germans, are seldom impressed by "le système D, on se débrouillera toujours" which, roughly translated, means "we'll muddle through somehow."

The British officers who guided us around the front and arranged interviews belonged to a class I had never encountered. I can see now that they were survivors of the generation that fought the first war, products of a richer, more assured Britain. They were intolerant, reactionary, and snobbish. They were also brave, generous, and alive. Most of them, those like Arthur Pilkington, Charles Tremayne, and Bobby Hartman, had been cavalry officers in the first war. They wanted to fight. Instead they had been given this odious duty of bear-leading correspondents. They found it burdensome and made only slightly lighter by the willingness of the correspondents, all of them on expense accounts, to pay for the best dinners and wines the country could produce. When the fighting started, they displayed a strain of contemptuous bravery. There were no better guides to war on the basic level.

Statesmen and soldiers have cursed the wasted months of the "phoney war"; for me they were not all waste. Because newspaper people are the most generous people, I received a great deal of instruction from men whose credentials were high. Daily in Arras after lunch I would pace the little park with Webb Miller and talk of the great stories he had covered and of how they had been covered. How this man or that had got it all, "the whole damned business," in one pungent first paragraph, how so-and-so had written a diffuse story on the Anschluss because he would not wait until the evening but felt he must file his story by noon.

The dullness of a nonexistent front was relieved by occasional trips to Paris. The train from Arras arrived at the Gare du Nord in the evening, the chill, sparkling evening of Paris in late November. Paris had recovered her spirit, as she always does. The gloom of September was gone. There was more people on the streets. The restaurants were full. In the government offices, in smart flats, in the great houses of the rich, and everywhere among the Communists and the others on the left, the plotting went on. But the silence on the western front had encouraged the French masses. Perhaps, after all, a war could be won by sitting tight. Evidently the dirty English were not doing enough. But the Americans were about to step in, and didn't the posters say "We will win because we are the stronger"?

So Paris reasoned, and a young man in uniform had a good time. There were small restaurants, smoke-laden and brightly lit behind the blackout, where conversations were easy to begin and where a persevering American could learn the words to "La Table Ronde" and "O, les Fraises et les Framboises" and other less innocent songs. There were long walks in the Bois de Boulogne and evenings in the flat in Passy with the picture of the captain of Spahis on the wall. In the early mornings the city was gray and wet, but it was no chore to walk in the drizzle.

One Sunday we, the correspondents with the British Expeditionary Force, were summoned in company with those accredited to the French army to meet General Gamelin, the Supreme

Allied Commander. He was then at the apex of his brief fame, a small, almost dainty, man with a soft, melodious voice. France, he told us, had gone to war to save Poland, just as once, long ago, it had gone to the aid of the infant America. All was going according to plan on the front. When the time came, the initial objectives would be taken. Meanwhile the Allies were gathering their truly formidable strength for the battle. And so on and so on. The soft voice wrapped us in a cocoon of complacency.

I knew enough French and enough French officers to know that Gamelin's pie in the sky was not to everyone's taste. The British, victims of wishful thinking in the prewar years, at that moment were far more hard-headed than their allies. Any complacency arising from Gamelin's remarks was eliminated a few nights later when we gathered in Arras to listen to Lieutenant General Noel Mason-Macfarlane, the Director of Military Intelligence for the British Expeditionary Force.

What Mason-Macfarlane, universally known as Mason-Mac, did was to treat us as intelligent people. He had been British Military Attaché in Berlin. He knew the Wehrmacht from top to bottom. In a cold voice he delivered the brutal statistics: so many panzer divisions, so many bombers, so many reserves. It was a lecture on the frightening proportions of the German war machine. Oddly, it shook the Americans more than the British.

After the general had departed, we were sitting in the Café du Commerce for a nightcap. The British were unmoved by what they had heard. I thought this was part of the famous British *sang-froid*. I know now that it was a kind of inbred racial reaction. The British since nationhood had *always* faced in their major wars nations that were stronger, better armed, and, superficially, of greater spirit. The ancestors of these men had listened to tales of Philip's Armada and Bonaparte's Grande Armée and the Prussian Guard of Kaiser Wilhelm. And each generation in its time had seen the small, handy ships of Drake, the thin, red lines of Wellington, and the battered Tommies of 1918 come out on top.

The year spun to its close. We visited the Royal Air Force at Rheims, we saw the huge stockpiles of equipment behind the lines. We gave a bibulous dinner to twelve officers of an armored-car regiment; all but two were dead in a year. We had our spy.

The spy was, as is proper in all spy stories, a woman, a Belgian with a beautiful body and the face of an intelligent Pekingese. She was, according to whichever story one heard, the mistress of the Bulgarian Ambassador in Paris, the divorced wife of a prominent French manufacturer, or the madam of an extremely distinguished brothel on the right bank. She was particularly attracted to young officers who knew what was going on at General Headquarters. Had her dear friend Alan Brooke arrived? She had known many Canadians in Paris; would some of those charming French-Canadian officers be with us soon and help destroy the boche? She was very patriotic and generous with her favors.

One young officer in his cups described the lady's soft, persistent questioning to Bernard Gray of the *Daily Mirror,* a hard-headed, hard-drinking veteran of many wars and many stories. Gray told someone in Intelligence. The someone in Intelligence told the French. She was a spy all right. They shot her one cold morning before Christmas, and some young officers heard some home truths from commanding officers. "By God," said one of the latter, "if you want a woman, I'll *give* you a fiver and you can go off to Paris."

News of the outside world filtered slowly into the dismal villages of the north. The Soviet Union attacked Finland, and Sir Philip Gibbs said portentously that "America will have to come in now, we can't fight both Germany and Russia, you know." Our interest centered on the minutiæ of garrison life; the arrival of a new type of field gun or brief tours by King George VI or Hore-Belisha were regarded as startling stories, and few of us could understand why they got so little attention in an America becoming bored with "the phoney war."

But always there was the dining room at the Universe at night with the wind whistling through the courtyard and a great fire of logs at one end of the room and the wine flowing free.

It was to this room one night that Philip Jordan brought the Chinese military attaché in London for dinner after a long, cold trip along the front. They had been friends in London and were talking quietly when a British brigadier approached.

The brigadier was attached to General Headquarters because in the first war he had become an expert on French railroads. If you wanted to ship a division or a tank or a mobile bath unit from Brest to Soissons via Toulouse he would route it. He was the very picture of a British officer of the old school. A round, red face, a white moustache, a shining belt, and three rows of ribbons. In addition, he was deaf. On his chest hung a small, black tin box into which one shouted.

While Philip and the Chinese were talking, the brigadier bumbled past, a great, brimming glass of port in his hand.

"General, I want you to meet the Chinese Military Attaché," said Philip.

"Oh," said the General, "Jap, are you?"

"No," Philip screamed, "the CHINESE Military Attaché."

"Ah, Chink, eh? Never could tell you yella buggers apart," said the General and departed.

The Associated Press called me back to London, for, obviously, there was to be no war that winter. I stopped in Paris for three days and said goodbye to the flat in Passy, to the hard, gilt chairs, to "grandemère's" Watteau, to the picture of "papa" in his uniform of a captain of chasseurs, to the unknowing captain of Spahis. When I came back in 1944, Nicole was dead, shot by the Germans as a member of the Resistance.

They talked a great deal about the war that winter in New York. A cousin in Wall Street kept repeating, "blood is in the saddle," as though he liked the idea. My friends seemed cheated; they had ringside seats for the goriest of battles and, to their ill-disguised anger, it was nothing but a sparring match. I met Evil-Eye Finkel, who subsisted in the fight game on his supposed ability to hex fighters; once, after a good many drinks, he told me that if them God-damned Nazis ever did start to bomb, I was to write and get his Special Double Evil Eye to protect me from bombs. In the confusion I forgot to write when the bombs started.

New York was prosperous and very gay. But I was glad to leave in February for Europe. No one seemed to take the war seriously, but I felt I should return. Sometimes you get the feeling something is about to happen.

CHAPTER 2

THE ROADS THAT
LED TO DUNKIRK

1940

War makes rattling good history,
but peace is poor reading.

Thomas Hardy

Memory is a bad guide on weather. In the mind's eye a certain period is a succession of golden days. Then the cold words of the diary remind you of rain, fog, heavy clouds. But the days in May of 1940 in France and Belgium were fair, and every memory is clear against the harsh sunlight or starry skies.

War came like a bomb. At midnight we had finished writing the story of the great House of Commons debate that drove Neville Chamberlain from office and led to the appointment of Winston Churchill; it was surely one of the most momentous debates in the long history of the House. At dawn Hugh Wagnon hammered on my door with the news that the Germans had attacked. By noon I was on a destroyer bound for France; by evening I was on a train bound for Arras. No time for more than a drink and a hurried meal in Paris. But Paris was serene. The girls' dresses were bright on the sidewalks, and the cafés were full. At the Gare du Nord was the war.

The Belgian reservists were headed home. Most of them were drunk. Their wives and sweethearts were crying. As our train pulled out, a tall blonde, big with child, ran beside the train shouting something to her man in the compartment. Then we rattled through the suburbs of Paris, and someone said that it might be a good idea to see if we could get a drink. No one knew anything about the battle except that it had begun. It was a long way away. It came closer in the morning.

Bill Stoneman and I shared a room in the Commerce. A light sleeper, he had been aroused by the sound of airplane engines and had dragged me from bed at dawn to watch a German bomber, flying very low, coming down over the railroad that ran through Arras north to Brussels.

Bill, known universally in the trade as "Doctor," is not a man with a quiet voice. Nor does his mouth suffer from mealiness. His shouts of "Jesus, here they come, Bud," and "Look out the other window, I hear more planes" woke the hotel. Soon we heard the rolling rumble of bombs in the distance, a few bursts of anti-aircraft fire, and then the Germans hurrying home. It was over. We dressed, packed, and went down to breakfast before starting for Belgium. We appeared to be the only guests.

A couple of nights later in Lille we met a Scots reporter, Dick M., who told us with profane vigor that we had not been alone. He had been in the room above us with Charlotte. She worked in the post office, a girl of undoubted beauty, but unfortunately, of the strictest bourgeois virtue. Until that night she, guarded by an imposing mother, had resisted all advances. Sporting young cavalry subalterns, middle-aged majors, ebullient American reporters, all had assaulted that fortress of virtue only to be repulsed by Charlotte and Maman. But Dick had succeeded.

Employing the argument that the war had really begun and that they must not waste the fleeting hours—I never figured out how he put that argument over, but he was a clever man—and exploiting Maman's absence in Douai about some family property, Charlotte, after a huge dinner, went very late to his room.

"She was damned timid," Dick recalled, "I had hell's own time getting her to undress. Then, just as she was getting into the spirit of the thing and dawn was breaking, you bastards started to shout in the room below. I thought the whole bloody Luftwaffe was on top of us. She put on her clothes a damned sight quicker than she took them off and ran like a hare. And when I got downstairs, I found you bastards had eaten the only bloody eggs and drunk the only bloody coffee and taken the only bloody car."

The British Expeditionary Force, in fulfillment of its part of the famous, or infamous, Plan D drawn up by Gamelin and his strategists at Grande Quartier Générale, had poured northward and then eastward into Belgium. We hurried to catch up with the war.

For the first time I saw refugees, a sight that was to become terribly familiar in France and later in North Africa and then, finally, and justly, on the uphill road that runs from Aachen in Germany into Brand. The first time is always the worst.

They came down the roads in farm carts and ancient cars. Every vehicle was piled high with household goods. People had snatched the first thing that came to hand: a handsome clock, a cheap vase, an enormous mattress, a set of china. The old rode, the young walked. We moved past in a staff car and then switched to a parallel road kept clear for military traffic.

We had a beer and a sandwich in the hot sun. There was a low throbbing, steadily louder. Hamer, our driver, said "Jerries," and we dropped in a ditch.

They came in very low on a line with the refugees' road. They were ME-109s. When they sighted on the refugees, they let go. You could not see the bullets. But you could see the gaps they cut in the refugees still on the road. Some ran to the fields. The MEs finished their run, rose, and turned in for another. Hamer kept saying, "Oh, no, no, you bloody bastards." They came down again and worked over the road a second time. Then they flew off to the east. When the sound of the motors died, you heard the wounded, human and animal. We ran over to the road to do what we could do.

There wasn't much we could do. The dead were dead. The wounded were being cared for by some British medics who had rushed across from the military road. Earlier I had seen a pretty girl pushing a baby carriage. She had dark hair and she wore slippers with big red pompoms. She was dead and the baby was dead. We went back to the car and started for the front. It was about ten in the morning.

We drove on past Brussels toward the line of the Dyle. The countryside was silent. The sun beat down on deserted farmhouses and empty villages. The map was no good. Finally we stopped at a crossroads and went into the estaminet.

Behind the bar stood a tall, gross man, wearing trousers and a blue-and-white striped shirt, very dirty. He had a heavy unshaven face and small black eyes, and he was very drunk.

"Our allies," he shouted, "here they are, the dirty British, too late as usual. Our country is in the shit and they come in their fine car. Have a drink, have a hundred drinks. This place is finished, Belgium is finished, we are all finished."

Two men were asleep at one of the tables. An old man, his eyes bleary, sat in a corner singing quietly to himself. There were pools of beer and wine on the floor and flies everywhere.

We got no sense from the drunken proprietor. He offered us brandy, wine, whatever we wanted. All he knew was that many British had marched past in the early morning, followed by guns, and that they were somewhere to the east. We left him and went out into the sun. From down the road there came the rumble of guns.

It was a good position. The British were dug along a ridge that rose sharply from the road. The guns were back beyond the road. They were Highlanders, and they wore khaki kilts. The slit trenches were well sighted. The men were quiet. At one place the ridge extended out to the right and then fell away, and a heavy machine gun had been placed at the extremity of the extension.

The ridge and the battalion looked out across a valley split by a stream. On the far side of the valley was a village. Some of the houses were burning.

"We think, we think, mark you, that jerry is in that village," said a major. "The gunners are looking for him. If he's there and comes out across the stream we'll give him a show. I hope he does, I hope he does."

British shells were bursting in the village. For a moment out of the smoke we saw, indistinctly, a tank. It nosed around the corner of a building, fired, withdrew. Then the smoke grew thicker. There were more shells. There was no firing by the infantry. In the slit trenches some of the men were asleep.

The afternoon wore on. We had some whiskey with the battalion commander. Occasionally shells burst in the village. A patrol went out and came back to report it empty. The major thought the Germans would come back. They didn't. Not that day.

This was the pattern throughout the fighting in May. The Germans—and these were the Germans of 1940, professional, confident, superbly equipped, well led—seldom wasted time in attacks on the stubborn British. Instead, they punched through the French to the right and the Belgians to the left and, inevitably, the British withdrew to maintain the line.

Very tired, we stopped at Brussels for dinner. The headwaiter in the restaurant of the Métropole would not change our money, neither French francs nor sterling. Shrugging his shoulders, he went out to consult the management. A waiter came over, a little, depressed-looking man. "That one, he is a fascist," he said. "Give me your French francs, I will change them." When the headwaiter came back, we paid the bill and marched out. We left no tip, and when the headwaiter raised his eyebrows Bill said, "You son of a bitch."

Four years and more later Bill entered the Métropole for dinner. Brussels was liberated, the Americans and British were the liberators. The same headwaiter was berating an R.A.F. pilot and an American lieutenant for an insufficient tip. Of the waiter who had changed our money there was no sign. The Doctor went out in search of a Military Policeman. He found one. The headwaiter, they discovered, had been one of Brussels' leading informers. They took him away.

The country east of Brussels was empty. We drove into Louvain. There may have been people behind the drawn shades and the lowered shutters. But we saw no one. The streets toward the east stretched wide and spacious. We moved up toward the library of the University of Louvain, the library that had been burned by the Germans in the first war and had been rebuilt partly with the money contributed by American school children.

The names of the schools were inscribed on the library. I looked for "P.S. 46," remembering the assembly and Dr. Pyatt, tall in a stiff collar, introducing a Belgian who thanked the school in English so heavily accented we could get perhaps one word in three. That was a public school in New York on 156th Street between Amsterdam and St. Nicholas Avenues. Here in the hot sun, amid the smell of rubble—the Germans had shelled the area—I searched for its name.

Past the library in a garage was a British antitank gun. The gunners were eating well. They had an enormous ham of a type not usually distributed by the British army. They also had some beer. We had a good lunch and went eastward toward the railroad station held by a battalion of the Royal Ulster Rifles. We ventured, on their instructions, out through an underpass into the suburbs to the east. There we met our first Germans dead.

They had driven their armored car down the road onto a mine. The mine had blown the car to bits and thrown three bodies out into the road. They lay there now in their congealing blood, their faces black. They were all young men.

The Germans left the Ulsters alone that day. But the next day they came back and took the station, only to be driven out by the Guards and the Ulsters in a fight as fierce as any in that campaign. After that they didn't bother Louvain again until the British drew back to maintain the line intact.

From then on the campaign dissolved into a series of isolated incidents. Years later I met a young Hussar officer who had fought through it in armored cars and, miraculously, survived. His comment was apposite: "Wasn't it confusing?"

There was the day we saw two nuns leading a column of children down a long, straight road. The Germans had command of the air then, but the nuns, confident in the protection of a Higher Power, marched straight ahead, and the children followed. They went off to the west, and we went on to where a Yorkshire battalion was resting on its arms. The Germans had tried them the day before, had been badly mauled, and had drawn off. The battalion had been heavily bombed by the Stukas, the ubiquitous German Ju-87 dive bombers, but they were unshaken.

There was the night we foregathered in Lille with the fighter pilots of the R.A.F. They were men who had met the preceding autumn—young, highly professional, the result of the exhaustive, testing training of the peacetime R.A.F. Now at last they were measuring their skill and their aircraft against the Luftwaffe, and they were encouraged. I stood on a balcony looking out over blacked-out Lille with Dickie Lee. He had shot down two Germans that day "for sure, maybe another, old chap." The R.A.F., he thought, had the better men and the better machines.

"Of course, we don't have enough, never do have in this bloody country," he said. "We can't help the brown jobs [the infantry] as much as we'd like. But we can kick the tripes out of the jerry in the air."

There was the morning back at Arras when the order came to start for the coast and evacuation. Little Major MacCormack told us the Belgians had "packed it in"; he poured us champagne and said, "To victory!" It seemed a hopeless toast. But we all drank. Privately Mac said, "I hope they give me a battery and let me kill a few Germans."

Just as there is nothing more exhilarating than an army advancing, so there is nothing more depressing than an army in retreat. Yet the depression was only in our minds. The troops we passed were cheerful, if frustrated, orderly, and even smart.

There was the night in Amiens when we ate very well indeed at Mère Marie's with an officer who had known *la patronne* well during World War I and found her perhaps sixty pounds heavier but still handy with the skillet. We ate and drank too much and, wandering through the silent town, found only one café open. Inside René MacColl, an R.A.F. officer, was playing darts with two very drunken Senegalese. We played for a while, drank more brandy, and went home. In the early morning we raced out of town, the Germans whipping us on with their shells.

Finally, we came to Boulogne. We did not know it, but the fight the British put up to hold Boulogne and Calais made Dunkirk possible. For had the Germans turned the flank at Boulogne and come up the coast road then, in that third week of May, they would have taken Calais before it was reinforced and rolled on to Dunkirk. But the British sent the Guards into Boulogne and the Rifle Brigade into Calais, and their people fought there through the hot May days in the burning cities. They fought long enough for the British to prepare the defenses of Dunkirk and to begin the evacuation.

By then the backlash of war had filled Boulogne with civilian refugees and the soldiery of four armies. In the square a column of Dutch troops, big, grave men, stood at ease. There were Belgians in twos and threes. And plenty of French from the rear areas to the south, where the Second Panzer Division of Army Group A had broken through to the sea at Abbéville. And the British, still workmanlike and soldierly in their battle dress, manning the anti-aircraft guns in the hills behind the town, and filing in measured steps up toward the positions around the town from which the Germans could not drive them until they were dead, dying, or wounded.

If defeat means anything in memory it means this: the wail

of children, the wide, staring eyes of women who have lost husbands and children, the petulant old, snatched from the fireside, weary and uncertain, the restless cattle and nervous horses shying from the staff cars, and the smells of unwashed bodies, stale wine, and manure. From this crowd there arose a sad cacophony of argument, sobs, children's cries, and the creak of wheels and rattle of carts on the cobblestones.

So sounds and smells defeat. It was a relief to reach the town major's office in a building just off the square. I did my business, which was finding someone to take a dispatch to England in lieu of telegraphic communication, and listened to a young corporal read from a tattered newspaper Winston Churchill's first speech on assuming the premiership. Blood, sweat, toil, and tears. Well, they were all there out on the square, and when the sun set and the bombers came there would be more.

I had started home from a restaurant just after nightfall. Before I found the street that led to the house in which I had been billeted, the first bombers came over. God knows there had been enough bombings and machine-gunnings and shellings in Belgium and France. But here, in this crowded city, it was worse. I made my way from doorway to doorway until I reached our billet.

By then the bombers had left. With a fair show of nonchalance I climbed to the room I shared with Bill. The windows had been blown out, but we lay down in the darkness. Suddenly a great band of light lit the wall behind the house.

Bill tore out the door, threw open the door of the only toilet and shouted, "For Christ's sake turn out that god-damned light you bloody fool." I heard a quiet voice murmur an apology. Bill came back to bed.

The bombers came back. Not, of course, because of the light but because the German High Command realized the value of Boulogne's destruction as a bar to British reinforcement. We stood in the gap where the window had been and watched the bombers turn in from the sea toward the town. They were very low, and the anti-aircraft fire seemed to have no effect. Suddenly, without the warning scream of the falling bombs, there were two close explosions. We rushed from the room onto the staircase that led around a large entrance hall to the cellar. Leaving Bill with the comment that he should take the stairs, I vaulted over the railing and landed ten feet below. We made for the cellar.

By that time bombs were bursting up and down the water-front. Our billet was on it. We crouched in the cellar with Dick MacMillan of United Press. There was an anti-aircraft gun on the bluff immediately behind the house. The firing shook the house over us. There was a long, rumbling, explosion up the street. Paul Bewsher, very drunk, wandered in, a bottle of gin in the pocket of his raincoat.

"They hit the Hôtel Impérial," he said and subsided in a corner. The Hôtel Impérial was rear headquarters of the B.E.F. and housed, among other notables, the Duke of Gloucester, younger brother of the King, a pleasant enough fellow of the huntin', shootin', fishin' type of Englishman. He had dearly loved his life with a Hussar regiment and disliked intensely the circumstances of his brother Edward's abdication, which had thrust him into a minuet of royal ceremonies and pageantry, which were his lot as the new King's younger brother and to which he was ill suited.

When the bombing and the fire were at their height, we had another visitor, Douglas Williams of the *London Daily Telegraph*. Bill and I were grimy and stank of sweat and, I suppose in my case, of fear. Douglas wore white silk pajamas, a maroon silk dressing gown and red morocco slippers, and his white hair was neatly brushed. He looked like a Noel Coward hero at the close of Act I, about to make some cynical and witty remark. However, he offered no comments on the situation. He said mildly that it had become "rather noisy" in his room and he had retired downstairs. He viewed with distaste the uninviting bed Bill and I had made on the floor and wandered off.

In the bright morning we returned to our room, to find it undamaged except for the absence of glass in the windows. As we dressed Bill wondered idly about the identity of the officer who had "left the God-damned light on in the john." He did not wonder long. At the head of one table in the dining room was the Duke. He looked at us with a chilly eye and then resumed breakfast. When he left, he paused at our table.

"You chaps here last night?"

We managed a strangled "yes" and he left. I consoled the Doctor with the thought that few people are favored by fortune to such extent that they can call a prince of the blood royal a bloody fool. He told me to eat my God-damned eggs and start thinking about how we could get our stories out.

But when we reached press headquarters, we found that the orders had gone out for our evacuation—in one hour. We made it. The next night I was at the office in Tudor Street grappling, somewhat ineffectively, with the eyewitness account of the evacuation and the fighting that preceded it.

A great deal of nonsense has been written about the evacuation of the British, and of a great many of the French, from Dunkirk, Calais, and Boulogne. The German generals put the blame for the British escape on Hitler. The French early decided that the British had ratted on them, overlooking, in the course of this congenial argument, that, when the British had withdrawn, tens of thousands of French emerged from the cellars of Dunkirk where they had hidden while the British held the lines outside the town with deadly courage.

The evacuation itself has been represented on the screen and in fiction as a triumph for the little ships of England, the cabin cruisers and such craft. In point of fact the skill and courage of the Royal Navy were the dominant factors on the sea. The bulk of the troops were taken back to England on destroyers and other naval vessels.

The central point, so blazingly clear that many have missed it, is that the evacuation was made possible by the discipline, courage, and skill at war of the British Expeditionary Force. This army was composed largely of regulars. The withdrawal to the Dunkirk perimeter and their defense of that perimeter demanded those qualities which the British Army then had in the fullest measure: skill at improvisation, a high standard of accuracy with rifles and automatic weapons, a refusal to be discouraged by the defeats of their French and Belgian allies, courage in the face of tremendous odds, and a positive ability to meet and outfight the Germans where they attacked. All these were given them to the utmost and, because they were, the army largely escaped to live and fight in Africa and Asia and, until it finally paid the Dunkirk reckoning four years later, in northwest Europe.

In a curious way Dunkirk was a stimulus to the British. If Churchill pointed out that "wars are not won by evacuations," there was still a glow upon the island over a startling and unexpected feat of arms. That the evacuation was in itself a strategic defeat of great dimensions worried few. I have often wondered why some professor of history (or, better yet, a psychologist masquerading as a professor of history) has not investigated the curious British trait of extolling defeat and discounting victory. He could start with the battle of Balaclava in the Crimea where, as everyone knows, the Light Brigade charged to its death, but where, as few know, the Heavy Brigade also charged and defeated decisively a much larger body of Russian cavalry.

For a week I resumed an incredibly normal life in London.

The air-raid sirens sounded occasionally. But the capital was little affected by the war. The wishful thinkers were at work again. Their touching faith in the French Army remained. Weygand, Foch's lieutenant, was in command now; he would reform the broken armies and inspire the *poilu*. I walked one summer evening through the Temple on my way to the Savoy and a drink. The courtyards were quiet and serene. War, what war? Had I been lying on my belly in a ditch two weeks ago hiding from a German plane? Was it I who had watched the German tank nosing through the flames and smoke of a burning Belgian village? Could this serenity be broken? Or would England sleep forever until one morning it awoke to find the long dream of glory gone?

I bought a carnation from a flower seller—"that's right, ducks, give 'er a treat"—and walked on.

The next day I was off again. There were still two British divisions in France. The plan was to reinforce them and help the French hold the line Weygand was patching together. This time the press party was smaller. Perhaps I was overly pessimistic, but all my kit was packed into a gas-mask case. I had thrown the mask away. The Germans didn't need gas to win this one.

We landed at Cherbourg and were sent to a transit camp outside the city. The camp was a collection of old army huts with little to recommend it but a large officers' mess with a well-stocked bar. It was a bright, sunny morning. There was no traffic on the white, dusty road that led south. I wandered out with a drink and sat in the sun. It was, I reckoned, two years to the day since I had sat in the sun on the hills above the Hudson and watched the Poughkeepsie regatta.

The sound, faint at first, of pipes roused me. Coming toward the camp on the road was a small column of infantry, Scots. They marched wearily behind the pipers through clouds of dust. Some wore the khaki kilt of war. Others had donned the gay dress kilts of their regiments. They were from all the Highland regiments. As they neared the camp, the officer at the head ordered "March at attention" and they came past, many wounded and infinitely weary but with their arms swinging high, rifles rigid. This was part of the 51st Highland Division, just about all that was left. Little groups had fought their way through the encircling Germans—the division had been with the French in the south when the offensive began—and had united and marched north. They were tired, they were shaken, they were undefeated. You could hear the pipes long after the dust from the road had hidden the troops.

All next morning we drove southwestward toward the line through the placid fields of Normandy. France was succumbing rapidly to the paralysis of defeat. In one village full of Moroccan troops we asked a sergeant whether we could speak to an officer. There were no officers. Here and there little groups of French soldiers threw together road blocks and trundled ancient 75s into place. Villagers watched them apathetically.

At noon in Lisieux we came across a British tank. With two others it had fought a swarm of German tanks and then, suddenly, the Germans had broken off the action and veered to the east. The young lieutenant reckoned the Germans had found a hole in the French line. What, then, was he doing in Lisieux?

"Why, the jerries got one of our tanks, and our orders were to withdraw when they sloped off. But we've only three good tracks between us. So I take this tank a way, unstrip one track, and send it back to the other tank. Then he comes up, passes me, and sends the track back. We've organized [stolen] a car."

He found the French "bloody unfriendly."

"Stopped at a farmhouse to get water for a trooper who was hit, and someone let go with a shotgun," he said reminiscently. "Last time he'll do that."

By midafternoon we were somewhere between Lisieux and Evreux. A busy brigadier said politely he didn't think we should stay.

"Like to have you and all that, but the fact of the matter is the boche has broken through the French all along the line.

We're withdrawing in conformity with them, which is bloody slow. You see, their transport is all horsed. Ours is mechanized. And liaison isn't frightfully good."

The brigadier had a few words with a conducting officer. As he did, shells began to fall near us. In a nearby copse a battery of 25-pounders slammed into action.

Major Hastings, our conducting officer, returned. He motioned us into the cars. "We're all right with those chaps," he said, "but the French are running on both flanks, and my orders are to get you people out before the roads are cut."

The British gunners waved cheerfully as we went past. Later we learned that the brigade had been outflanked. But it was a regular brigade, and it had smashed through the Germans across its rear and continued to fall back to the south and west.

We drove for Le Mans, taking back roads. Oddly, the German bombers and fighters left us alone; there was bigger game afoot than a single car. We met a British battalion recently withdrawn from the battle. The viewpoints of the rank and file were the same as those of the brigadier, although they were put more colorfully.

"Fucking French scamper as soon as they see a jerry tank or plane," said a lance corporal. "Officers first. The noncoms is all right. So's some of the troops. But they ain't got no stomach for it. Queer, ain't it, it's their country. The sods, they even try to pinch our transport."

Le Mans, when we reached it, was quiet. As we drank beer in a café, we looked out on a little square baking in the first close, still heat of the French summer. A Paris taxicab drove up. Two whores got out and walked into the café. The man behind the bar said, "There it is, monsieur; in the last war the taxicabs of Paris carried troops to battle, now they take whores to safety."

I was billeted in a pleasant enough house and fed abundantly by "grandmère," the real head of the establishment. Her son, a man of thirty, was an engineer in one of the factories. As I ate, he gloomily contemplated a large battle map, one of those given away at the start of the war by the Paris newspapers. A black tape still showed the battle line along the Somme. I ventured that it was a bit out of date. He said sadly that he had not the courage to adjust it, it was a thing of such incredible disaster that he could not face it. I said lamely that perhaps the tide would turn. "With what?" he asked. "We are beaten, the British have gone, all but a handful, the Germans are too strong everywhere, the politicians have let us down and murdered our army." He went on and on as I ate. That night we could hear the guns to the north, and the next morning we drove out toward Brittany. It was the 15th of June.

Now France stank of defeat. When we halted for gas or water, we were greeted with surly looks and monosyllabic replies; *sales anglais.* It was not until evening, when we halted at the village of St. Aubin d'Aubigne at the base of the Brittany peninsula, that we found the heart of France still beating. A priest guided us to a schoolroom where we could cook our rations and, after a brief absence, returned with a bottle of Cheval Blanc. It was, he apologized, all he had. But there was wine at the inn. We explained we had been refused beds there. The priest went off and presently returned with the local policeman, a large elderly man, who explained in soldiers' English that he had fought beside the British in the first war, that he had spoken seriously to the innkeeper, and that we were now welcome there.

In the morning, amid much handshaking and after a parting glass of champagne, we left. Four years later I came back.

That night we reached Brest. The French had sued for an armistice, and the last of the British Expeditionary Force were leaving. I met Hal Denny of *The New York Times* in a bar. He was much provoked. The barman had refused to sell him a glass of beer. But a French officer had ordered the sale. The officer had then told the barman and the proprietor that, although the British might be leaving now, they would return. I said I was glad someone thought so.

"He told me a good deal more than that," said Hal. "He told me their whole army is in ruins, that the only thing he and others can do is get away to England and continue to fight. He doesn't think the English will quit. Neither do I."

We walked down the sidewalks to the ship. Down the middle of the streets marched the last of the British Expeditionary Force, arms swinging, heads high. The French stood on the pavement watching. When children ran out to march beside the soldiers, as they always do, their parents pulled them back and slapped them. No one wanted to have anything to do with the dirty English.

There was a French battleship in the harbor, festooned, as seems customary in that curious navy, with drying laundry. We stood aft, ate cold stew out of the can, and watched the light die on the water. With the night we left. From the sea we heard bombs in Brest. But no antiaircraft fire. France's long night had begun.

CHAPTER 3

EYEWITNESS TO WAR: The Battle of Britain, the Bombing of London, and the Struggle for the Atlantic

1940

It was not part of their blood
It came to them very late
With long arrears to make good
When the English began to hate.

Rudyard Kipling

I

The war was moving toward that great trial of strength between the British and German air forces that we now call the Battle of Britain. No one in late June of 1940 thought of it in those terms. The French were defeated; the British, except for the Royal Air Force, in disarray. America, for all of President Roosevelt's verbal support, was far away and, as yet, unaroused.

Life in England changed but slowly. The train that took us from Plymouth to London passed through stations on which yokels straight from the pages of Punch gaped at the soldiers. The dining car was crowded, and the talk was still of local happenings, the fête at the church, the cricket match, young Geoffrey's new job at the bank. When we got to Paddington, the old familiar roar of London enveloped us. Among the hurrying commuters I felt out of place in uniform.

Everything Britain had feared at the time of Munich in 1938 and on the declaration of war in 1939 was now about to burst upon her: the continued bombing, the thousands of casualties, the disruption of normal life, the mass reinforcement of the fighting services, the rationing necessary in an island under siege.

The future, mercifully, is hidden. Did the British even guess what was in store? They had ample warning. Every newspaper, every BBC broadcast, told what had happened to France.

The British tended to ascribe their ally's defeat to moral corruption. This was facile and hypocritical in a people not yet exposed to heavy bombing and never to experience the shattering psychological effect of enemies' armies moving at will across their country. Yet, in a sense, there was something in it. Military, economic, and political weaknesses, many of them rooted in or arising from the traumatic experience of 1914–1918, were the ostensible causes of France's defeat. But each of these weaknesses was exacerbated by a corruption of the national will, by skepticism and cynicism over the reasons for fighting, by doubts, in many cases not misplaced, about the ability and integrity of leaders and, above all, by lack of faith in France.

It is fashionable nowadays to blame the French defeat on the Right. This is an oversimplification. The antiwar sentiment of the Left, particularly of the Communist Party, contributed seriously to the national malaise that left the French unprepared for the efforts and sacrifices demanded by a prolonged fight for survival.

Walking about London in late June and early July, before the Battle of Britain began, it was permissible to wonder whether a similar malaise would affect the British when their trial came.

I cannot say that my anxieties on this score overcame my instinct for a good life. The irritating inability of some of my colleagues to grasp what war would mean when it really came to Britain was balanced by the joys of savoring life in London. Walking from Tudor Street through the Temple to the Savoy on a summer evening, I occasionally wondered what would happen to these ancient buildings, that couple kissing in the twilight. But I hurried on to meet my date at the Savoy.

Although the French capitulation shook Winston Churchill and his government and, indeed, all those who thought seriously about the war, it had an oddly exhilarating effect on the mass of Britons. One evening I noticed that a newspaper vendor had written on his placard, "In the Final—Alone."

The great voice in Downing Street had begun its instruction and elevation of the British. What surprised me most then, and even more in retrospect, was how thoroughly Churchill took hold. To many of those I knew, particularly working-class folk and the bright young people who flirted with Communism and voted Labor, the Prime Minister was anathema. He was everything they detested: a sprig of the nobility, a war minister discredited by Gallipoli, the epitome of a governing class that knew nothing about the people.

Some of this, indeed a great deal, was true. But now in that summer, even before the first bombs fell, Churchill began to mold a unity that was to survive years of defeat, disaster, and anguish, until the final victory. I believe he was able to do it because, although in some measure all the things his critics called him, he enjoyed, as few leaders of any nationality have done, an empathy with his people.

Here was a man whose daily life was far removed from theirs, who never travelled by subway or bus, who shared few of their interests in sports or entertainment, whose life was concentrated on Westminster and the great houses of the rich. Yet this fine flower of Edwardian society was able to communicate directly with every class in a stratified society. Why?

Because he had an insight into the people of Britain that amounted to genius. He knew the stimuli to which they would respond. And he, himself—by turns overbearing, petulant, dangerously adventurous, intolerant—possessed in great measure those qualities which they themselves cherished and which had lain unexploited during the years of appeasement: physical and moral courage, furious energy, and the desperate will, not simply to survive, but to conquer. By osmosis this became the national will in a time of unrivalled peril. Years later he said that his was merely the voice through which the British lion roared. He was too modest. He taught it to roar again.

During that terrible and glorious year one of the most striking experiences was to watch the Prime Minister in a crowd. One day he went down to the East End of London among people with whom, in theory, he had nothing in common. But in ten minutes theory fled, and you saw that the leader and the people had in common a basic quality: Englishness, I suppose, is the best description. When they shouted "Give it to them," he nodded in agreement. He knew, none better, how slender were the resources for retaliation. But he would do his best, and they knew he would. And when he walked through the shabby streets between the rows of shattered, tiny houses, where Union Jacks were stuck pathetically in the rubble, the tears streamed down his face, and they knew he cared, and they were cheered by it.

The moral atmosphere created by Winston Churchill owed something to that rejection of the idea of defeat that is, or perhaps was, so strong an element in British character. He was not alone in his conviction that the war must be carried on and eventually won. The admiration, almost the deification of Churchill, by the majority of the British has resulted in a tendency to skimp the contributions of those who served with him. Attlee, Eden, Bevin, Sinclair, all were strong men and, when the test came, none failed.

When the test came, Britain was better prepared for it than most watchers overseas believed. In the quality of its aircraft and pilots, in the technical means of defense—radar and combat communications—and in leadership, the Royal Air Force was superior to the Luftwaffe.

The British, unknowing, enjoyed another great advantage. The Germans of 1940, apparently all-conquering, all-powerful, supremely confident, were driven by doubts about the best strategy and tactics to follow. They were served by pitifully inadequate intelligence officers, who often were misled by the British. It does not matter now that some of the stories of new weapons and the reports of nonexistent divisions put about by the British do not seem apt to fool a bright child of ten. They fooled the Germans in the summer of 1940 which, of course, was what mattered. In June, at one point, the Germans put the number of complete divisions in England and Scotland at ten; there were three.

The Luftwaffe's problem was far more difficult than that of the R.A.F. It had to win command of the air over the area in which the army and navy would invade Britain. This meant destroying Fighter Command of the R.A.F., for only then could German bombers prevent the movement of British troops and ships to the invasion area.

The British task was clearly defined. The Fighter Command must inflict losses so grievous that the Germans would abandon their attempt to win command of the air over southeast England.

I have not mentioned London as an objective in the Battle of

Britain. This is because the bombing of London, about which so much was written and which probably did more than any other single factor to arouse American sympathy and support for Britain, was a strategic aberration on the part of the Germans. There was some, but not much, military reason for the elimination of the port of London but none for the bombing of areas of the West End and Buckingham Palace. Indeed, if one wishes to select the date upon which the fusion of people and government became complete, it was the Sunday that the Germans dropped bombs on the Palace. Then the people were sure that it was, as Churchill had told them, a war in which each had a stake.

The German bombing of London had the effect of inspiring the British. The people of London were very brave, and they went on being brave for a long time. By being so, they inspired to similar bravery those whose calvary was yet to come: the people of Liverpool, Glasgow, Coventry, and a half-dozen other cities.

The bearing of the King and Queen was an important element in this time of troubles. The monarchy became a focus for patriotic fervor. The King and Queen were no braver than their subjects. But, like them, like the clerk from Streatham who stumbled to his office through broken glass and piles of rubble every day after working all night at a first-aid post, they remained at their jobs. Each day saw the King or the Queen at the site of some particularly bad "incident," as the British, with characteristic understatement, called severe bombing destruction. It became known that the King would never leave England and that the Queen had said that, if he would not go, she and her daughters would stay.

To people condemned to stay and take it and aware that many of the well-to-do had sent wives and children to the United States and Canada, this was a tonic. Excuses could be, and were, made for these evacuations: fewer mouths to feed on a beleaguered island, for example. Yet those who could not send their children to safety were heartened by the royal family's example.

The Battle of Britain and the bombing of London, militarily different operations, are now enshrined together in British folk history as "the blitz." The outcome of these two events influenced powerfully what happened thereafter in the European theaters of World War II and, consequently, the lives of untold millions far from the scene of battle. Each was essentially a contest of will.

Any description of the Battle of Britain, no matter how abbreviated, must take into account the odds that faced the British. The Germans deployed against Britain three Luftflotte consisting of 2,355 bombers and fighters, including 998 long-range bombers, 702 single-engined fighters, and 261 twin-engined fighters. The R.A.F. Fighter Command could muster only 600 fighters, Hurricanes, Spitfires, and Defiants, and some Blenheims; the last were much too slow for combat with the German fighters.

This numerical advantage, however, was offset by other factors. The British had radar. The fighting showed that, generally, their pilot training was of a higher standard. Their leadership, both in the air and on the ground, proved cooler, more flexible.

The Germans in the early summer of 1940 suffered from an understandable but ultimately disastrous overconfidence. They had broken the French and driven the English from Europe. When the battle began, realities that conflicted with this overconfidence were discounted. The outrageous claims of Luftwaffe commanders, made perhaps with the purpose of placating that dæmonic figure in Berlin, were accepted and tended to warp operational judgment.

The only exception to this general euphoria was found in the Luftwaffe itself, particularly among those squadrons that had fought the R.A.F. over France and the beaches of Dunkirk.

One summer evening in Wiesbaden in 1945, when the war was over, I talked to Captain Erich Lattman, who in 1940 had been an infantry lieutenant in a division assigned to the invasion. He recalled his shock at the attitude of the pilots he met in a squadron in which one of his cousins was an officer. The squadron was at an airfield near Lille. France was finished. All that remained, they were told daily by German propaganda, was to invade England. The English, who had run away from France, would capitulate, and final victory would be won.

"Do you know," Lattman said, "not one of them was happy about the prospect. My division had seen no British planes. They had seen too many. They thought they would win, but they knew it would cost much. They told me we could take our time about invasion preparations. It would require the best part of a year to knock out the R.A.F. It was very puzzling for me. Much different from what Berlin Radio said."

The Battle of Britain was a drama in form and content. Ambition, resolution, courage, pride, improvisation, desperation: all these were elements of the drama. There was an overture and three acts. When in September the curtain fell on Act III, Britain was saved from invasion and for the long march to victory.

The opening notes of the overture were the high scream of Stukas diving on shipping in the Channel and the rolling crash of their bombs. The voice of Hitler provided a surprising counterpoint. His conscience was hurting him, he told the Germans and the world, he was "grieved to think of the sacrifices" the war must claim, he appealed to "reason and common sense in Britain."

Reason and common sense, the reason and common sense of men like Neville Chamberlain and Sir John Simon, had been replaced by that unremitting belligerence the British call bloody-mindedness. In that atmosphere the nation's will said "Fight on." Everyone had a good laugh at the idea of Hitler's having a conscience.

The bombing in the Channel gave the Luftwaffe the first taste of what was to come. It also provided a spectacular view of the war in the air.

You could lie on your back in the grass on Shakespeare Cliff near Dover and see the Germans come in: a squadron of Stukas, perhaps, with two squadrons of fighters flying escort above them. Then, as the Stukas peeled off to dive at the merchant ships plodding up the Channel, the British fighters appeared. They were so few.

Some would go for the Stukas, if they caught them, it was all over. The eight machine guns of the Hurricanes and Spitfires simply cut the ill-armed German bombers in half. Others, still climbing, would engage the German fighters. The Luftwaffe formations suddenly dissolved. Half a dozen or a dozen engagements were fought. Through field glasses you could see an orange blob appear on a plane's fuselage, a puff of smoke grow into a cloud. The noise of the engines and the rattle of machine-gun fire was very faint. When it was over, you went back to London.

The first act began on August 8. This day had been chosen as *Adler Tag*, "Eagle Day," by Reichsmarschall Hermann Goering, a day of massive onslaughts. However, the weather was unkind. The raids on August 8 were on a small scale, and *Adler Tag* did not come until August 13. On that day the Luftwaffe flew 1,485 sorties and was badly mauled. Luftflotte V, the air fleet stationed in Norway and Denmark, made the long flight to England's northeast coast. It did a little damage but paid heavily. Attacks on airfields and radar stations in the south told the same story: severe losses and little damage. There was a pause. Act I was over.

Everyone knows now that the war by then had reached a critical phase. Few Britons realized it then. Despite everything that had happened in Europe and to their army, the British displayed a remarkable detachment. They had lost their foothold in Europe. The ports of Norway, Belgium, the Netherlands, and France were open to German submarines, and week by week the losses of merchant shipping mounted. Yet sober confidence pervaded the government and permeated public opinion.

Years later I asked Lord Beaverbrook how Churchill, he, and other members of the cabinet were able to maintain this confidence in the light of what they knew about the state of the country's defenses and German strength. It was, I argued, reasonable enough for the general public to be confident; people did not yet know the full extent of the losses of materiel in France, nor were they aware that there were no more than three fully equipped infantry divisions on hand to fight invaders. But how could the government be anything but desperately worried?

"You forget that most of us had been through much worse times in the first war," Beaverbrook said. "We were never as close to defeat in 1940 as we had been after the Somme, when many of us thought the army would crack, or in 1918, when the German offensive came close to driving us into the Channel. Things were bad in 1940, yes; but we had seen worse. And don't forget what Churchill had done. He'd united the country. But he'd also taken control of the armed forces as well as the government. There were none of those rows between GHQ and Downing Street. Churchill was boss. And he, too, had been through the worst of the first war. No, no, we were much nearer defeat in the first war than we ever were in 1940."

Act II displayed Nazi Germany's military capabilities in the air. But, as the act moved toward its climax in a crescendo of bomb bursts and machine-gun fire, Hitler, Goering, and the High Command committed a strategic error that had the gravest consequences for Germany and that affected significantly the future course of the war in the West.

The Luftwaffe resumed the bombing assault in strength on August 24. The targets, chosen with foresight, were the seven sector stations and airfields in southeast England where the cream of the R.A.F. fighter squadrons was based: Tangmere and Debden, Biggin Hill and Hornchurch, Kenley, North Weald and Northolt. The German strategic objective was to knock out these airfields, their control and communications systems, and other facilities. Once the Fighter Command had been driven from these forward bases, the Luftwaffe would be able to control the air above the landing beaches during the invasion. This control was essential to a successful landing.

For the remainder of August and into September the Germans stuck to this program. Of 33 major attacks, 23 were on the complex of airfields. Both ground staffs and pilots suffered casualties. We came to Biggin Hill one day just as they were carrying four girls, members of the Women's Auxiliary Air Force, out of a wrecked communications building. Bomb blast had killed them. They looked like children asleep.

Fighter Command was losing men and planes at a ratio that boded ill for the future: 15 British planes lost to 14 German on September 1, 16 to 16 on September 3, 17 to 25 on September 4.

German bombs had seriously damaged five forward airfields. Reserves of aircraft and of pilots were dangerously low. At 85 Squadron I found old friends among the pilots tense, strained, unutterably weary. Many good pilots had "bought it," the R.A.F.'s euphemism for death in action, in the last few weeks. When you got away from the excessively cheerful public-relations officers and the professionally confident senior commanders, you had the feeling that the whole fragile structure of Fighter Command was near the breaking point.

This period, late August and early September 1940, was one of the worst phases of the war. Then suddenly the Germans made a gross error. Some Frenchman said once that the Germans, at war, make only the biggest mistakes, never the small ones.

On the night of August 24–25 a few German bombers attacked London. The raid was not particularly heavy, nor did it do much damage. A few nights later the R.A.F.'s Bomber Command sent a small force to Berlin in retaliation. Hitler and Goering were enraged.

The latter called a conference to discuss strategy on September 3, the first anniversary of Britain's entry into the war. If it is possible to pinpoint the day that Germany's chances of defeating Britain began to diminish, then that day, in 1940, is the day. The Reichsmarschall, apparently convinced by exaggerated intelligence estimates of British losses in men and planes and of destruction of forward airfields, decided to switch the German attack to London. This, he hoped, would bring the weakened R.A.F. to battle. He was not denied his wish.

In the late afternoon of September 7, our elderly office boy clattered down the stairs at 20 Tudor Street from the roof.

"Germans," he shouted, "hundreds of the buggers coming up the Thames."

The curtain was rising on Act III.

From the roof we could see the tight formations, clusters of small black crosses against the blue sky. Already thick columns of black smoke were climbing from that vast area of London known as Dockland. A mile or so away we felt the shock of the explosions: Bermondsey, Poplar, Woolwich, West Ham, the mean little streets, the huge warehouses, the cheerful pubs, were shattered and seared that lovely September afternoon. They were not unavenged.

For now smaller, brighter crosses were tearing into the German formations. One German went down, then another, a third, a fourth. The German formations broke up. A Ju-88 dove straight into the river. We could hear people cheering on the roof across the street.

For seven days the Germans pressed the attack on London by day and, with increasing force, by night. The climax was reached on September 15, a Sunday, a bright, sunny morning.

No one knew, of course, that this was *the* day, the highwater mark of the Germans' daylight onslaught. Dressing that morning, I knew that the day would be like those of the past week:

a trip to an operational base, talks with any pilots who wanted to talk, then back to London to write the story; so many areas, always described in carefully vague terms, bombed, so many German planes down, so many British down, the number of pilots saved.

The Germans came early. They came from airfields at Saint Omer and Laon, Wissant and Amiens at Crécy-en-Ponthieu and Alençon, from Montdidier and Clairmont, from Eindhoven, Brussels, Lille and Beauvais—Heinkel 111s, Dornier 17s, and Junker 88s. By that time the Ju-87, the once-feared Stuka, had been discarded as too vulnerable to British fighters. As the bombers rose, they were joined by the Messerschmitt 109s and 110s flying above as fighter escort. Along the English coast the radar sets began to register. The Germans were headed for London. But before they reached it, they had to cross the old aerial battlefield, about eighty miles long, thirty-eight broad, and five or six high, over southeast England, where most of that summer's fighting had taken place.

On British airfields pilots noted that a thick, low cloud was developing: the weather had "duffed up." When the alert came they were ready. The Spitfires and Hurricanes rose to the challenge. The fate of Britain flew with them.

There is no way to mark the exact turning point. The Germans flew about 700 sorties that day. Goering had hoped to provide sufficient fighter cover to protect the bombers, but in many cases the escorting fighters flew too high, and the Hurricanes and Spitfires savaged the bombers. As the day wore on, Air Vice Marshal Sir Keith Park, commanding No. 11 Group, threw in squadron after squadron. By midafternoon he had to inform Mr. Churchill, impassively watching the progress of the battle at Group Headquarters, that there were no more reserves. But the crisis had passed.

Battles are contests of minds and wills. Sometime, during those hundreds of dog fights, somewhere over the vast aerial battlefield, the R.A.F. established superiority. By nightfall the Germans had lost fifty-six bombers to British fighters and four more to the anti-aircraft guns. This was almost a third of the German bomber force engaged. The British had lost twenty-six aircraft. This was victory.

II

Fighter Command's victory could be measured in terms of planes and pilots lost by both sides and in the changes in the German High Command's attitude toward invasion. The victory won by the people of London during the bombing from September 1940 until May 1941 is less susceptible to military accounting.

Osbert Lancaster once remarked that God surely was an Englishman, since the shortage of liquor, which grew acute later in the war, did not coincide with the blitz. Looking back, it is remarkable that in the midst of death and destruction so much pleasure could be won from life.

Nightly, as darkness came, the sirens would start their mournful ululation. From then on, sometimes for eight hours and sometimes for more, there was the queer arrhythmic hum of German motors in the air, the scream of falling bombs, the crash of anti-aircraft guns, and most terrifying of all sounds, a building collapsing. Often at the office or at home the rooms would be alight with flames.

Someone always had a party going; restaurants had not run short of food; dance bands blared above the noises of the blitz.

Quentin Reynolds and Bob Lowe lived in a magnificent flat in Berkeley Square. We would gather there late at night, drink, and discuss the war. Once a bomb fell on the north side of the square. The blast blew Bill Stoneman across the room onto the chair where his future wife was sitting. He explained carefully that he had crossed the room to save her.

"A Nightingale Sang in Berkeley Square" was popular. Reynolds and Lowe, dissatisfied with the saccharine words of the original, wrote their own. The refrain ran:

The Abri at the Ritz
Was full of shits.
There were Heinkels aloft in the air.
There were six miscarriages under Claridge's
When a screaming bomb fell in Berkeley Square.

I found it almost impossible to sleep during the bombing. But I could go out in it. It was unbearable to lie in bed and listen to German motors. The government was prolific in statistics that proved that your chances against a single bomb were one in a million. Or was it one in six million? What comfort this might provide in daylight fled with the sirens at night.

My trips around London during the bombing took me one night to Spitalfields in the East End and a bomb shelter presided over by a dwarf. It was November, and the cold east wind, that makes London's climate hellish in that month, blew across the city. The bombing was no worse than usual when I arrived at Spitalfields and was directed to the shelter by a bobby.

When I pushed aside the curtains at the top of the steps leading to the shelter, I saw at the bottom a tiny man standing in a cone of light. His name was Micky. He told me to come on down and close the bloody curtain.

Micky was an optician in ordinary times. Within him, never stifled by the monotony of lower-middle-class existence, there dwelt a genius for organization. Appointed an air raid warden— more as a joke than anything else, he said bitterly—he had taken over the shelter, made it habitable and hospitable for the people of Spitalfields, who flocked to it each night, bedding in their arms, when the bombers came.

Each family had its own area; single men and single women slept in widely separated sections. There was always hot tea, and each night Micky organized some sort of entertainment. They sang, but not, the sentimental will be sorry to hear, "There'll Always Be an England" or "Rule Britannia," but the songs of their class and kind, such as "Knees Up Mother Brown" or "My Old Man's a Fireman."

To the eye they were in no way heroic. The women were heavy and bloated, with great, round, red faces. The men, most of them laborers, were dull-eyed and worn. The children slept fitfully. One woman, younger than the others, soothed a little girl. Father would be home, she told her. No, perhaps not in the morning, but soon.

"Where was Father?" I whispered to Micky.

"He was at Calais," he said, "missing, presumed dead."

"It was bad here until we got it organized," Micky said. "Now they're sending us some more cots, first-aid stuff, a doctor looks in every night. But if you want to see how bad it can be, come along."

We went up to the street. The cold wind, so penetrating earlier, was welcome after the steamy, sweaty air of the shelter.

Down the street stood a church. We could hear planes and the heavy crash of guns from a destroyer in the river. In the crypt of the church the cold bit to the bone. The walls were damp.

Along the sides of the crypt were a number of old, stone coffins. In one lay a mother and two children. They were asleep. She lay awake with wide eyes staring at the room. Every coffin was filled. An Air Raid Precautions worker passed around with a pot of tea and an enameled tin cup. We talked in the vestry.

Did I think that "we" would "give it 'em back?" he asked. I said I didn't know, that Berlin was distant, that I had heard that the first raid, which enraged Hitler, had not been a military success.

The man did not want to hear about what the United States was doing, or said it was doing, as Mickey did.

"Treat us like we were kids at the dentist," he said, "telling us how good we are. Tell 'em not to talk so much, let 'em do something."

I said good-night to Micky at the entrance to the shelter.

"Come back in a month or so," he said, "you won't know the place from the Savoy."

The raid was rumbling away in north London. The underground had long since stopped. I walked toward Fleet Street. As I turned into it from Ludgate Circus a bobby grabbed my arm.

"Not that way, sir," he said, "a land mine has got caught in the wires up by the *Daily Telegraph*. The army's coming to get it down. If it goes up, there'll be hell's own mess."

He had the soft accent of Ireland's south. I asked him where he was from.

"Cork, sir."

"Keeping out of the war, eh?"

"Yes sir, someone says that to me twenty times a day."

The land mine was an ordinary sea mine dropped from a German bomber. Its particular virtue, from the German standpoint, was that it did not penetrate and explode but exploded on contact with the first object it hit. Thus it had a wider lateral blast then ordinary bombs.

We sheltered in the door of the tobacconist, the bobby and I.

A man across the street shouted, "The trucks are there, they're starting to cut it down."

We waited a long hour. The east was growing gray when, almost simultaneously, the "all clear" sounded and the truck rumbled away with the land mine. I went back to the office and wrote my story. I did not mention the land mine. The censors had a "stop" on any mention of these weapons. Besides, such things happened every night.

Sometimes the night was terrifying. You found yourself looking down a street lined by rows of buildings in flames. Or you were flung against a wall by blast.

One night they hit a small, old, very select apartment block in St. James's. By the time the first engines arrived the fire had taken hold. Someone was screaming in the building's upper stories. Two Air Raid Precautions men tried to get across from the next building. The flames were too much for them. Gradually the screaming lapsed into a liquid coughing.

London's problem was how to keep the largest city in the world functioning while under attack. The anti-aircraft guns and the night fighters, then a rather haphazard force without the electronic aids that later cost the Germans dear, could do little more than annoy the bombers. And, since the bombing was largely indiscriminate, a bomber captain, driven away from the docks by the anti-aircraft guns, was content to drop his load on Wandsworth or Stepney. The change of target did not matter to Hitler, who wanted to bring the Londoners to their knees. What mattered to the British was keeping the city going.

Railroad stations were prime German targets. It is a reflection on German inefficiency and on the efficiency and courage of the British repair crews that London's great termini operated without prolonged interruption through most of the blitz.

If you wanted to see what Kipling calls "two o'clock in the morning courage" you visited one of the great railroad stations. At Waterloo I spent a couple of hours in the little room above the tracks outside the station with the men who controlled traffic. It was a particularly bad night.

The Germans had hit the line outside London. A freight train had caught fire somewhere else. There were fires on both sides of the Thames. Death and destruction were taken casually and dealt with efficiently. Voices were low. No one was excited.

Phones rang and were answered. Such and such a junction was clear. Incendiaries had fallen on a suburban station but had been put out by the stationmaster, his wife, and two commuters. An important train—ammunition or tanks, I supposed—was making the circuit of London without difficulty. Blackfriars station reported a "near miss."

"Must have been really close that one," said one of the men, "blew old Arthur clear off his stool."

Later Warren Chetham-Strode, from the Ministry of Information, and I went to one of the Lyons food factories out past Kensington. Lyons provided food for innumerable tea shops, and we watched the process. We had both had more whiskey than most people would have said was good for us, and the manufacture of individual fruit pies was not an edifying sight. But, again, people were going about their jobs. Women in smocks, tired-looking men checking shipments, truck drivers lounging in doorways.

We decided to walk home. As we came to Storey's Gate, at the St. James's Park side of Whitehall near Downing Street, a car drew up. A stout figure in a square-topped derby emerged. Warren, an officer in the first war, saluted. I took off my hat.

"Evening, evening," said Mr. Churchill, "another night gone, eh? Still [he pronounced it "shtill"] here."

It would be inaccurate to say that there were no panics, no cowardice. Of course there were. But they were incidental to the general performance of the Londoners.

One night I stopped at the Savoy for a drink with Douglas Williams. A frantic crowd was milling around the Embankment entrance. A stout, bald man was lecturing two assistant managers, both dressed in dinner jackets.

They must, he said, let the crowd into the Savoy's shelter. The poor had nowhere to go. It was criminal that the rich should be safe and the poor in danger. Much more about inequality and the selfishness of what would now be called "the Establishment."

This was before the Germans turned on their Russian allies. The Communists—there were not many of them—did their best, however, to weaken the Londoners' will.

The two assistant managers were courteous but firm. A bobby came up with the inevitable "Move along, please, move along." The crowd began to disperse.

The Londoners could do only one thing: take it and wait for the tide to change. They did it superbly.

Morning after morning I walked home through streets littered with debris, past shattered buildings and burned-out homes. You could not believe, you could not even imagine, that life could go on. The army was beaten, the R.A.F. had not yet found the means to cope with the night bombers, the Navy was remote, the losses in merchant shipping mounted, and every convoy to Britain was under attack by submarine and bomber. How could they go on?

Occasionally the army took correspondents on "sorties" to see Britain's defenses. We saw two things: desperate improvisation and the new men who would lead British armies of the future.

Montgomery: exciting and excitable, talking continually of the British infantryman as a pearl of great price, confident of the ability of the "P.B.I." (the Poor Bloody Infantry) to defeat the best German troops. Someone asked about antitank guns. The quick, foxy face grew sober. "Not enough, not enough," he said almost to himself. "These politicians."

Alexander: handsome, controlled, courteous. Pointing out in convincing detail the enormous losses the Germans would suffer in an invasion unless they had command of the sea and air. The same question: did he have enough of this or that? "No general ever *thinks* he has enough," he answered. "Successful ones make do with what they have."

The Prime Minister had ordered the organization of the first commandos. This was not unpopular with regular officers. Every battalion commander was eager to send all his hard cases, his drunks, his incorrigibles, to the new formations. These men were, of course, just what the commandos needed. For when they were used, those qualities that had made them bad soldiers in regular regiments enabled them to singe Adolph Hitler's moustache as effectively as Drake had singed the beard of the King of Spain.

Once we went north to Scotland. The Highland Division, the 51st, had been decimated and captured in France. In the Highlands every farmstead had a black knot of crêpe upon its door. In the pubs they would not talk about it except to say that a new Highland division was forming and that it would not be found unworthy. Nor was it.

As the bombing continued, the war contracted. There was little daylight fighting in the air. What mattered was what happened each night, what was hit, how many had been killed or wounded. The war was honed down to one dimension: the blitz. Sometimes you saw it from an anti-aircraft battery on Primrose Hill, sometimes from the roof of an office building. But the crash of bombs, the crack of anti-aircraft guns, the hum of German motors—*that* was the war. Other cities were punished now: Coventry and Cardiff, Liverpool and Southampton. But the war meant London.

In November I saw another battle. After the Germans occupied the ports of Norway, the Low Countries, and France, the Battle of the Atlantic intensified. In the autumn of 1940 it ranked, in the opinion of Mr. Churchill and his military advisers, as the greatest threat to Britain's capacity to continue the war. From their new bases on the Atlantic coasts packs of German U-boats were taking to the Atlantic and to the coastal waters around Britain in increasing numbers. Dornier bombers were ranging out into the Atlantic to bomb convoys and to report their location to the submarine commanders.

Like most things in war it seemed depressingly simple. Get enough U-boats built, sink enough shipping, and no amount of rationing and sacrifice by the islanders would suffice to keep the war going. It was not, of course, simple. The Germans' industrial output was not unlimited.

H.M.S. Vanquisher lay alongside the dock in Liverpool. She was a four-stacker of the "V" class built in 1917, one of the scores of destroyers turned out in the British counteroffensive against German submarines in World War I. Her captain was Commander Adrian Northey, a big, burly sailor with a loud voice and a jovial manner. We sailed in the *Vanquisher* with a British corvette and a Free French *contre-torpilleur* as escort for fifty-six merchant ships. The job was to escort them halfway across the Atlantic, where the convoy would break up and the merchantmen head for ports in the New World; three ships to protect fifty-six.

When we turned westward at the head of the Irish Sea, the weather grew worse. The sea, the wind, the cold that swept down from the Pole; here were the constant enemies. I have never been seasick. But I found the job of staying on my feet or in my bunk or climbing to the bridge physically exhausting. Once on the bridge I stayed until I found myself dropping to sleep. Northey was always there, railing at his young navigator, whom he called "Vasco" after the great Portuguese da Gama, instructing me in the art of escort, or swearing with splendid vigor at merchantmen that wandered from course. He ate and slept on the bridge.

There were the usual rumors. The most persistent was that the German battle cruiser *Scharnhorst* was at sea. I asked Northey what he would do if the convoy encountered the *Scharnhorst*.

"Oh, try and get close enough to send a torpedo up her ass," he said cheerfully.

But there was no *Scharnhorst*. We plowed westward day after day. There was nothing to see but the convoy, the gray sea, and the gray sky. One night, calmer than most, the lookout spotted a light. As we drew nearer, we saw a lifeboat with three men aboard. Northey brought *Vanquisher* up to the lifeboat.

"Number One," he shouted to his lieutenant, "we'll have to stop to bring them aboard. I want it done quickly."

It was. But everyone felt better when *Vanquisher* again gained speed and raced after the convoy. The three men were the captain and two seamen from a Greek freighter torpedoed three days before. They were tough and revived quickly with mugs of rum and tea. I asked the Captain what he would do when he got back to port.

"Get another ship," he said and launched into an obscenely picturesque description of the Italians who, that autumn, had attacked Greece.

The day came when the escort left the convoy. We watched the faster merchantmen increase speed and make off to the west. We watched them a long time.

Almost all the members of the crew came from ports which, at that stage of the German air offensive, were under attack from the Luftwaffe. Every morning on the BBC they heard that Portsmouth or Plymouth or Liverpool had "caught it." They knew what could happen to wives and families and girl friends. They showed no emotion. I spoke to Northey about it.

"It's almost unnatural," he said. "You know they do care.

But they feel that to talk about it only makes it worse. So no one says anything. And, you know, most of them are seamen, either R.N. or Merchant Navy. It's a tough life, and they learn young that talking about the dangerous things doesn't do any good. Oh, they grouse about things all right. But if I told them now, 'There's *Scharnhorst,* we're going to have a go at her,' I know I could count on them."

The sea looked very empty for a couple of days. The wind rose, and the *contre-tropilleur* rolled even more villainously than before. The corvette bumped along through the gray seas. On the bridge, while Northey slept beneath a tarpaulin, I talked to the young officers. They were interested in London, looking forward to their next leave. They never betrayed the slightest doubt that Britain would win the war. They were not particularly interested in whether or not the United States would come in. They had, to a supreme degree, that confidence that a century and more of world supremacy had bred into Englishmen of their class. To them the question was whether the war would be long or short, not who would win it.

One morning we raised the hills of Scotland and then, in brilliant sunshine, we came down the Irish Sea again. I had a drink in the wardroom and said goodbye.

"Sorry we couldn't raise *Scharnhorst* for you," Northey said, "it was a damned quiet trip, and I must say I'm not sorry."

In March of 1941 I started home on vacation. The effect of coming out of a war zone was not unlike that of leaving a particularly bloody bullfight and entering a church. The three or four days in Lisbon, where I was to board one of the American Export Line's ships for New York, had an unreal quality.

The voyage to New York brought me one inestimable gift, the friendship of F. Raymond Daniell, one of the truly great reporters I have known. He and his future bride, Tania Long, herself a most able reporter, were in Lisbon after nine months of war in London, where he had been Chief of Bureau of *The New York Times* and Tania a member of the *New York Herald-Tribune* staff.

During those long, quiet days of the passage westward and at night I learned more about the newspaper business than I could have done in four years in a school of journalism. Ray had a profound knowledge of the craft. He had read enough of my stories to be a forceful but never captious critic. His advice then, and for years afterward, helped me over many a tough spot. A year later he was instrumental in hiring me for *The New York Times,* and two years later he was best man at my wedding. It was a fortunate trip.

I was born in New York and was reared there and in the suburbs. But, that spring, I was lonely. My friends were there. I went to the theater. I spent weekends in Connecticut and New Jersey. For three days in Washington I talked to people in the State and War Departments. I found, somewhat to my surprise, that, as a reporter who had seen something of the German Army, more of the Royal Air Force, and much more of the bombing of Britain, I was an object of interest if not a person of importance. Still, I was lonely.

Friends said it must be frightful in Europe. But they did not know—how could they?—what it really meant. One night I met an Englishman, a R.A.F. officer, whom I'd never particularly liked, in a bar in New York. But I liked him that night, for his first words were, "It's all bloody unreal." We sat drinking until the light filtered down Madison Avenue and the reality was recaptured, the ungainly outlines of Ju-87's as they turned to dive, the crackle of flames as you retreated through a burning village, armored cars nosing through an orchard in Normandy. I was lonely for the war.

Many of my friends were upset by what they considered the appalling slowness of the United States in "getting into it." This was combined with, to me, an equally appalling exaggeration of America's strength. You did not have to spend much time in Washington to learn just how weak we were. Yet American confidence was working overtime. We would fix it. Just let us take a crack at those Germans. And we'd attend to the Japs at the same time.

That spring of 1941 was an age of innocence. Not since then has the world seemed so simple, so much the American oyster. There were, of course, those who didn't want us in the war. But their reasons usually had nothing to do with military strength. I was buffeted by slogans and plagued by argument. Men would lead me into corners at cocktail parties to explain that the only thing needed was a really tough statement by that man in the White House. A firm-mouthed midwestern lady lectured me about Roosevelt's sell-out to the Jews. I was told that America would be "saved" by helping the Allies or that America "came first." Much of the chatter was irrelevant to the war I had left. It didn't matter what the President said or they said. What mattered was guns, planes, tanks, and ammunition.

I lectured at the University of Alabama. Someone asked me what would happen if the Germans landed five divisions in New Jersey. I said they would be in Washington in a couple of days. There was no outcry. No one took me seriously.

I sailed from New York one bright May morning. London had suffered the heaviest of all the raids the night before. I stood by the rail, oblivious of the matchless panorama of lower Manhattan rising from the sea, and thought of the shattered streets. The fires set the night before would still be burning, and there would be the clang of fire apparatus and the taste of smoke in your mouth. I was glad to return to the war.

As the *Excambion,* great American flags painted on her sides, plowed eastward toward Lisbon and the war, there was a good deal to think about. It was a time for reflection. Since September 1939 I had lived in a whirlpool of events. Physically intact, I found my mind in a ferment, my emotions drained. As alone I walked the decks—for obvious reasons the passenger list was small—one question recurred: How would Americans have reacted to the situations in which France and Britain had found themselves in 1940?

The survivors of my generation, people in their late fifties, accept rather complacently Scotty Reston's view that "they have been over the hurdles." A depression, World War II, two Asian wars, the clamant problems of race and cities, have confronted us with difficult issues, hard choices. None of these has been a crisis of the proportions that faced the French in mid-June of 1940 or the British a month later when they found themselves alone.

We have debased the word *crisis* as we have debased so much else. A crisis is not a series of race riots or a fall in the stock market. A crisis is when the whole fabric of society crumbles under the foreign attack, as it did in France, or when a country, like Britain in 1940, finds itself facing a foreign foe of infinitely superior strength, vulnerable to his attack, and without powerful allies.

The question I asked myself in 1941 can be asked appropriately today. What would Americans do in the situations that faced the British and the French? Most of us do not understand what has happened to Americans since 1945. Yet, except for a few short intervals, this has been a time of troubles. But it is not so much the origin of the troubles, which was largely, but not entirely, in our follies, or the manner in which we dealt with them that should be of concern: it is the moral stamina of the people.

Clearly, there has been an erosion of the sense of duty owed the Republic. Pointless, really, to argue why. It's there. Equally pointless to contend that, were a foreign enemy to threaten invasion, Americans would be prepared for sacrifice. This is a doubtful proposition and, in any case, the time for sacrifice and self-discipline is before danger is real and imminent.

The erosion of the sense of national duty has occurred when the formal political commitments of the United States still extend around the world. Richard Nixon's administrations have sought to reduce these commitments and, to some extent, they have succeeded. But in the larger sense of America's political commitment to freedom and democracy and of the economy's increasing interdependence with the economies of other countries we cannot withdraw from the world. It is neither morally justifiable nor economically sound.

But are we willing, are we able, to pay the price our position in the world demands? A large number of Americans are unwilling to fight further small wars in far-off countries. Very well. As long as they understand that tyranny, instability, and hostility in the Third World will in time affect them. Are we prepared for the hard thinking and austerity that the coming energy crisis will demand? Would we go to the aid of an ally if she were in mortal danger? Would we help the British against Russia, or Israel against an Arab world that has the oil we need?

The thoughtful must have serious doubts about the answers. For thirty years a great many Americans have enjoyed an ease and affluence unmatched elsewhere. Have we considered that history may ask us to pay, as she has asked others to pay in the past? Are Americans prepared morally to pay that price?

No one with any knowledge of history can ignore the signs of decadence. Vast expenditures on military enterprises far from our shores, enterprises bungled by civilian and military leaders alike. The widening gap between rich and poor. The disappearance of the middle class, which, with all its faults and virtues, was essential to the flowering of America. Great corporations and interests becoming states within the state. Corruption rife in business and politics. A wave of preoccupation with sex, including the exaltation of homosexuality. Old standards mocked, old values discarded.

Providence has given us no special dispensation that will allow us to wallow in self-indulgence and avoid the cost of it. There is nothing Americans cannot do when their resolution matches their energies. But does it, today?

Our society could face dangers from abroad that will make our present internal problems seem minor. Nothing in the record of our leaders since 1952 engenders confidence that they can avert such dangers. Nothing in the record of the Soviet Union, our continuing adversary, encourages the appealing idea that the wars are over and that we can devote ourselves to the pursuit of pleasure.

My mind goes back, today as it did in 1941, to the frightened French looking north along the roads down which the Germans raced. They were ready, at any cost, to save themselves, and to hell with their country. Would that be the American choice? Or would we rise to the sacrifice and danger necessary to the survival of the United States?

The time has come for hard thinking about ourselves. Unless we can return to the essentials that made this country great, we are on the road to disaster. We cannot continue as we are and celebrate the two-hundredth anniversary of the birth of the Republic with a good conscience.

CHAPTER 4

THE AMERICANS IN ICELAND, THE CANADIANS AT DIEPPE

1941-42

A great country can have no
such thing as a little war.

The Duke of Wellington

The second summer of the war was a curious period, as odd, in its way, as the "phoney war" of 1939–1940. The war was real enough, but it was moving away. The German air raids dwindled to intermittent small-scale attacks. The sense of living under siege gradually disappeared. There wasn't any complacency—the realities were too obvious for that—but there was a feeling of accomplishment. If we had got through "that," meaning the bombing of the past fall and winter, people said, we could get through anything.

The situation might be easier at home. Abroad all was dark. The army in the western desert, after some initial victories over the Italians in Libya, had been driven back by the first elements of the German Afrika Korps. A new name, General Erwin Rommel, crept into the headlines. An expeditionary force sent to Greece had been driven out by the Germans and its survivors badly mauled in Crete. The Axis now ruled Europe from the English Channel to the Ægean Sea, from Sicily to the North Cape.

The newspapers and the politicians, taking their cue from the driving force in Downing Street, spoke of victory. But how could the British, even with American arms and the help of the Dominions, defeat the Germans and the Italians? However, in the summer of 1941, just as in the previous summers, events that would contribute to the final victory were developing.

Under conditions of war and censorship the sixth sense, which all reporters have, works overtime. In Lisbon on my way back to London I sensed that something was stirring behind the bleak panorama of the war.

A constant stream of travelers flowed through Lisbon. The city was a center of espionage for the warring powers. Before long I began to hear reports that the Germans were preparing to attack the Soviet Union. There was nothing particularly secret about this. Nor was there solid evidence. But you heard the reports in bars and restaurants and embassies. Even the Associated Press's Portuguese stringer—he kept a pet goose and was the politest man I've ever known—knew of them.

At the outset I was skeptical. Such a report, it seemed to me, was exactly the sort of thing that an alert military intelligence department would spread in neutral countries about its enemy. British Military Intelligence at that time, and not without cause, was accorded a reputation for devilish ingenuity. Still, my sixth sense kept warning me that there might be something to it. The United States Embassy seemed to think so. An Englishman, vaguely connected with cultural affairs at his embassy, was even more certain. But there were no facts. Without facts there was no story.

On June 6, after I had returned to London, I was summoned with four other correspondents to see Anthony Eden, back in his old post as Foreign Secretary—a role he filled with consummate distinction. Eden went to the point. The British government "knew," he said, that the Germans were preparing an invasion of the Soviet Union (I have found that when a British cabinet minister or diplomat says in a flat, no-contradiction tone that he or his government "knows" something, he is speaking on the basis of secret intelligence). The Russians, Eden said, had been warned but appeared to pay little attention. The invasion would begin about June 21. As evidence he named a number of German divisions that in the last four weeks had moved eastward.

Diplomatic reporting can be a dull business: long, frustrating discussions between reporters and diplomats, who are natural enemies, and, in any case, hours of reading reports, speeches, and government documents. But it has its moments. This was one.

The sun's rays caught the high varnish on the table in the Ambassador's waiting room. Eden, handsome and vigorous, warned of what was to come. We wrote our notes with a sense of history: this was not simply news, it was the promise of an elemental change in the balance of the world.

Occasionally reporting is lifted out of what, to the reporter, is commonplace, and he is face to face with an event that molds an era: two old men, Konrad Adenauer and Charles de Gaulle, vowing to end the ancient duel between Frank and Teuton, or American infantry and British fighter planes combining to smash a German counterattack, and Mark Watson and I, in our fox-holes, knowing the Germans are beaten in Normandy. I have driven up the Khyber Pass into the world of feuds, torture, and spontaneous poetry. I have watched the old, now dying, Africa slide past along the banks of the Charri river in Chad. I have seen the sun set over Mandalay and the moon rise over the Pyramids. I have seen battles and riots, heard noble speeches, listened to great men. But that afternoon in the familiar, old Foreign Office clings to memory. Such moments make it all worth while: the frustrations, the separations, the weariness.

The invasion came as Eden predicted. But it came at least a month later than the Germans had originally planned. The delay resulted from a combination of events that individually meant little. Later they became hideously important to the Third Reich.

The Italians had invaded Greece in the autumn of 1940 with, even for them, singular ineptitude. In April 1941 the Yugoslavs refused to allow Hitler to occupy their country on his move east and threw out a government bent on appeasement. Infuriated, Hitler moved against Greece and Yugoslavia. The British, hard pressed in the western desert, deeply committed in Ethiopia, facing the Vichy French and their Nazi directors in Syria, and worried over the pro-German party in Iraq, were asked for help.

The decision was the cabinet's. Eden's was the strongest voice for intervention: at best a desperate military risk, at worst the prospect of complete defeat.

After the war Eden explained the reasoning behind the decision. "We couldn't let the Greeks go down without trying to
help," he said. "We had committed ourselves to the defense of
small nations against the Axis. What value would this commitment have for others if we stood by and Greece was overrun?
We didn't have enough troops or enough equipment. To fight
in Greece meant reducing our forces in the western desert. But
we were pledged to act against the dictators. So we had to act."

Intervention was a failure. The British, Australians, and New
Zealanders were too few, their weapons were inadequate, their
air support was meager. However, the campaign in Greece and
the assault on Crete did divert the Germans from the Soviet
Union, their main objective. The Germans suffered some losses
on the mainland, and their best airborne units were badly
mauled in Crete. The campaign was over in one month. The
Germans were victorious, but they had lost far more than thirty
days.

The German attack on Russia thus began a month later than
planned. Had it been launched in late May, against a Red Army
no stronger and even less prepared psychologically for an attack
from its "allies," the Germans would have been within striking
distance of Moscow a month, perhaps five weeks earlier. The
snow and cold that froze their December offensive would have
been less of a problem. The reinforcements that stiffened Russian
resistance had not then reached the capital.

Had the German Army arrived in front of Moscow in late
October or early November, it would have taken the city because, at that time, it was the best army in the world. Moscow's
fall would have had incalculable consequences. Russia would
not have been defeated. But her road back would have been even
longer.

Here, as in the Battle of Britain, is a turning point of history.
Again we see Hitler's strategy governed by emotion, in this
case his fury over Yugoslav and Greek resistance. And time, the
most precious commodity in war, was wasted on a sideshow. As
in the decision in the Battle of Britain to strike at London rather
than the advanced airfields, Germany's foe benefited from the
Fuehrer's emotions.

General Eisenhower, although he believed the German diversion to the Balkans contributed to their initial check in Russia, thought that the true turning point of the war came on Good Friday, 1942.

A Japanese fleet of aircraft carriers, cruisers, and destroyers stood off Ceylon on that day. Its objectives were the naval base of Trincomalee and the port of Columbo. The result would be the establishment of Japanese naval power in the western Indian Ocean, including the approaches to the Red Sea, the Suez Canal, and the Persian Gulf.

Ceylon's defense had been bolstered a few days earlier by the arrival of three Hurricane squadrons from Britain. These attacked the Japanese aircraft when they attempted to bomb its targets. The Japanese command, in what now seems an excess of caution, retreated after doing severe damage to the British naval forces.

"If they'd taken Ceylon," Eisenhower said in 1944, "the results would have been enormous, catastrophic. This would now be a true world war with a world front. The Japs in Ceylon would have threatened the British in Egypt and the Russians in the Caucasus. Japanese pressure might have forced the diversion of troops from the desert and the Caucasus just when the German offensive reached its climax. It was close as it was. I tell you, the British got those fighters to Ceylon just in time."

Eden's prediction was fulfilled with terrible consequences, first for the Russians and ultimately for the Germans.

In Britain the military and political character of the war changed overnight. From that day the Germans were continually in combat with a large, resolute enemy on the eastern front. It still was difficult to see how the war could be won. But it was more difficult to see how it could be lost.

The political change was more subtle. It may be that by allying herself so quickly and so completely with the Soviet Union Britain lost much of her claim to moral leadership in the West. Until that alliance Britain's position was high. She had gone to war for Poland, a small nation attacked by a larger neighbor. She had intervened in Greece in an attempt to save another small state from aggression and tyranny. Now, because of the exigencies of war, she was allied with a dictatorship as cruel and ruthless as that in Nazi Germany. The Arabs say, "My enemy's enemy is my friend."

The reaction of the British to the new Nazi aggression had little to do with moral values. It was one of unabashed relief. Another major power was in the war on their side. Someone else would share the burden. The reduction in the number and strength of German air attacks—the last "big one" had been on the night of May 10, 1940—might continue. To most Britons the Communism of the new ally didn't matter a damn.

Of course, in the upper reaches of British society the word "Establishment" had not then been revived, and many hoped that the two great totalitarian powers would exhaust each other. Some were indiscreet in voicing such views. The Communists and their left-wing allies were shocked by such forthrightness, although I have never understood why. Had not Moscow in 1939 hoped that the capitalist world would tear itself apart and so allow international Communism to pick up the pieces?

The Tory government that ruled Britain until May 1940 was strongly anti-Soviet. Premier Neville Chamberlain evinced much greater enthusiasm for a proposed Anglo-French expedition to help the Finns against the Soviet Union in the winter of 1940 than he did for pursuing the war against Germany. The coalition formed by Churchill, including some of the ablest men the Labor Party ever produced—Clement Attlee, Ernest Bevin, Herbert Morrison—could not be called pro-Communist by any stretch of the imagination. Indeed, men like Bevin had spent most of their lives fighting Communists in the trade unions. And, since taking office, they had been engaged in a war in which, until June 1941, the Soviet Union was an ally of Nazi Germany.

In the months and years that followed, however, sympathy, admiration, and relief combined to produce an enormous reservoir of good will for Russia and the Russians, if not Communism, in Britain. This generous outpouring of friendship naturally was exploited by the native Communists and their masters in the Soviet Embassy for their own ends.

The "Second Front Now" campaign was born of this temporary alliance between the natural, spontaneous sympathies of the British and the Soviet government's desire to divert the German armies, no matter what the cost, to the British and Americans.

In total war public opinion is at its most vulnerable. Because of censorship it is not informed. It is even more emotional than in ordinary times. The British government knew that a second front was beyond its means. Even in the summer of 1942, a year after the German attack on Russia, the British were hard pressed to hold their positions in Libya and Egypt. They had been driven out of Malaysia and Burma with cruel losses.

But the government could not say why a second front was impossible. It could only point to the damage that R.A.F. Bomber Command was then, allegedly, doing to German industry and communications and advise the Russians to wait. For Churchill to disclose the inadequacies of military equipment, which were the principal reason the British could do nothing more ambitious than raid the coasts of Europe, would have been politically disastrous. British rearmament really began in the summer of 1940. In time it became an industrial wonder. But to expect a landing in Europe a year or eighteen months later was folly.

The soft-hearted and the softer-headed pleaded for an attack into Europe to relieve the strain on "our Russian comrades in arms," forgetting that six months earlier those comrades in arms had been hand-in-glove with the Germans. Politicians on the left and a few on the right parroted the cry "Second Front Now." Lord Beaverbrook's newspapers threw their weight behind the idea, even though their proprietor was a member of the cabinet and a friend, even an idolator, of Winston Churchill.

The Beaver was one of the most remarkable men I have known. Some thought him evil. I found him amoral. He was a political maverick, coldly calculating in many respects but prone to violent enthusiasms. He was a man of great energy, callous mental brutality, a passion for intrigue (sometimes, it seemed, for intrigue's sake), and a vast generosity. People with only a tenuous claim were given financial help. Employees who ran afoul of the law found the Beaver in their corner.

On British internal politics he was acute. On international affairs he displayed a baffling ingeniousness. Once, aboard the Queen Mary, when I was correspondent in Germany, he questioned me closely about the revival of right-wing parties in the Federal Republic. I said there was a chance of such a revival but that forceful measures by the American, British, and French high commissioners could prevent any real growth. I was whistling in the wind. The Beaver spent an hour attempting to convince me that nations never change. He told me that my efforts to expose neo-Naziism were weak and were influenced by my fear of the Truman administration. When I protested that the extent of the catastrophe of 1945 probably had changed the Germans and certainly had created a political and moral climate in which change was likely, he brushed aside my arguments.

Television and changing fashions in news have made the Beaver's slam-bang reporting and his "hit him again, he's still breathing" editorials out of date. His newspapers, the *Daily Express,* the *Evening Standard* and the *Sunday Express,* still prosper. But something of the old devilish ingenuity has gone. While he lived he made a stir, and Fleet Street has not been the same without him.

The Beaver's eclipse as a historical figure cannot be blamed on the loyal cohorts who hymned his praises in life and death. They have managed to establish the image of Lord Beaverbrook, Minister of Aircraft Production, as the man who made the Spitfires and Hurricanes that saved Britain. Tripe. Given the time it took to produce a Spitfire or a Hurricane in 1940, the planes that fought and won that battle were already built, their production largely unaffected by the Beaver's spirited and successful efforts to raise output. His real achievement was to push production to the point where the losses in the Battle of Britain were met and the foundations established for the truly amazing production record of the last years of the war.

He gave me hell once, during the same voyage on the Queen Mary, for failing to attend church on Sunday morning. He had, I knew from the lady concerned, spent most of Saturday night and Sunday morning unsuccessfully trying to get the wife of a very prominent movie star into his bed. He knew I knew it, but he didn't give a damn.

Beaverbrook's antithesis was Anthony J. Drexel Biddle, former Ambassador to Poland, and in 1941 President Roosevelt's envoy to the governments that had taken refuge in London after the Nazis had occupied their countries. Tony Biddle was a decent, honorable, and engaging man. He was, a cockney friend said, "by way of being a gent." He was a man of almost overwhelming charm—gay, handsome, immensely likable. His range was wide: he could discuss with insight the intricacies of the policies of the refugee governments to which he was accredited, and he could spend an amiable evening talking about Philadelphia Jack O'Brien and the young Jack Dempsey. Many thought his wide and unabashed interest in people and their lives was false. It was not. He was interested. He did remember.

One afternoon Tony was walking along Hill Street balancing in his mind the competing claims of his guerrilla governments for American help. Suddenly he realized that a pretty girl had smiled at him and that he, the most courteous of men, had failed to tip his hat. He turned back, apologized and, thinking that she was someone he had met at a dinner party the night before, chatted easily about the evening and the hostess. Finally the girl got a word in.

"Oh, please," she said, "it wasn't me. I'm just a tart."

Interest that summer in London centered on the Russians and what they would or would not do to hold the Germans. Military opinion at the War Office was more optimistic on this score than that in Washington. But neither government nor parliament lost sight of what was now Britain's main interest, which was to see the United States involved in the war.

A few thought that Britain and the Soviet Union, helped by risings against the Germans in occupied Europe, could defeat the Germans with only peripheral help from the Americans. This view lost some of its luster when the Germans began, as Bill Miller, a cockney friend, said, "to kick the tripes out of the Roosians." Generally, however, the British—government, parliament, and people—wanted the United States "in," not solely because they believed American participation would shorten the war, but also because, even then, statesmen were speculating on the appetite a triumphant Russia might bring to the peace table. The British wanted the United States in the war: from the standpoint of their national interest they were perfectly right to do so. But nothing was said about this publicly. The public line was "Give us the tools and we will finish the job."

Meanwhile Eden embarked on the difficult task of extending the military alliance to political cooperation. He got along well enough with Ivan Maisky, an intelligent, cultivated man, but he found some of the boorish diplomatic assistants at the Embassy and the military representatives hard going. "After all," he remarked philosophically, "it's not surprising. If you tell people for twenty years to come in through the servants' hall, you shouldn't be surprised if they spit on the floor when they come in through the front door."

At the same time Churchill worked on the military connection with the United States. There were many Americans in London that summer as the administration, if not the people, moved closer to involvement.

Destroyers of the U.S. Navy began cooperation with the Royal Navy in the convoy system. A brigade of U.S. Marines was sent to Iceland, which had been occupied by the British in 1940. The 10th Infantry Regiment of the U.S. Army prepared for duty in Iceland, freeing the British garrison for more important and dangerous service elsewhere.

Early in September 1941 I was sent to Iceland to report on American activities there. It was my first encounter with the forces of my country. It is curious to recall that in the twenties and 'thirties the army and navy, which now, with the air force, represent such a vast conglomerate of political and military power and influence, were almost an unknown quantity to most Americans.

The services are going through a bad patch at the moment. They are paying the penalty not only for an unsuccessful war in Vietnam but also for their arrogance in the years when they ate high off the hog. I have encountered the stupidity, narrow-mindedness, and boorishness of the professional military in many countries. Their conduct abroad, not as fighting men but as occupation forces, often has been inexcusable in its crassness, its ignorance, its intolerance of other governments and peoples, and its blindness to the great tides of change that have swept the world since 1945.

Having said that, I contend that the high professional competence, the foresight, and the valor of the regular soldiers, sailors, and airmen, who were there when the bugles blew in 1941, established a debt of gratitude that this country can never repay. It was the regulars who trained the army, navy, and air force and got the three services through the first terrible years of battle.

We are lucky people. The treatment given the services by the Congress and people of the United States in the period between the two great wars was so disgraceful that the logical

result should have been an officer corps of outstanding medi-
ocrity. Instead, from the tarpaper posts of the West, the ancient
barracks of crumbling forts, the overage destroyers, came a
generation of officers of great distinction.

Their pay had been reduced. Their weapons and equipment
were allowed to become obsolete. Their warnings of war were
ignored and their plans and projects pigeonholed. Yet their
loyalty to their country and their pride in their profession out-
weighed all. Finally, given the resources, they wrote pages of
military history that an American can read with pride.

The Marine brigade awaiting the arrival of the infantry in
Iceland was in good shape. The officers gave me a hospitable
welcome. They were professionals and, since the original British
Expeditionary Force in France had been largely professional, the
differences were not as great as I had anticipated. I visited the
Marine posts, I watched their company of tanks maneuver in
company with the British, a battalion of the Durham Light Infantry, a very fine regiment, and dined and drank with the young
officers. We sang "The One-Eyed Reilly" and "The Muffin Man"
and escorted Icelandic girls to dances and to bed.

After Pearl Harbor the Marine regiments sailed for the Far
East. I never saw any of those gay and generous fellows again.

The army arrived with great panache. After all, this was the
first contingent of the U.S. Army to enter what was recognizably
a war zone.

It did not take long to learn that a high proportion of the
officers and quite a few of the men detested service in Iceland
and were violently critical of the government that had sent them
there.

I mentioned this cautiously to an artillery colonel one night.
"Hell, they're talking treason. I know it. But I'm damned if I
can do anything about it now. But we'll be in this thing before
long, and things will change then."

Iceland was hardly a welcoming sight to the G.I.'s aboard the
transports. A tumult of land thrust up from the North Atlantic,
almost treeless, very rainy, it left those who had bitched about
camps in the United States speechless with rage. Aside from the
very bad local beer and the local bootleg spirits, known genially
as The Black Death, Iceland was dry. The women, true, were
handsome and free. But the Marines and the British had staked

out their claims. The 10th Regiment was not impressed by Iceland.

Nor was the regiment, after those weeks at sea, particularly impressive. In the autumn of 1941 the expansion of the army had not yet adulterated the old units to the extent that prevailed a year or so later. There were plenty of seasoned noncommissioned officers in the ranks. There had to be. For the troops with whom I came in contact were on the whole undisciplined, sullen, ill-kept and, to use the modern word, unmotivated.

A soldier from Bayonne, New Jersey, spent a good half-hour one night complaining about his billet, a Nissen hut turned over by the British, about the food, the lack of suitable entertainment, the idiocies of military life, and the general fat-headedness of the officers. I interrupted his tirade to say that, while it might appear tough to him, at least we weren't being bombed.

"Bombed," he shouted, "Jesus, nobody's going to bomb us. Why, Christ, we're not even in the god-damned war."

But of course they were.

They were a sorry lot when I compared them with the German prisoners I had seen or the British infantry. It is to the eternal credit of their officers, commissioned and noncommissioned, that they took this unruly material and in a few short years made it into one of the finest armies the world has ever seen. In standards of education and physical capacity, of course, the Americans were well ahead of most of the European armies. But they were psychologically unprepared for the army, let alone the war. They could not understand the reason for discipline or the methods by which it was taught.

Normal soldiers accept a rational order. To achieve discipline, however, troops must be obedient to seemingly *irrational* orders on no more authority than the next link higher in the chain of command and on no more information than comes with the order. The reason is that battle is an irrational business. At the rifle-company level battles do not follow the pattern laid down by higher headquarters, although the results, often due to haphazard, irrational actions, may convince those headquarters that "everything went according to plan."

Disciplined men will stand when the better part of wisdom seems to be to run and when undisciplined men will run. The former have learned obedience to the seemingly irrational and, if they have been in action long enough, they also will have learned that to stand more often leads to survival and victory than does running away.

In Iceland the officers and noncommissioned officers of the U.S. Marines and the British, who understood discipline, watched with a mixture of scorn and apprehension as the Americans began to whip their unpromising material into shape.

The first American commanding officer I met was Major General Charles H. Bonesteel II. His was a type now familiar: lean, gray, courteous, very "regular Army." He was a bit too old for field command in the war that was to come, but he knew his business in Iceland, which was training troops. The Army and the country owe much to him and others like him.

The General's aides were two young professionals, Captains Charles H. Bonesteel III, his son, and Theodore W. Parker. They were West Pointers. Disparagement of West Point and its products is fashionable nowadays, usually among people with only a remote knowledge of war. What I found then and have found since in West Pointers is a high level of professional accomplishment and cold courage untainted by self-advertisement.

The two aides were intelligent, erudite, and broad-minded. Their views on the war were knowledgeable and perceptive. They discussed economics and history, politics and social problems, with insight and understanding. Each won high professional distinction. Tick Bonesteel ended his career as Commanding General of the United States forces in Korea. Ted Parker retired in 1969 as Chief of Staff at Supreme Headquarters Allied Powers Europe.

The Battle of the Atlantic was going very badly on Reykjavik's doorstep. The U.S. Navy had entered the convoy business and, since this was war, not maneuvers, it was getting hurt. In late 1941 the Navy suffered from a superiority complex that had to be heard to be believed; they could take care of the Japs in a couple of weeks and the Germans in less.

Drinking one night with a young officer from the destroyer *U.S.S. Greer,* I learned that on a recent voyage the ship had depth-charged a German submarine. My story, when published, set the doves fluttering in Washington. President Roosevelt said indignantly that nothing of the kind had happened. The Associated Press asked for verification. I stood by my story and heard no more.

The outcry in America over the *Greer* puzzled me. My reaction to the incident and the reaction taught me a bit about myself. The destroyer captain's action seemed right and logical to me. If you were a captain at sea and there was a submarine about, you dropped depth charges. What else? What the hell were people hollering about? Did they think the Nazis would leave us alone if our ships were withdrawn? Two years of war, most of it on the losing end, had made me callous and intolerant of those who did not see the war as I did. In a war you see things in black and white, victory and defeat. Perhaps this is part of its appeal. You see the gray only after considerable exposure to war.

Pearl Harbor and the declarations of war by Germany and Italy elated me. I knew we would win now, and at that stage, with my experience, winning was the only thing.

We got drunk in the British headquarters mess on the night of Pearl Harbor: British, Americans, and Norwegians—there was a Royal Norwegian Air Force squadron on the island—soldiers, sailors, and airmen. A young Royal Navy officer had been aboard one of our cruisers when the first flash from Pearl Harbor arrived. It was followed, he said, by an order to carry out Plan Yellow, which called for the arrest of all Japanese in the vicinity.

"There they were," he said, "stuck in a bloody fjord, thirsting for revenge, and all they could do was arrest nonexistent Japanese."

At the end of the evening an American lieutenant-colonel appeared. For two months he had quarreled bitterly with the British. He was a patriot who saw no good in any other nation. The musket smoke of Bunker Hill clung to his nostrils. That night he was crying. They tell me that a lot of the regulars, knowing the full extent of the shame and the humiliation, cried that day.

One of the English, a burly captain, no less patriotic, went over and gave the American a drink and touched glasses. "I drink to our gallant allies," he said. After Pearl Harbor, Iceland became a backwater. The army settled down to intensive training. I bombarded the London office with messages imploring a transfer. In late January I was told to return to London. It was a long, slow trip in a liner built for the South American run and consequently as cold as even the English might wish. I did not mind. I was going back to the war.

Back to London again. The atmosphere in early 1942 was far different from what it had been the previous spring when I returned from the United States. The grand alliance had been formed. People didn't think about winning the war. Instinctively they knew it would be won. What really concerned them was how much more they would have to pay before final victory.

"Look, people can't take that much more, not when they're not under fire too," William Ridsdale at the Foreign Office told me, "the loss of the *Prince of Wales* and the *Repulse,* the fall of Singapore, getting nowhere in the desert, the losses in the Atlantic. This is very hard to take. When they were being bombed, it was different. Now they're starting to ask questions. Makes it bloody difficult for the government."

The morale of the people of Britain and, specifically, of London was a key element in the European war. The public attitude was never more questioning, never more unsettled, than in the spring and summer of 1942. The Germans were on the move again in the Soviet Union, plunging toward Stalingrad, the desert war was going badly, the Battle of the Atlantic took a high toll of tonnage and lives, rationing was tighter. I was optimistic, but I had by own dark moments after Dieppe.

The names of accredited war correspondents were on a rota and, when a commando raid was planned, so many names, representing the British press, the Commonwealth press, and the American press, were drawn from a hat. My name came up for the raid on Dieppe, the biggest, costliest, and most ill-starred of all combined operations.

The attack on the seaport was to be carried out by five thousand of the Canadian infantry supported by tanks and assisted by British commando units.

Canadian army divisions had been in Britain since late in 1939. One division had been scheduled to go to France in 1940. But France collapsed before they could embark. Since then they had trained intensively, bitched incessantly about their inaction, and earned deserved reputations as drinkers and wenchers.

To preserve secrecy, correspondents assigned to cover the raid left London four or five days before the attack. On the train to Bath we changed our war correspondent badges for British officers' insignia. I drew a major's crown. We were not a very military looking lot, but a regular major told us that "compared with the odds and sods that are becoming officers these days, you chaps are quite presentable."

We spent some pleasant days in Bath. Then we drove eastward, the whole of a day, through lush August countryside toward the coast. We were delayed by a breakdown, and when we reached Newhaven, the commando I had been assigned to accompany had gone. The second best was Motor Launch 127, not much bigger than a big cabin cruiser, armed with an Oerlikon gun and two Lewis machine guns. We set out in the summer twilight for the French coast. It was August 18, 1942.

The sea was glassy calm. Until we neared the coast, it was very quiet. As it grew light, we saw bombs bursting when the R.A.F. hit German positions. The sailor at the forward Lewis gun was whistling cheerfully. There was a burst of fire from two diving Focke-Wulfs and a spurt from the Lewis gun. The kid who had been whistling sat down suddenly on the deck. There was a red smear on his thigh.

"Christ," he said, "my fucking, bloody Christ."

Except in very exceptional circumstances, battles have no pattern for a man involved. That is why the description of Waterloo, given by the confused Fabrizio in *Le Chartreuse de Parme* is as true a description of experience in battle as one can read. Battle is formless. In retrospect the outlines of what happened can be put together, mistakes discerned, praise and blame apportioned. But not then, not on the day.

Dawn found us bouncing toward Dieppe. The motor launch ran efficiently, although the officers were a bit unconventional in dress. This was true of all who commanded on what the Royal Navy called the Light Coastal Forces: motor and steam gunboats and torpedo boats and motor launches. Our captain wore dirty white sneakers, worn gray flannel trousers, and an old white shirt. An amiable New Zealander who looked after the gunnery wore white duck trousers and a football jersey. We passed another motor launch commanded by a figure in shorts and a pajama jacket. No one wore a helmet. It was a very in-formal operation.

The smoke from the bombs and the shell fire of the support-ing destroyers obscured most of the shoreline. We could see, above the gray-white smear of smoke, the upper floors of a long line of hotels facing the sea. Little pinpoints of light jumped from window to window.

"Snipers," the captain murmured, "snipers and machine guns. Looks as though they were all ready for this party."

I wondered what they were firing at. The Canadians, if they were anywhere near schedule, should be well beyond the hotels and into the town by now. Then, through a gap in the smoke, I saw two figures in battle dress rise from the beach and start for the hotels. One fell. The other went on. The smoke closed in.

The captain was studying the signal flags of a Hunt class destroyer. A big, young officer who had left Eton to join the Royal Navy Volunteer Reserve was in high good humor.

"They'll have to rewrite the bloody Michelin guide after this," he said. "Have to absolutely, bloody well redo the bit about Dieppe. 'Exclusive seashore resort. Healthy climate. Mod-ern hotels. Golf. *Plage*.' Won't do now. Not so bloody exclusive. Lots of jerries and Canadians lowering the tone of the place. Probably a lot of mixed bathing. Oh, the Michelin guide doesn't know the half of it."

The sailors grinned. Most of them had never heard of the Michelin guide. But men will follow and serve the man who cracks a salty joke as fast as, and often faster than, they will the man who speaks in the name of The Flag or The King or der Fuehrer.

The captain turned around. "Some ass wants us to pick up the wounded off the landing craft and take them to one of the destroyers. What landing craft? What destroyer? Damned if I know."

We turned inshore. A wave of German fighter bombers swept down to attack the destroyers supporting the attack and the landing craft. They came low out of the sun. A bomb fell close, but they were not after us. We heard the machine guns and the cannons as the Germans strafed the ships. Our Oerlikon opened fire on a twin-engined Messerschmitt off to port. A wisp of smoke, then a gout of flame appeared on the German plane.

"By Christ," said the New Zealander in awed disbelief, "we got him."

As we moved in we could see nothing through the smoke. There was heavy firing from the direction of the town. It did not sound as though the Germans had been driven out or killed.

We found the landing craft wallowing a hundred yards off shore. She was down at the bow, and the big doors through which the attacking infantry had rushed ashore were still open. I clambered aboard behind the launch's party. One of them shouted "She's empty." Then he muttered something and dropped into the well of the landing craft.

Seven men lay where they had fallen as they started off the craft. The water that had washed in through the open doors was tinged with red. A corporal pointed feebly at the body nearest the doors. "He was alive a minute ago," he said. The man was dead. He had been hit in the shoulder by a machine-gun bullet. He probably had drowned in the foot or so of water. The New Zealander shouted "Any use?" I said no.

We bandaged the three wounded men and started them back to the motor launch. The corporal shouted "Look out!" and we fell flat. There was a crash and a mighty thump on the side of the landing craft. I looked up for the plane.

"It's not planes, it's guns," a sailor said.

We got the wounded off. The sea was a little choppy. The Germans were dropping a shell our way every two or three minutes. One man fell and began to scream. The New Zealander, who had been a medical student, bent over him with a hypodermic syringe.

"Why the hell should jerry be shelling *us?*" the Etonian asked. "He must take us for a bloody battleship. Fucking waste of ammunition."

I was in battle dress and terribly hot. I gulped some tea as we neared a Hunt class destroyer, *H.M.S. Fernie.* We passed the wounded aboard. I saw Quentin Reynolds's big, red face staring down. I called, and he waved a hand large as a ham as we pulled away.

Above us raged the greatest air battle in the West since the Battle of Britain. We still could see nothing on shore. We got little chance to look. As the launch turned inshore again, four

Dornier 172s came over, headed for the landing ships. They flew at about six thousand feet in echelon through the flak bursts. Every ship fired. Even our own Oerlikon. Someone in an excess of spirit let go with the Lewis gun.

"Leave off that machine gun!" the New Zealander bellowed.

The leading bomber swerved slightly. Out of its belly tumbled the bombs, looking like small, dark pencil smudges against the sky.

"Short, they're short," murmured the captain.

The bomb explosions shook the motor launch. The first Dornier was in trouble. Like a hawk in a chicken yard, a Spitfire caught her. The Dornier burst into flame and turned over. Two more Spitfires hit the other Dorniers. Another German plane hit the sea. We could hear cheering from the people on the destroyers.

Another motor launch, dripping from the shower of water thrown up by a near miss, came along. Her captain, the man in the pajama jacket, hailed us.

"I say, will you go in and fuel that M.G.B. [motor gunboat]? Chap's almost dry."

"No drier than I am," the Etonian said.

We moved to within a half-mile of shore. The M.G.B., commanded by a big man with a piratical red beard, ran alongside. He began to chat, and aft we ran a hose over to the M.G.B.

The New Zealander came up. "Machine-gun bullet through the electric pump," he said. "We'll have to do it by hand."

The two captains continued talking. I leaned on the rail and sweated. The air was thick with gas fumes. I was very frightened. I thought of what would happen if we were strafed and a tracer got the gas. Foolish, of course. Imagination, a good companion on most occasions, is a bad one in battle.

Two sailors, one from the motor launch and the other from the motor gunboat, took turns pumping the gas. The pump handle moved about eighteen inches. I thought it was a damned primitive way to fuel a ship at sea.

The two captains chatted about the idiocies of the regular navy.

"Bloody two-striper says, 'And what excuse do you have for the condition of these guns?' I said, 'We've been playing about with two E-boats [German motor gunboats, heavily armed] and just made port, we didn't have time to clean them.' Then he says, very high and mighty, 'That's no excuse, this is the Navy.' What did he think *I* thought it was, the bloody P. and O. line [Pacific and Oriental, a first class service from Britain to the Far East]?"

The redhead scratched his beard and said they were all like that. "Think you can keep these things like a bloody battleship."

From the shore we heard field guns firing and occasionally the flat, never-to-be-forgotten, crack of 88s. Our captain said it sounded like big stuff: "How the hell did they get it here if the commandos knocked out the batteries?"

"Thought you knew," said the pirate. "We bumped into one of their convoys coming in. Sank the convoy all right. But they knew we were on the way. Hard on the brown jobs [soldiers], eh?"

I asked how the Canadians had done.

The red-headed captain shook his head. "Didn't have much chance. Waiting for them. Some of the tanks got in, but a lot of them bought it when they came off the landing craft. Like shooting birds let out of a bag. I heard the infantry was pretty badly chewed up."

A seaman said, "Fueling completed, sir."

We moved off. The captain said he was glad it was over. So was I.

Four British destroyers were shelling the hotels. As I watched, the buildings changed shape. The shelling dumped their upper floors on the snipers, machine-gunners, and mortar crews that had sheltered there. It was too late to help the Canadians now. The air battle went on above our heads. I have thought often that had a similar battle been staged for the same length of time in a movie, the audience would have been bored. We were not bored.

Twelve British planes fought seven German planes just above us. Even in that continuous shower of noise the sound of their machine guns and cannon fire came through. A Spitfire turned over and plunged down. Just before she hit, a figure fell from the cockpit.

Two Ju-88s came in from the sea. A fighter jumped one. I

wiped my glasses hurriedly. The fighter wore the insignia of the U.S. Army Air Force. The pilot closed the Junkers, and one began to burn.

A Messerschmitt came in very low and strafed us. We fell flat. The bullets killed a sailor and wounded two others. The seaman at the Oerlikon shouted, "I think I hit him, sir." A smudge of smoke came from the German's engine. Then the plane blazed and hit the sea.

"Good work, Jenkins," said the captain, "that's 100 Players."

"I give 20 cigarettes for a hit, 35 for each damaged and probably destroyed, and 100 when we see a plane is destroyed," the captain explained. "If this keeps up I'll have to go on the black market."

The Etonian came up to the bridge. "Cannon shell just above the waterline. We can cope. I say, Jenkins is getting bloody good with that Oerlikon."

We ran alongside a landing craft. There were eight badly wounded soldiers aboard. One man, his left arm nearly torn off by a shell splinter, died as we worked on the others. Another was delirious, talking about his farm and his horses and his wife. A bomber let go as we worked. I heard the bombs whistling down, and my stomach contracted. I looked up. Everyone paused, frozen, as when the film stops in a movie. To this day I can see the New Zealander, his face red from the sun, bending over a Canadian private, whose battle dress was dark with blood, a sailor, his jersey ridiculously white, handing the New Zealander a bandage, a Canadian, who was not badly hurt, holding a water bottle to his mouth, another looking up with very blue eyes in a brown face at the sky. Then the bombs burst, the landing craft shook, and someone said, "Christ, that was close."

We took the wounded to a destroyer. I was still very hot, my lips were dry and cracked, and I was hungry. It was about one o'clock in the afternoon.

We headed in again. As we did, the Etonian handed me an enameled mug. "Water, lemon, and whiskey," he said, "mostly whiskey. Tell me you Yanks are weaned on it."

He handed the captain a mug. The captain bowed and said, "Kiss me, Hardy," which, supposedly, were Nelson's dying words. The Etonian said, "I looks toward you."

We were looking for landing craft in trouble. Our friend in the pajama top, who, apparently, commanded the motor launches, told us to escort one landing craft coming out from Dieppe. We found it, and as we did, something went "plonk" in the water: a mortar bomb.

The wounded in the landing craft had been stunned into lethargy by their experience. A lieutenant vomited briefly. "It's this God-damned sea," he explained. I asked him what it had been like ashore.

"You may well ask," he said slowly. Then he shook his head and repeated the words with an interval between each one. "You . . . may . . . well . . . ask." A sergeant held a finger to his lips. I went off and gave my field dressings to two of the wounded. "Lieutenant's had a bad time," one said, "got knocked ass over end by a shell. Not a scratch, but, Jesus, he's shaken up.

"Christ it was horrible. We were in the second wave, see, and the bloody jerries were waiting. Fucking first wave had left them when they went in and they opened up on us. Those bastards left them there. So god-damned anxious to get into the town.

"*We* caught it. Machine guns at fifty yards and mortars *and* mines. They had road blocks to stop the tanks. The engineers tried to blow them, but no dice. One wounded guy blew a hole, and some of the tanks got through. We couldn't move. When we tried, they blew hell out of us."

He sounded American. "Worked in Detroit for a while. Wish I was there now."

The other man talked slowly. "It wasn't a question of bravery. It was just a question of whether you wanted to die moving or lie there until the mortars hit you. The officers were good. Then some shells hit the Germans and we tried to rush them. Another machine gun started up on the flank."

There was an air of hopelessness about them. But one said, "Next time, we'll use a whole bloody army." At that point "next time" seemed years and years away.

The launch left the landing craft and pulled up to another lying motionless in the sea.

"Bloke wants us to tow 'im 'ome," a sailor told me, "make a bloody fine target for the fucking Stukas, we will."

The motor launch secured to the side of the landing craft, and we started home. The sea was very choppy now, and clouds obscured the sun. As we moved slowly westward, "like a mouse escorting an elephant," the New Zealander said, two towering columns of water arose from bomb bursts ahead of us: the Luft- waffe's farewell gift.

It was the third time I had left France in defeat. We were not attacked again on the return trip. But that was little solace. It was very late when we made Newhaven. I ran into Johnny MacVane of the National Broadcasting Company.

"You're the last correspondent back," he said. "We thought you'd bought it." How had it gone? "Well," he said, it doesn't look good." We had a drink and started back for London.

The next day we saw Lord Louis Mountbatten, then head of Combined Operations and, simultaneously, a lieutenant-gen- eral, a vice-admiral and an air vice-marshal. It was his first major operation, and it had been a disaster.

No one could ever question Mountbatten's courage. He was, a Royal Navy captain told me, "the best fellow you can think of to get you out of a scrape and the surest to get you into one." That day he was shaken but honest. He did not try to hide the extent of the failure. He did say that some "useful" lessons had been learned. He did not take the distant attitude toward casual- ties that some senior officers adopt as, I have always believed, a mental shield against thinking about the consequences of their orders to the men who serve.

Walking back to the office, my basic optimism fought mis- givings. The Russians were reeling under new German blows. The news from Africa was bad. And, when I went into the Associated Press, Cliff Daniell said, "Did you know there were some of our Rangers with the commandos?" I said I did not.

"Well, some damned fool of a P.R.O. [Public Relations Offi- cer] has given the impression that they fought the whole battle and the Canadians and British weren't good enough. This sure is a screwed up war. Well, write what you have."

Later, when I had written all I had, I went to the Connaught for dinner. We were joined by Alan Kirk, who had been U.S. Naval Attaché early in the war and had now returned. He played a distinguished part on D-day as the United States naval com- mander and, later, was an equally distinguished ambassador in the Soviet Union and Belgium. We sat and talked about the war and drank the last of the Connaught's celebrated bock. It was a good dinner, and by the time we left I had forgotten about the three Canadians in the landing craft except for the one who screamed as the seas shook the ship and his shattered leg.

My fortunes took a turn for the better that summer. Ray Daniell asked me to join the London staff of *The New York Times*. It did not take me long to decide. *The Times* did not enjoy the solitary eminence that it does now; London was full of able correspondents from the *New York Herald-Tribune,* the *Chicago Daily News,* and half a dozen other newspapers. But the decisive factor was Ray himself. He was brusque, impatient, and contentious. Beneath lay a singular sweetness of character. Besides, taking him in all aspects of his professional life, he was the best reporter I knew. If I were to continue to learn, Ray would teach. I have never been sorry that I joined *The Times*. I have often been sorry that it has not given me the opportunity to use my abilities at full stretch.

I had eight weeks in London. Again, the war had entered one of those periods of deceptive calm. I had on *The Times* more leisure than on the Associated Press. I got away for weekends. I made more money and paid off debts. I learned my profession from Ray. I covered the Allied bombardment of Germany, then finally getting under way.

One evening Ray called me into his office.

"There's a big landing coming," he said, "American and British. I can't tell you where it is, I don't know myself. But I've named you to be one of *The Times* correspondents. All I can tell you is get plenty of warm clothes."

The next day I stocked up on long underwear, which I had not worn since boyhood, and British battle dress. At that time this rather unattractive uniform was by far the most practical military dress yet devised. I could have saved myself time and *The New York Times* money, though, for the expedition was "Torch," the Anglo-American descent on French North Africa at Casablanca in Morocco and at Oran and Algiers in Algeria.

I suppose some German agents, learning that war correspondents were buying stocks of heavy clothing, took the bait and advised their masters that the Allies were preparing for an attack on Norway. They were often fooled by less tangible reports. At any rate, the long underwear and the battle dress came in uncommonly handy the next winter. For North Africa, whatever it is in spring, summer, and fall, can be damned cold in winter.

On the day I was due to leave I had a long lunch at the Connaught. I was always leaving for some place. It no longer seemed odd to look around a well-appointed restaurant and think that in a few hours I would be in a ship or a plane or a truck on my way to war.

It was one of those golden days London sometimes gives you in autumn. I wondered idly when I would see the old place again. The bomb damage was still all too visible. People seemed more strained than they had been a year earlier or even under the bombing. They still had that marvelous, gay bravado, though. When I came out the door in uniform, the taxi driver said, "Well, mate, where to? Egypt, India, or bloody France? I'll take yer."

CHAPTER 5

MILITARY VICTORY AND POLITICAL FUMBLING IN NORTH AFRICA

1943

> It is no doubt a good thing to conquer
> on the field of battle, but it needs
> greater wisdom and greater skill to
> make use of victory.
>
> Polybius

I

The convoy passed the Straits of Gibraltar at night. For more than a week we had sailed westward, to confuse German U-boats and scouting aircraft. Then the long column of ships turned eastward toward the Mediterranean, the African coast, and the opening of a new front in French North Africa. The wind blew from Africa, and I caught the sickly-sweet, heavy breath of the continent. A young captain talked interminably, criticizing the singing of some tenor at the Met. In the morning we turned north, and the mountains of Spain, raw and broken, stood stark off port.

The *U.S.S. Samuel Chase* carried the First Battalion, 39th Regiment, 9th Division. The battalion's job was to land at An-Taya, a village east of Algiers and the easternmost point of the invasion, march to and take from the French the airfield at Maison Blanche so that Spitfires of the R.A.F. from Gibraltar could land there and provide air cover.

Life aboard the *Chase*, a converted passenger ship of the

Grace Line, was pleasant. The convoy or, at least, our section had proceeded unmolested. The battalion was better trained than those I had seen in Iceland and strikingly willing to learn. They had stopped in Scotland to maneuver with two Highland battalions, and the experience had been salutary. They had learned that there were other infantry as tough, as smart, and as durable.

The enemy's first strike came at dawn twenty-four hours before the landing. A German torpedo bomber from God knows where came down the column of transports and put a torpedo into the *U.S.S. Thomas Stone,* carrying another battalion of the 9th. The *Stone* stayed afloat, and the battalion got off in landing craft and headed for Algiers. This was nothing to what happened that evening.

By then the transports were closer to the African coast although still out of sight of land. North lay Force X of the Royal Navy, battleships and carriers, cruisers and destroyers, *Rodney, Nelson, Renown*—names awakening memories of battles long ago.

In the dying sun the ships in their camouflage slipped into the background of the blue-gray sea. For a few moments one could see them clearly—great islands of power moving inexorably into the twilight.

Italian and German bombers flew in from the darkening east. The northern horizon twinkled as hundreds of antiaircraft guns went into action. Across the miles of water the sound of guns was muted and mixed into a steady roll. A Royal Navy lieutenant shouted that the British carriers had sent up fighters. We saw a great, orange spasm of flame ahead of the first carrier. Gouts of water, tiny at that distance, rose around the battleships and the carriers. Night fell, and we could see only gun flashes.

The Axis had committed a tactical error. The planes had attacked the battle fleet and had been badly shot up. The transports should have been their target. Losses to the escorts of Force X would not have diverted the landing; sinkings on a large scale among the transports would have done so. The *Chase* plowed on through calm seas. The wind from Africa blew strongly as though in welcome.

In the early morning gun flashes and searchlights showed faces taut and intense. Landing craft nuzzled against the side of the

Chase. In ours, sitting aft, I could see rows of steel helmets and rifle muzzles ahead. The transport grew smaller in the distance. The coastline loomed black before us. Above, the African stars were bright. There is a bluff above the beach at An-Taya, and on it stood a two-story building of white stone, our landmark. I thought of other landings, Dieppe mostly, and hoped to God that the information was correct, that this would be an unopposed landing.

A shadow emerged from the shadow of the bluff: a major of French artillery.

"You gentlemen are late," he said.

In the village was a small square surrounded by white houses and palms. Two Frenchmen stood watching as the company formed and marched off. Far from the west we heard the tap-tap-tap of a machine gun. The column flowed through the village and onto the road toward the airfield. I hitched a ride in a jeep and followed as far as Rouiba.

That first morning in an invaded country: what do you remember? Chiefly the personal things: the wet uniform, the eyes dry from lack of sleep, the sharpness of every sight and sound. Rouiba's town square was filled with people, many still in night clothes. Some called to the Americans and laughed happily. Others stood silent. A man pushed a bottle of cognac into my hand. We went on to the airfield.

Maison Blanche was taken without a shot. If God does look after fools, drunkards, and the United States, He did well by us that day. The infantry filtered into the fields around the airfield. A light machine gun chattered, coughed, and was silent. Then the French surrendered.

The French troops, slovenly as always, clustered around the Americans. Their officers glared. Slowly the mists that had shrouded the airfield cleared, and we saw rows of Dewoitine fighters on the apron. Then, from above, the high, shrill keening of a Spitfire. It landed perfectly, and a blond, slim pilot clambered out. He asked for a cigarette, got one, and said the whole business had been a piece of cake. We watched while the other planes of the squadron came in. When the Germans came over to bomb the Allied shipping, that squadron destroyed eight of twenty Nazi planes before the awed eyes of thousands of French and Arabs watching the battle above their city.

The battle for Algiers had only begun. Some French troops, led by officers who were pro-Vichy or, perhaps, fanatically nationalist, fought on at Fort de l'Est and Fort de l'Eau. The forts were squat, thick, and gray. The Americans had only heavy machine guns and mortars to support the attack, and they did not get far. Colonel Ben W. Caffey, commanding the battalion, called for naval support. Two cruisers left Force X.

From that distance, lying in the rank and heavy undergrowth, the cruisers seemed to approach deliberately, their mottled camouflage bold against the blue background of the Mediterranean. Salvos rippled from turret to turret. The sound hit us, and chickens in a farmyard scattered and pigeons rose and circled across the sky. But the shelling was not enough. When the Americans went forward again, the machine guns resumed their chatter.

When it was quiet, I walked toward the American positions. Something popped from the fort, and I scrambled into a ditch where two soldiers crouched beside a machine gun. A jeep came down the road, and the driver shouted that some of the self-propelled 75's had landed and would soon be there. When they came, the cruisers resumed their shelling and fighter bombers from Maison Blanche hammered the forts. The French marines came out. They had fought very well. Our people told them so. The French were regulars, surly, unimpressed.

The battle for Algiers rested on a razor's edge that night. In Rouiba the French didn't know it. The bar of the hotel was crowded, and there were toasts to the Americans, to the British, and to the Marshal. Pétain's dignified, stupid face with its watery eyes looked out from a portrait above the bar. The French seemed content. The Americans and the British who, as everyone knew, were foolishly generous, were here. The grasping Germans and Italians were gone.

Algiers fell the next day. In the morning the Americans and British came ashore. They were not in great numbers. But they looked impressive. The commandos made an impact on the French. They wore American flags sewn to the shoulders of their battle dress. The idea, proven wrong at Oran and in Morocco, was that the French wouldn't fire on Americans. I asked a commando officer if his men minded wearing an alien flag.

"They don't give a bugger," he said, "if it saves lives, they'll wear the bloody Chinese flag."

I had envisaged entering Algiers with long columns of troops and tanks. Two or three of us went in by trolley. By late afternoon I found myself at the Hotel Aletti confronted by Bill Stoneman of the *Chicago Daily News*. He was standing guard over a laundry basket full of Scotch, gin, brandy, and vermouth. He had, he said virtuously, found these goodies being taken from the hotel by a newsreel photographer who had discovered them in the suites formerly occupied by the German and Italian Armistice Commissions. Stoneman had warned the photographer that he was in imminent danger of being shot for looting, so the photographer fled. We took the loot, selected a suite, and settled down to write. Around us the Americans and British poured into the city. There was no firing. Admiral Darlan had made his deal with the Allies, and the North African French, as far as Darlan's writ ran, were with the Allies. Or so they said.

Algeria and Morocco were not Gaullist then. Nor did they ever become so, except nominally, during the war. The French in those countries were intolerant bourgeois, extremely reactionary. Darlan knew this. But Darlan was an opportunist. He had double-crossed the British in 1940. He double-crossed the Germans now.

General Dwight D. Eisenhower was criticized for making a deal with Darlan. Eisenhower spoke no more than the truth when he said that he had agreed to appoint Darlan French political and military commander in chief because he was the only officer in French North Africa who could persuade the French forces to stop fighting. And although the fighting had been on a small scale at Algiers, it had been heavy at Oran and in Morocco.

Eisenhower's error was not the deal with Darlan. The mistake was the failure of the Allies to recognize that the French officials, businessmen, and farmers, with whom they dealt in North Africa, were basically opposed to the ideals for which the Americans and British supposedly were fighting. The French were ready now to give oral support to the Allies. Why not? Alamein had been fought and won. The Germans had been ensnared at Stalingrad. Take to the winning side. But don't accept this talk about democracy. So the Allies blundered along, supporting General Giraud and closing their eyes to the near-fascist totalitarianism that still dominated French North Africa under the Stars and Stripes and the Union Jack.

General Mark Wayne Clark was Eisenhower's deputy in Algiers. He was arranging cooperation between Giraud and Darlan, an arrangement complicated by Giraud's belief that he, as a veteran, but not particularly successful, French general should be given command of all the Allied forces. We saw Clark one morning at the Hotel St. George, then and later the Allied Headquarters.

Of the many soldiers I have known only two—Clark and Field Marshal Alexander—physically fitted the popular conception of a general. Alexander, of course, was a general of the first magnitude: modest, brave, subtle, generous, discerning, and decisive in action.

I felt almost sorry for Clark. Here he was, natty in his boots and breeches, and miles out of his depth. He was so anxious to prove that everything had been smoothed over, and he was so obviously confused and appalled by the intricacies of French politics. He clearly did not like or understand the French. He had, he said, with the grin of a comedian telling his best joke, sent a message to General Eisenhower that the "Yebsobs" had come to terms. This, he explained with a smirk, was a West Point term for "yellow-bellied sons of bitches."

Algiers lapsed into the minor excitements of a garrison city. The British First Army had landed and was pushing east into Tunisia, where the Germans had landed powerful forces. The war lay to the east, and one morning I started for Tunisia.

In the Atlas mountains the R.A.F. station wagon went dead. I rode into Bougie in a truck filled with gasoline tins. In the morning five ships lay sunk or disabled in the inner harbor. Outside were the burned-out remains of two more.

A colonel of the Buffs, the Royal East Kent Regiment, offered me a lift on one of his trucks. The back of the truck was filled with cases of mortar bombs and machine-gun bullets. I lay looking out the back, hoping no stray German raider would strafe the trucks, *my* truck. The road is beautiful, running between the Mediterranean, which was whipped that day to fury by a gale, and a wall of cliffs. We slept the night on the dusty stone floor of a cork factory in Djidelli.

The convoy began to climb next day. It was cold in the mountains. Outside Phillipeville we halted. There were oranges on the trees in a grove on our right. The Buffs got out and ate them. A sergeant said it was the first orange he had tasted since he had gone to France in 1939. We shared a drink and stood shivering in the twilight. To the east, west, and south the mountains loomed. Phillipeville was a white smudge on the horizon. Behind us labored the remainder of the convoy: Bren gun carriers, anti-tank guns, 25-pounders.

The Buffs dropped me the next morning twelve miles from the port of Bone. It had been bombed, and there were few civilians about. Walking through its empty streets, Bone reminded me of the towns in Belgium and France in 1940 when the Germans were on the move. This time, I kept telling myself, we are on the move. I found a room in the Grand Hotel de Nice and waited for my rendezvous with Bill Stoneman and Bill King of the Associated Press. They arrived next day, having nursed an ancient Ford over the mountains. We picked up Ned Russell of the United Press, and started for the Medjerda Valley in Tunisia where everyone said there was heavy fighting.

Souk-el-Arba was the temporary headquarters of a French artillery battery that had come out of Tunis although the French commander had ordered them to stay and help the incoming Germans. We ate sardines and hard-boiled eggs, chicken, beans, and lamb, and drank deep of Tunisian wine. While we ate, three German bombers attacked the nearby airfield. No one turned a hair, although three officers did go out to watch. The colonel said that nothing in war was as important as eating well when it was possible.

All that afternoon we drove into Tunisia. A long hill took us into Teboursok. Below lay a long valley, the floor brown except for the shiny green of olive groves. In the valley we met a patrol of Spahis. Later a platoon of British. They advised us to head for Beja. They thought the town had been taken that morning by British parachute troops.

We set out for Beja. It was raining heavily, and we could hear guns in the hills. We climbed out of the Medjerda valley, now completely lost. Finally we saw a battered signpost marked "Thibar." We turned that way.

Thibar was to become the headquarters for the correspondents in Tunisia for the next seven months. The village's one street runs along a hog back that rises from the valley where it turns north near Beja. One end of the street trails off into wheatfields. The other enters the courtyard of the monastery of the White Brothers of St. Joseph who came to Tunisia in the 'eighties as missionaries. The houses are of stucco painted white or pink. The people are simple and good. We went into the tiny hotel that night and were made welcome. We sat by a fire and ate well. The rain beat on the windows. Often we heard guns.

A quarter of a century later I went back to Thibar. There is an agricultural college where the prisoners-of-war camp stood, and the inn is a hostel for girls at a domestic-science college. The quiet sunlight was the same but nothing else. Too many ghosts. You remember Charlie Wertenbaker, Randolph Churchill, Evelyn Montague, Arthur Pilkington, all the good men gone. I got into the car and drove to Tunis. You never really go back.

In the morning it was clear, and an Arab boy said there were many soldiers on the road into the valley. Yes, they were singing. We knew this must be the British 78th Division. As we left, a cannonade began in the hills. The road to war had ended at Thibar.

The campaign in Tunisia remains more vivid in my memory than other, greater, battles. I asked Ernest Hemingway why this should be, one winter's night in Paris when the war was won. He said that everyone cherishes one episode of a war in his mind and that this remains so clear in memory that all others, often more important, seem secondary. I find that I can recall those next weeks in Tunisia as though they had occurred last week and that the sound of men's voices, the smell of dust and decay when we were bombed in Tebourba, the taste of fear as I dove to escape a strafing German plane, are with me forever.

Nothing is worse than strafing when you are alone and unarmed. A German caught us once on one of the hills around Beja. You lie face down in mud and listen. The machine guns beat the air. The ricocheting bullets sing off the road. This was only one car. The Germans attacked it twice. When they came the second time, I rolled to the other side of the ditch. I wondered what would happen if I met a snake.

Medjez-el-Bab was the Allied objective. We slept the night before the attack in a barnyard just off the road and started on foot in the early morning. The farm was being taken over as headquarters for the British 78th Division and a major peremptorily ordered us out; apparently he needed our straw.

The moon set, and in our faces was the glare of a new day. The eastern hills were black against the dawn. Somewhere ahead a British 55-pounder opened fire. We moved out into the valley and the war. That day it was like this:

I lay in a foxhole with British infantrymen, looking down the road to Medjez. They had accounted for German patrol that morning with a Bren gun and their rifles. The Germans, they said wonderingly, had come on "like bloody Guards on fucking parade." As they talked, German fighters came over and strafed. One dropped an anti-personnel bomb, and we could hear someone crying in the next trench. . . .

Nick Stoma, a corporal from Brooklyn, gave me a cup of strong black coffee. His American antitank company had been engaged for a day. They were tired but confident. They respected Germans and "the god-damned limeys" who had gone in to clear out two troublesome machine-gun positions. . . .

In the late afternoon a column of General Grant tanks stood on the road waiting to get into Medjez. Their shells were bursting in the town, and in the twilight the British infantry went in and took the place. But Longstop Hill, the commanding ridge beyond, was untaken. It did not fall for another five months.

Next day the little Allied army poured down the road out of Medjez-el-Bab toward Tebourba. Tebourba was dusty and empty. Life existed only in the Hotel de France facing the square. Three Italian laborers had taken it over. The proprietor had left them in charge, and would we not have some brandy? We went out into the town just in time for an attack by Ju-88s. No Allied fighters were visible. That day was the climax of the first Allied attack to take Tunis.

We slept in the courtyard of a farm. The Northamptonshire Regiment and the Hampshire Regiment were in line. The American tanks had suffered badly. So had the British infantry. An American battery was in action a mile or so away. In the afternoon a sergeant drove up in a jeep. "Drag ass outa here," he shouted, "there's thirty German tanks comin' this way."

The rest of the day was very bad. As we left the battery there was the flat, heavy blast of a 25-pounder and then a long burst of machine-gun fire. Men of the West Surrey regiment were moving into line with Brens, mortars, and antitank rifles. In the sudden silence you could heard the clipped, precise voices of officers and the roars of noncoms.

Another long burst of machine-gun fire. We dropped into a ditch and made our way around the town. It was four in the afternoon. I was wet with sweat. A German tank stood eighty yards away on the road into the town. The crew paid no attention to us. The guns started again, and we heard the crack of grenades. The Germans must have been very close.

There was a British observation post on a hillside. Tebourba lay on our right, and a second wave of German tanks moved across the plain toward the town to reinforce those already fighting there. The tanks were dusty gray-brown against the brown of the fields, the dirty white of the roads, and the green of the olive groves. Shells from the British 25-pounders and 12-pounders, antitank guns, fell among the tanks. I could not see any hits. When the tanks fired, there a gray wreath of smoke, almost like a smoke ring. Night fell, and we lost sight of the tanks. On the way back to the farm we were shelled by British tanks.

The next day the tanks fought on the plain in back of Tebourba. We got, we thought, five of theirs and lost three of ours. The Americans were using Grants; the British, Crusaders. I started back toward the farm. But the one I headed for, which I found later was not the right one, was suddenly attacked by six Stukas. The ground jumped. Earth and debris shot skyward. But the farm was still there.

Mining was not extensive in that part of Tunisia then. I made my way across country to a group of farm buildings held by three 25-pounders and a 6-pounder antitank gun and their crews. German tanks appeared on the crest of a hill to the left of the farm. They swung away, then turned back. The captain, a little fellow with highly polished boots and a crease in the trousers of his battle dress, told the crews to fire at six hundred yards.

The Germans mixed their cannon fire with machine-gun bursts. They got one or two gunners each time. Soon the guns were being served short-handed. There was a dead man in front of one gun. Each time bullets hit the body, the body jumped. The action lasted seventeen minutes by the captain's watch. To me it had been an hour. There were five tanks burning across the valley.

"We had another one of the bastards," a gunner said, "Knocked his tracks off and 'e 'ad to stop. Two of them 'opped out and fixed it while we wus firing. Takes a bit of doing, that," he added reflectively.

I got back on the road and hitched a ride behind a courier on a motorcycle. We were machine-gunned and lay in a ditch. I spent a lot of time in Tunisian ditches. When the fire lifted, I reached a British command post.

While I scanned a map, a Grant tank towing a half-track from a tank destroyer company came down the road. The 75 on the tank had been knocked out. The half-track had a shell fragment through the engine. A British major came up.

"Look here," he said to the sergeant commanding the tank, "I'm taking some chaps, gunners, engineers, and odds and sods around to catch these buggers on the flank. Will you give us five minutes' start and then start down the road? You'll draw a bit of their fire but we'll winkle them out before they can really get to you."

The sergeant said, hell yes, he'd be glad to; Allied cooperation.

The tank came back, and I clambered into the back of the halftrack. It ran through some German fire on the way back, but there was no great damage. Henry Sobelman, a soldier from the Bronx, slapped me on the leg. "Couldn't hit the ground with their hats, these bastards."

Outside Medjez the tank and the half-track turned into a repair depot. I started on foot for the division's headquarters where I could write and perhaps get a story off to Algiers by courier.

A blue Chevrolet covered with dust stopped in the road. The driver was Darryl Zanuck, then a colonel in the Signal Corps. I had met him that summer in London. He was making a movie about the campaign. Zanuck, smoking a fat cigar, was cheerful.

He was tired, but he was having a wonderful time. He waved his cigar largely in the direction of Oued Zarga. "Little bombing up the road," he said. "It's over now. You want a lift?"

"We've had a hell of a time, a hell of a time," he said. "Got some great shots of those dive bombers. Wish I had more equipment. I'd make a picture they'd never forget."

At headquarters it was quiet. The staff officers were clean and rested. A French liaison officer, very smart in riding breeches, shining boots, and the light-blue kepi of the cavalry, sipped a gin and lime. He didn't offer me a drink but asked me how things went at the front. I said they didn't go at all. He shrugged his shoulders.

The French in Tunisia were not de Gaulle's Free French but regulars of the colonial army. They had come over to our side at Darlan's command. Most of them disliked the British, and they held Americans in arrogant contempt.

In another room I met a British major I knew and told him what I thought of the Frenchman who hadn't the decency to offer me a drink. He led me to a mirror, and I understood the Frenchman's coolness. I got my drink and stood with the major in the sunlight in the barnyard. Now, at noon, it was hot, and the dust from the road was in my throat, nose, and eyes.

That was the way it was when the Allies made the first try for Tunis. They tried again on Christmas Eve, but the Germans and the mud were too much. The Americans and the British lost a lot of good men. Bill and I drove back to Thibar in the early morning of Christmas Day. At dinner in the home of a friendly farmer we heard that Darlan had been shot. Early in January 1943 I drove back to Algiers. The soldiers said there would be no new offensives until spring.

The Allied reverses in late 1942 were dreadfully serious, then. Had the Allies broken through, however, they would have taken only ten or fifteen thousand prisoners and would have been too few themselves to have moved against Sicily. In the interval between the first battles and the final offensive in May 1943 Hitler poured thousands more troops into Tunisia. Of these approximately three hundred and fifty thousand were killed, wounded, or taken prisoner in the victories of April and May 1943. A greater triumph grew out of the initial setbacks.

II

Algiers in January 1943; gray skies, gray streets, gray buildings, cold wet nights. This dull city was the stage for the first clash in the long contest over occupation policy that continued in Italy, France, and occupied Germany and that was not to end until the late 'forties.

The point of this contest, to generalize on so complicated an issue, was this: Should American and British occupation policy retain and support those politicians, officers, and officials who could run the government services and the industrial structures of the occupied countries, in the knowledge that most, if not all, of them had been enemies, had collaborated with the Axis powers, and might still, in their inner hearts, wish them well? Or should the occupying powers eliminate them and turn government and industry over to those who swore so fervently they were loyal to the Allies and bitter opponents of the late régime?

The cast of characters in Algiers included Generals Eisenhower, Giraud, de Gaulle, and Bedell Smith, Ambassador Robert D. Murphy of the United States, Minister of State Harold Macmillan of Britain, a collection of Vichy appointees now protesting their loyalty to the Allies, a large number of Frenchmen who, if not members of the Communist Party, were certainly far to the left of anyone in the Allied camp, a small group of dedicated Gaullists, and sundry intelligence officers of all the parties concerned. The noises off stage were provided by such disparate characters as Franklin D. Roosevelt, Winston Churchill, their cabinets, the leaders of the left in Britain and the United States and, to add a touch of comedy, the Comte de Paris, pretender to the nonexistent French throne, who thought he saw an opportunity to insert himself into the making of the new France. He was wrong.

At one time or another I came in contact with these people. It was instructive. In addition to the then President and Prime Minister, the cast included future Presidents of the United States and France, a future Prime Minister of the United Kingdom, and others who have left their mark, for good or ill, on the history of our times.

With Darlan's death General Giraud had taken his place as the Frenchman recognized by the Allies as the leader of French

North Africa, meaning in this context Algeria, Morocco, and Tunisia. He was a lion-hearted, empty-headed old man. But he had one incontestable advantage in the struggle for power that was now opening with the Gaullists. Algiers and Algeria and, to an even greater extent, Morocco were pro–Pétain, anti–de Gaulle, and indifferent or hostile to the Allies. There were naturally some fervent patriots, including some Communists, who hated the Axis. But the Establishment—and the Establishment is more important in a colonial society than elsewhere—strongly supported Pétain.

This position was expressed by continued discrimination against the North African Jews. Philip Guedella, that gifted, if florid, historian told me with tears in his eyes one night that he was ashamed of the uniform he was wearing—he was in the R.A.F. at the time—because his government winked at the continued repression of "my poor coreligionists."

Officials in Algiers and Rabat, the Moroccan capital, continued to support the Marshal in private, whatever they said in public. General Auguste Nogués, the Resident General in Morocco, told a friend, a friend he apparently lost, that the Americans were "simpletons" and that he could handle them and their silly ideas about democracy and de Gaulle. It is interesting to think that in those days liberal American opinion considered de Gaulle a democrat, a Wilsonian from St. Cyr.

Giraud clearly did not know what the row was all about. When we questioned him, at a news conference he was foolish enough to hold, it was quite clear that this honorable old soldier had only one aim, to defeat the Germans. This was laudable but, in the situation, insufficient. He made light of the imprisonment of Gaullists, Jews, and Communists, then incarcerated in a camp in the Sahara where conditions were so bad that the prisoners killed and ate snakes. He made it only too clear that he considered all the opposition Communist and couldn't understand what the reporters were getting at. In any case, such matters were better left to the French. He was brave, he was single-minded, but he was not up to the job. In retrospect it is easy enough to see why Roosevelt supported him. To the White House and to Secretary of State Cordell Hull this simple soldier was preferable to the imperious, devious de Gaulle.

Moreover, political reporting to the State Department at that time said, quite accurately, that Giraud and his High Commission and Imperial Council had the support of the North African French. The question was whether they had the support of the Resistance in France. As General Walter Bedell Smith, Eisenhower's Chief of Staff, later admitted, the support of the North African French was all well enough for the moment, but the Germans would have to be driven from France, and when that campaign opened, the support of the Resistance would be important. We will meet Bedell Smith later. At this point in the war Smith displayed one of the more balanced approaches to the problem among the American generals.

The importance of the French Resistance in the future was modified, to some extent, by another consideration, the degree of Communist control of the movement. I am not concerned here with the effectiveness of the Resistance in France. But in early 1943 reports out of France indicated that the Resistance, even when it was most violently pro-Gaullist, had strong Communist tendencies and that some groups—and these were among the most effective—were entirely Communist. The Allies did not intend to liberate Europe for the benefit of international Communism.

The Gaullists in Algiers were a minority—active, intelligent, forceful, but still a minority, living under constant police surveillance. They knew, however, that there were powerful forces in London and, less powerful but still vocal, groups in the United States supporting their leader and their cause. Their best card was not the personality of Charles de Gaulle nor his achievements as the leader of Fighting France, which were minor, but the character of the men Giraud summoned to his side to rule North Africa and to offer a facsimile of the future France. They were a sad lot.

For example, there was Marcel Peyrouton, who had been removed from government office by Pierre Laval, a circumstance that commended him to the Allied High Command because it had learned that Laval was bad, as indeed he was. Peyrouton, a gross reactionary, hated by the Arabs, replaced Yves Chatel as Governor General of Algeria. The pouches under his eyes would have held at least a pipeful of tobacco. Noguès in Morocco, sly,

highly intelligent, was out of the same stable. They were, of
course, men who knew how to make French North Africa run.
That was their temporary salvation.

The atmosphere in Algiers grew steadily more reactionary.
Youth groups, organized under the Pétain régime, marched
through the streets, singing songs of praise for the Marshal. The
opposition, meaning the Gaullists, met reporters in shabby
hotels. Some were arrested for "complicity" in Darlan's assassination. Those who, like myself, believed the war was not being
fought to restore the same old, corrupt gang to power in France
were disheartened. I could understand the arguments against
de Gaulle. But I had a visceral feeling they were wrong.

The one ray of light to pierce this murky situation was provided by a middle-aged, then almost unknown, British politician.
His name was Harold Macmillan, and he talked to us one afternoon. Macmillan, tall, elegant and eloquent, had not at that
time perfected the casual manner with which he later treated the
most important matters of state. That afternoon he said roundly
that Britain had not gone to war, as indeed she had not, to per-
petuate the fascist mentality. The imprisonment of Gaullists and
others was an abomination. It should and would be ended.
France was a partner in the war and, as such, would have to
subscribe to the common goals of the Allies. Much more of the
same, tough, uncompromising antifascism. When we left the
conference, a friend whispered, "Why in hell haven't we heard
that from the St. George?"—that is, from Allied Force Headquarters. Macmillan had reminded us that the war still had a
moral element.

Those were fascinating, busy days. For a correspondent there
were always three or four stories: the political struggle in Algiers, the military situation in Tunisia, which had to be "rounded
up" and explained, the air and naval offensive against Italy now
gathering strength as the North African bases came into use, and
the smaller events of life in Algiers, such as the invasion of the
Casbah by Red Cross girls bearing powdered milk (the Arab
women were extremely suspicious of the milk, and they didn't
think much of the girls, either).

I worked ten to fourteen hours a day. It was not hard to do so.
It was a hell of a story. There was also a psychological factor.
Any war correspondent knows how infinitely lucky he is to be

in his job and not in a rifle company. He understands, if he is worth his salt, that it is incumbent on him to give his best as a sort of thanks offering. There were good correspondents in North Africa in those days. John Lardner, Charlie Collingwood, Bill Stoneman, Ed Beattie, John Macvane, to name only a few of the Americans. Reading the old papers I think that they laid down a report superior to anything offered American readers earlier in the war and, in some respects, better than anything that has been done since.

In that sort of life there is very little time for relaxation. My warmest memory is of a dingy room in the Regina Hotel, headquarters of the British Public Relations office. The men who presided were not the smooth, eye-on-the-main-chance public-affairs officers of the later years of the war. John ("Little Mac") Maccormack, "Noah" Flood, and Ted Billett were what they called "serving soldiers," barred by age or infirmity from playing what they considered their proper part of fighting the enemy.

In that room at about six each evening they dispensed liquor and wisdom in equal parts. Often it was cold and rainy outside. Inside there was a snug homeliness. We sat and talked and learned.

"You had better keep your eye on southern Tunisia," Little Mac (he was just over five feet in height) advised one night. "The brass hats may think that they've got the jerries bottled up, but I doubt it. If Rommel comes as far west as southern Tunisia he'll turn around and give your [the American] troops a hell of a knock."

Mac was a splendid raconteur. He had enlisted in the Royal Horse Artillery before the first war, fought through it, been commissioned in the field, and won a Military Cross. One night I told him that it had been very rough in Tunisia in November. He was an Ulsterman with that breed's tricks of speech.

"Aye, war can be rough. I mind now in 1914, or was it 1915, I had come to a corps headquarters with my battery commander. I was waiting for him to come out of a meeting when a chap I knew from the (Connaught) Rangers said, 'Come in and have a bite, Mac.' So I went in, and a bloody great German shell burst in the courtyard, killing the horses and making me spill my stew.

"Another shell fell on the headquarters, 'twas a chateau but a bit shabby, like some houses you see in what they call the Republic of Ireland—Republic be damned—and then a galloper comes pelting in from one of our batteries.

" 'We're firing at the Prussian Guard over open sights,' he shouts. The generals come out on the steps of the chateau. One of them was Haig, looking like he'd just come off guard at Buckingham Palace. They start for their horses, which are wild with fear at the shelling, when a major rides in. One arm is useless, and he has a bandage on his head.

" 'It's all right,' he hollers, 'Fitz-Clarence has restored the line.' It was the end of October in '14, I think. So don't get the idea that things aren't tough in all wars. Someone very high up told me once that if Fitz-Clarence—and a wild, dashing soldier he was, too—hadn't restored the line, it would have been all up with us. But, of course, a soldier never knows at the time."

Suddenly we were hauled out of the Algiers story. The public-relations officers rounded us up, put us on a C-47, and told us nothing. We flew east, taking a few shells from the anti-aircraft batteries in Spanish Morocco—they killed a Canadian broadcaster in another plane—and we landed in Casablanca, filled with the rear echelons of the American army and buzzing with rumor. Bob Murphy, the State Department representative at Eisenhower's headquarters, took some of us to dinner, and we learned finally why we had travelled across Africa. Churchill and Roosevelt were to meet outside Casablanca. We ate young wild boar and drank claret, elated at the prospect of a major story.

The political situation in Algeria was bad, but there were faint signs of improvement. In Morocco the situation was odious and, apparently, hopeless. General George S. Patton, Jr.—Hemingway called him "a lucky Custer"—had succumbed to the Vichyites. His ego, inflated by a victory over the French, was flattered by the attention paid him by General Nogués.

As the war progressed, Patton demonstrated certain military abilities and, in some situations, considerable strategic insight. He was a babe in politics, easy game for clever men like Nogués.

As a result of Patton's support Nogués and his followers continued to rule Morocco much as they had before the American landing. The French who had prayed and worked for the landing found themselves suspect, in some cases imprisoned. They saw the U.S. Army support officials they knew to be traitors to

France and the Allied cause. They watched Patton and other officers mingle with collaborators and Vichyites.

Patton's support enabled Nogués and his henchmen to stifle the Republicans, usually shopkeepers, and small independent farmers on behalf of the Establishment which, in Morocco as in Algeria, included the Army, the civil service, the Church, the rich landowners, and the industrialists. In Morocco, as in Algeria, the Establishment cried "Communism" to defend repression. Even then some of its members regarded the occupation as a passing phase, and a Pétainist official instructed his followers, "Remain loyal to the Marshal and the true government, and await the day of liberation."

Supporters of the Allies who were indiscreet enough to let their feelings known were detained in concentration camps. The largest was at Al-Ayasha, five miles from Casablanca. Prisoners there could see the Stars and Stripes flying over American installations.

The correspondents' part in the Casablanca Conference was limited to a news conference held by the President and Prime Minister after their discussions had been concluded. The conference was unexciting until, midway through his remarks, Roosevelt introduced the phrase "unconditional surrender." This, he said, was to govern the Allied governments in their reactions to any suit for peace by the Axis powers, individually or separately.

The phrase was damned by some and praised by others. Deep thinkers in New York, Washington, and London considered that it would only make the Germans fight harder, and, in fact, Dr. Goebbels did make much out of it in internal propaganda. Unconditional surrender, Allied critics said, would blight any chance of resistance in Germany to Hitler, although, as the bomb plot of June 1944 demonstrated, it did not.

The President, when he made the statement, gave no sign that he regarded unconditional surrender as a matter of great moment affecting grave issues. In his manner was the genial glow of a politician who has just produced an ear-catching slogan. Mr. Churchill soon took up the burden of the conference, picturing "this sombre and repulsive panorama" of the war. He did not look particularly pleased with the President's phrase. But he was, he said, the President's "ardent lieutenant."

Twelve years later, sitting in the Cabinet Room of 10 Downing Street, Churchill, again Prime Minister, referred to that afternoon at Casablanca.

"Did I look surprised?" he asked. "Well, I was, most certainly. It had not been discussed between us. There were obvious arguments for and against it. It was the sort of pronouncement that should be discussed at length with every political and military advantage and disadvantage weighed and every repercussion scrutinized. But, he was a great man."

Casablanca produced one of the great Churchill stories. As Harry Hopkins told it, General de Gaulle there met the President for the first time. De Gaulle gave Roosevelt the full treatment: he was the only man who commanded French loyalties, the Free French could save France. Then he saluted and strode from the room.

Enter Churchill, chewing on a cigar.

"Well, Mr. President, what'd you make of him?"

"Why, Winston, he really does think he's Joan of Arc, doesn't he?"

"Yes. And my bloody bishops won't let me burn him."

The President and Prime Minister spent much of their time trying to persuade de Gaulle and Giraud to cooperate. In fact, Roosevelt said at the news conference, they had been "brought together."

This was true only in a physical sense. The two generals, smiling weakly, shook hands for the benefit of the photographers. Subsequent events proved that they remained worlds apart politically.

In the next few weeks in Algiers it became clear that Giraud had finally been convinced that the Americans and British meant what they said about the necessity for reform in his régime. He had been told that the Vichy laws, still being applied rigorously through Algeria and Morocco, must be jettisoned and that support for Pétain and Vichy's form of fascism must end. It was not necessary to say "or else." Giraud and his cronies knew that de Gaulle was in London and that, to some extent at least, his quarrel with the Americans had been patched up.

Giraud and the Vichyites around him moved much too slowly, however. They would not accept the urgency of the situation. What was the uproar in London and in the United States to them? Blinded by years of power and corroded by their internal fears about Communism they procrastinated, playing at reform. Prodded by Macmillan and Murphy, Giraud replaced the Imperial Committee by a War Committee and chose the title of Military and Civil Commander-in-Chief. Café wits commended his choice as shorter than "Duce." Slowly Vichy officials were replaced. Some of the lesser turned their coats and with varying degrees of enthusiasm embraced the Allied aims. Political prisoners were freed. Restrictions against Jews and Freemasons were lifted.

There was little real enthusiasm for reform. The Giraudists' attitude toward the Allies cooled noticeably in February when Rommel mauled the American II Corps at Kasserine. It warmed again after the German threat was broken. While Giraud played at reform, in London and Washington they were beginning to realize that de Gaulle was the only leader recognized by the Resistance, whether anti-Communist, Gaullist, or Communist, in France.

In late April of 1943, when I returned to Tunisia for the last offensive, Giraud's day was done.

III

The military situation had altered out of all recognition. The British First Army and the American II Corps had been joined by General Sir Bernard L. Montgomery's Eighth Army, which had rolled westward across Africa since Alamein, driving the Germans and Italians before it. Into Tunisia had flooded the equipment and supplies so desperately needed in that first wild grab at Tunis the preceding fall: thousands of tanks, trucks, and guns, hundreds of bombers and fighters, airfields and depots, adequate communications—it was a military bonanza staggering to those accustomed to the poverty of the last three years.

Like Fighter Command of the Royal Air Force in 1940, the Eighth Army has become a legend. Strikingly successful, it developed, as successful veteran forces do, a character of its own.

Victories, especially Alamein and the Mareth Line, had endowed everyone from the commanding general to the ordinary tommy with supreme confidence. Although predominantly British, this was not a spit-and-polish army. Junior officers were strangely and wonderfully clad: desert boots, corduroy slacks, a sweater, and a uniform cap. Few wore helmets. The men, hardened by long exposure, were tan and lean. The Eighth was a family affair. Men had fought in its ranks since the old days when it had been called "the Army of the Nile." Everyone knew everyone else. Cooperation between units and between the army and the air force was casual but efficient.

The Eighth with its air of victory, its informality, and its "family" atmosphere was in sharp contrast to the First Army and the II Corps, both of which had struggled through the cold winter in Tunisia. But they, too, were confident. Under General Omar Bradley the II Corps had emerged from the winter as a competent, aggressive force. The French XIX Corps had been strengthened by Moroccan and Senegalese units. The First Army, its rough spots smoothed by the winter fighting, was fired by the condescension shown it by the Eighth, to prove that Britain had other fighters in addition to the men from the desert.

By mid-April General Alexander who, as Eisenhower's deputy, commanded the Allies in Tunisia, was ready. He placed the French on the extreme left of the Allied line, moved II Corps to a new sector between the French and the British First, and brought the Eighth up on the right of the First. This was the situation when I returned to watch the largest and last offensive of the war in Africa.

At two o'clock in the morning of April 21 in the broken country east of Medjez-el-Bab the infantry of the 1st and 4th Divisions of the First Army were moving out in the moonlight, throwing shadows on the white dust of the roads. I heard the drone of many motors. Six months before I would have looked instinctively for shelter. Now no one worried. They were squadrons of American bombers; there seemed to be hundreds of them. Off to the right two squadrons of Spitfires swept down a valley toward Kournine.

The fighting in the hills was savage. The Germans counter-attacked whenever they could put a force together and harassed the British with mortar and machine-gun fire. They fought well, but by nightfall the British had driven them off three hills and the Germans had withdrawn.

Longstop Hill was the next barrier on the road to Tunis. The Germans had defeated an Anglo-American attack there on Christmas Eve. They were still there, well dug in. When the shelling and the bombing ceased, they emerged dragging their machine guns and mortars and met the British in one of the sharpest encounters of the war. Through the glasses you could see the British moving forward, small figures against the gray-green and brown of the hill. The rattle of fire carried very clearly, and you swore as you saw the British go down. The attack came to a halt.

The Medjerda valley was at its best on April 22, the second day of the battle for Longstop Hill. The sun shone on the poppies in the hills and the blue flowers growing in patches on the sides of the mountains higher up. When the wind rippled the blue flowers, these patches looked like ponds set in the gray rock. The air was very clear, and sound carried a long way. I could hear the guns of the II Corps pounding away in the north.

The Argyll and Sutherland Highlanders had been chosen to lead the attack, supported by a squadron of Churchill tanks. The tanks labored up the hillside, rooting out machine-gun and mortar positions, and the Argylls finished the work. They lost, in the process, Lieutenant Colonel Andrew MacNab, who had been on the First Army staff but who had wangled a transfer back to his old regiment for the final offensive. He was a big, genial fellow who looked like Robert Donat. He died leading his old battalion against the Germans. When he was hit, they propped him against a tree and he said, "All right, get on with it."

By dusk the Germans were off the hill. They came back in the night. Counterattack after counterattack; bitter fighting with grenades, rifles, and bayonets. The Argylls were just strong enough to hang on. In the morning another British battalion arrived and with the remaining Scots swept the hill clear of the enemy. By noon the road to Tunis through Medjez was open.

Longstop Hill was the key to the advance to Tunis. Hill 609 was the most important position on the front of the II Corps driving for Bizerte, Tunisia's largest port and an important French naval base. The Germans had held Hill 609 for months. As on Longstop, they had entrenched themselves. Later I saw some of the dugouts blasted from the rock. Each held twenty men and their weapons, and the Germans retired into them when the bombers came over and the shells fell.

On a Saturday morning the 34th Division attacked the hill, held by the Barenthin regiment.

As the barrage lifted, the G.I.'s went forward into the fire of the German machine guns and the "whop-whop" of mortars. They held their rifles across their chests, as men have held them since first they had the weapon. Under their helmets their figures were curiously foreshortened.

From some Arab hovels came a steady, deadly fire. The American artillery ranged ahead and smashed the pitiful buildings. The infantry resumed their progress. New German machine-gun positions came into action. The Americans went forward in little rushes, sheltering behind rocks, taking snap shots at the enemy. Slowly they forced their way up the hill until from the summit they saw the white roofs of Mateur and, beyond it, shimmering in the heat haze, Lake Bizerte and a white smudge on the horizon, Bizerte itself. Another road was open.

These were the Germans of 1943, hardy, tenacious fighters. They had to be cleared from the reverse slope of the hill, and little pockets of resistance fought on behind the advancing infantry. It was a long day.

Now the roads were open, and the Allied armies poured forward. The last attack on Tunis and Bizerte was being prepared. Of course, there were other actions just as harsh during the days that Longstop and 609 fell—at Ken-en-Nsous and Bald Hill and Jefna—but the keys were in Alexander's hands.

I seldom felt exultation in the war. Fear, often; acute physical discomfort, yes. Exultation came sparingly and fleetingly. This was one of the times. In the next few days, seeing the thousands of tanks and trucks, hearing the almost uninterrupted roar of *our* bombers, *our* fighters, listening to the big guns pounding in the night, I felt at last the taste of victory. At the outset of the war I had not hated the Germans. In the intervening years my attitude had changed. I had seen, heard, and read too much about the Germans. Now I knew they must be beaten, here, in Europe, anywhere they fought. I don't believe I was bloodthirsty. My feelings struck me as entirely natural.

I left Thibar each day in the early morning in a station wagon with three or four other correspondents. Driving was difficult and dangerous because the roads were filled with trucks and tanks and jeeps moving forward. Once I was rewarded by a battle laid out before me as on a stage, something very rare in war.

A big, square, white house stood in the middle of a grove of orange trees. From its porch I could see, a half-mile or so ahead, a thin line of American infantry advancing across the marsh in front of Djebel Achikel, a vast hill rising solitary out of the plain. To the right seven American self-propelled 105-millimeter guns fired at German positions in an open-face mine on the lower slope of the mountain. To the rear, and again to the right, 155's were searching for German mortar positions and infantry along the top of the mountain. Farther to the right lay the Ferryville road. Around it American medium tanks were moving. They had broken through a German tank screen, and the action was sputtering to a close. Beyond the retreating German tanks German guns shelled the American vehicles and guns shelling Achikel. The German guns were firing from the grounds of a hospital easily distinguished by the big red crosses on the roof.

The Germans fought stubbornly and skillfully. They had been told to hold Achikel. As long as they could use its observation posts, their guns dominated Mateur and the road leading out of it through Ferryville to Bizerte. The German machine guns sought the American infantry crossing the marsh and, in turn, were hunted by the American mortars and guns. The action changed constantly.

A file of German prisoners, very young most of them. Wounded, American and German, lying in back of the white house. The G.I.'s were closer to the mountain now. The German fire weakened under the pounding of the guns. A major named John Wynne said he thought "the krauts have had about enough, they'll pull out in the night." They did.

The end of a campaign, like the end of a marriage, is likely to come with a rush. This happened in Tunisia. It had been hot, very hot, in the day, but at three o'clock in the morning of May 6, 1943, on the hills beyond Medjez the wind was cool, almost cold. I could just see the figures of the gunners a couple of yards behind our party. The eastern sky held the first faint hint of dawn. Then four hundred guns opened fire, and the climax began.

Sound has its terrors. Hammer strokes struck my ears, my

chest. I wanted to lie down, to dig a hole, to do anything that would allow me to escape from this incessant, punishing clamor. The endless din went on. More and more batteries joined. They told us later that the noise rolled forward beyond the targets to Tunis and Bizerte, bringing families to their doors.

As the sun rose, the bombers came. Bostons and Baltimores, Mitchells and Marauders, even a few Fortresses; the U.S. Air Force and the R.A.F. Minutes later we heard the rumbling explosions on the German positions. Two British armored divisions, the 6th and the 7th (the latter the Desert Rats), and two infantry divisions, the 4th and the 4th Indian, came out of the *wadis* [valleys] and the olive groves and the ruined farms that had sheltered them for the night and started up the valley toward Tunis. The last attack was on its way.

Dust was an enemy. People talk about General Mud and General Rain and General Cold. General Dust has a role too. The dust rose from the roads and from the fields. It ascended in clouds whenever a gun fired. It sifted into the engines of tanks, trucks, and jeeps. It was light brown in color, bitter to the taste. In the late afternoon the valley was a sea of dust. A battery of 25-pounders was hammering away. I could see the flare from the muzzles and that was all. Ahead I saw a sudden red glow on the horizon that lasted fully four seconds. Someone said, "That's the way the jerry ammunition dumps looked when they blew up in '18." The dust continued. Ten divisions, perhaps a hundred and fifty thousand men, were on the move.

The next morning found me between Massicault and Saint Cyprien. Meaningless names now. We entered a farm and saw the remains of a German battery. Oberleutenant Kopf had commanded the battery, and in the farmhouse was all of Oberleutenant Kopf left in the world: a bundle of letters from his wife, passionate letters through which ran a stream of anguished fear; another bundle from someone named Luise in Darmstadt, equally passionate but no fear there; some photographs, a tall, erect old man holding a child of about two.

A big north countryman came up. He had been in the action.

"Some of them tried to get away through the wheat," he said, "but we got them as they left the guns. I suppose this bugger"— he gestured toward the letters I held—"is out there. Might be with his guns, though. Mostly the officers didn't run."

He turned away. The Eighth Army had seen a thousand positions overrun.

In Saint Cyprien there was a smithy by the road. Bill Stoneman and Charlie Collingwood pounded stakes into the ground
and began to pitch horseshoes. I played for a while but I was
rotten. I climbed a rickety staircase until I reached the roof. I
put my glasses down the empty road, then swung them to the
right and nearly dropped them. There were thirty-two British
tanks beyond the road starting into action. The first troop
rumbled down the road and into the fields. The camouflaged
tanks melted into the hillside beyond. As they rounded the
shoulder of the hill, the tanks stopped and fired. Wreaths of
smoke blossomed around the turrets. Far off I heard the ugly
crack of a German 88.

We followed, watching the tank battle. The British had spread
out and were moving across the fields toward a low hill. One
tank was on fire. The sky grew darker. German shell fire burst
harmlessly in the fields behind us.

The road curved to the left around another hill and then
dropped into a shallow valley dominated by a ridge toward
which the British tanks headed. The German gun was still firing.
As we watched, a shell burst among the tanks. The tanks lurched
forward.

The magnet of Tunis pulled us along. I remember thinking
this was a damned dangerous way to approach the city, on foot
and behind a handful of tanks. Finally I reached the brow of
another hill. Through the glasses I could see Tunis on the horizon. I rejoined Bill and Charlie and our station wagon, and we
went down through the heavy rain toward the city. There was
still firing on the right, but the tanks had disappeared. There
were fires in the city now; the Germans were burning their
stores.

Single guns held out, firing to the last at the British tanks
coming down the roads. It was all gray and brown now: gray
roads, brown houses in the rain. An unknown brigadier came up,
took a long look through his glasses, and said mildly that he
thought they could go in now. A column of tanks came out of
the fields and suburban side streets and moved into the city.

As the column went deeper into the city, more and more
French came out of the houses: old men wearing the ribbon of

the Legion of Honor, harassed mothers trying to keep their young in the houses, and tattered, scared Arabs. The children danced around the tanks. So Tunis fell, and the campaign reached its last hours.

By May 11 there was no gunfire in the hills. I wrote my last dispatch and headed for the airfield. There were many working in the fields, and on the roads refugees trudged toward Tunis. Peace had returned to the Mejerda.

IV

Algiers again. I went up to the Hotel St. George to see Eisenhower, bearing Oberleutenant Kopf's Luger. The General was still a little surprised by the completeness and finality of the victory.

"You know what it was?" he said. "We just outfought them. It wasn't overpowering superiority in any one weapon. They're good soldiers. But we beat them, fighting it out. Those kids of ours on 609, the British at Longstop. They outfought the Germans, and when they put the pressure on, really on, the Germans couldn't stand up to us. We've got them now."

De Gaulle came in May. Young, slim, aware; a different de Gaulle from the head of the Fifth Republic.

His battle was won without a serious encounter. Giraud maneuvered. De Gaulle maneuvered. The latter had drawn to him many who, at the outset of the campaign, in November 1942, had seen in the Darlan-Giraud axis a legitimate base for the recovery of the homeland. They were not Vichy people. They just wanted to fight Germany and Italy. De Gaulle now offered greater promise of French victory than Giraud.

De Gaulle had the manner, he had the words. He could make a speech of five minutes that made Giraud's long, carefully prepared oration seem empty and meaningless. His speeches then had less of the Delphic tone they assumed during his Presidency. I never fell under the spell. Some good men did. To me, reared by my father's harsh practicality, all too often de Gaulle, then and later, talked of a France, a Europe, that no longer existed.

The de Gaulle of those days, off duty, was far from the majestic figure of 1958–1969. We lunched one day in the rather ordinary villa allotted him. He said all the expected things about the Free, or Fighting, French (I never could tell which adjective he favored). Toward the end of the meal he relaxed. We talked, my diary recalls, about the difficulties the American armies would have in Europe.

Not the obvious military difficulties, but those involved in coming to terms with populations unprepared for the totality of America at war. This time, I said, we would not be a small army that was part of a larger Allied force but, if all went well, the largest component of an Anglo-American force. He nodded agreement.

Sticking his cigar in the side of his mouth, he acted the average Frenchman's idea of the average American. His head went back, he parodied the French of the visiting American. His staff, shaken by this sudden change from his normal manner, quite clearly didn't know what to do.

"Evidently," he said, nodding that long, impressive head, "it will be necessary to teach our people that the Americans are not men from another planet but those who have come to help them. It will be difficult. All will depend on your policies."

We returned to politics and the General's belief that Europe and America must learn to live with each other. One impression stands out: he did not, nor did anyone, except perhaps Churchill, envisage the ruin Europe would be in after the fighting had halted. De Gaulle seemed to think that the nations of Europe after Germany's defeat would resume the place they had held in the world before 1939.

His basic theme was simple. France was a great power. The Resistance was performing marvels. The Americans and the British must realize this. An aide interposed that the British planned to establish themselves on the continent after the war. I said that this was nonsense, or words to that effect. The General agreed. Although he clearly was not in love with the British, they were, he pointed out, a great empire and would have all they could do to hold it together after the war without worrying about Europe. "Europe," he said grandly, "is for us, the Europeans."

A last night at the Regina, when someone rang a bell and gave the closing call of all pubs, "Time, gentlemen, please." I

climbed aboard a plane and headed for Marrakesh with Elmer
Davis, head of the Office of War Information, the only other
passenger.

I like to recall that, having landed in North Africa, cold with
the sweat of fear and wondering whether machine guns were
on that bluff above the beach, I left on the wings of laughter.

Elmer and I were housed in the elaborate villa that had been
Winston Churchill's residence during his recent illness. We were
invited to dinner at the home of Josephine Baker, then living
with a Moroccan prince. Our guide was a lieutenant of Spahis,
disdainful of these nondescript Americans. Elmer was in a
rumpled tropical suit, and I wore a desert uniform that had seen
some wear. The lieutenant drove his jeep through the native
quarter. It was the hour after prayers, and the streets were alive
with people, listening to story tellers, watching snake charmers
or acrobats, or sitting and gazing vacantly at the passersby. It
had the tremendous vitality of Africa. It always hits you hard,
in Cairo, in Fez, in Dar-es-Salaam, in Lagos. There is life, almost
gaiety, in the air. These people had nothing by our standards.
But they had lived that day and might live another.

I have seen enough Arab homes in Morocco and elsewhere to
know now that the home of Josephine's prince was extraordinary:
large and cool in the hot August night. We dined in the Moroccan style and dined very well. As we relaxed on our cushions,
dancing girls entered. They were not my idea of dancing girls
nor, as I learned later, Elmer's. They were about sixty pounds
overweight for a start. They sang in Arabic, and the lieutenant
translated: "They are the gazelles and you are the lions who
hunt them." I made a mental reservation that this lion was to
be counted out.

Later we were given whiskey in another room as novel to me
as the one in which we had dined. Scattered around the wall
were seven pinball machines. Elmer and I wanted to play but
we had no coins. The Prince, an affable enough fellow, said he
would fix that. He hauled up the front of his long Arab robe.
Swinging from a belt around his middle was a heavy purse. I
noticed that in that heat he was wearing long underdrawers. He
pulled a handful of coins out of the purse.

"Please play," he said, "it is one of my amusements."

CHAPTER 6

NORMANDY TO AACHEN: The Last Campaign

1944

Ev'n victors are by victories undone.

John Dryden

I

Although not, at that age, an introspective person, I realized in the fall of 1943 in London that my attitude toward the war had changed. In all its aspects—military, political, and 'social—the war still filled my life, but I had become more objective. I no longer felt the old, belly-tightening excitement. I could see how the war would be won. I could see, too, how it could be lost. I had no great faith in the Russians. In my encounters with Soviet diplomats I found they put national interests first. This was understandable in view of the losses they had suffered and the extent of their commitment. But I wondered whether this same concentration on national interests might not lead the Soviet Union to separate peace negotiations with Germany. After all, Stalin had made one deal with Hitler; why not another if, by so doing, he could save his country the terrible losses certain to follow a Soviet invasion of Germany? Could the West win then? I didn't know then and I don't know now. I do know that a Soviet switch would have been a terrible setback for the West.

I was roundly abused, for voicing such thoughts, by those of my friends who then regarded the Soviet war effort as above question and retailed stories about genial old Uncle Joe in the Kremlin.

There is evidence now that Stalin in 1942 and 1943 did consider a separate peace with the Germans and that Soviet and German emissaries met in Stockholm. But even had this been known at the time, it would not have much dampened the puerile enthusiasm of the Left in Britain for the Red Army or diminished the exaggerated picture given by the newspapers and the BBC of Soviet progress.

The management of the war had changed during the year I had been in the Mediterranean. By the end of 1943 the United States was applying the enormous industrial and financial resources that were the basis of eventual victory. It followed that the military and the diplomats who represented those resources would assume direction of the war.

In London this was done with discretion. Necessarily so, because the British, the only western ally that counted militarily, still disposed of powerful armies, fleets, and air forces scattered around the world, more numerous, experienced, and skilled than those then deployed by the United States. Moreover, the coalition government headed by Churchill included many exceptionally able men. Neither in Washington nor in Europe did I meet American political leaders the equal of Attlee, Eden, and Bevin, to name only three. Their ability and the commanding stature of Churchill enabled Britain in the last two years of the war to play a part in its direction that was more important than the global British military contribution justified.

The American takeover thus was more real than apparent. London remained the capital of the war in the West, even though basic decisions might be made in Washington under the direction of General George C. Marshall's penetrating intellect. In London people still talked of the "Imperial" armies; the laurels of Alamein were unwithered; the great air offensive of the R.A.F.'s Bomber Command held the headlines. All this tended to obscure the reality of a country that had spent blood and treasure on three continents and was now fighting on material and financial resources increasingly furnished by the American ally.

I had friends in various ministries and in the fighting services who understood what the exertions of the next two years would do to Britain's position as a world power. No great expertise or imagination was necessary to recognize that victory, whenever and however it came, would leave Britain financially spent and incapable of maintaining her position in the world. Yet those who saw this reported it without bitterness. The thing to do now was to beat Hitler. This was the reality.

The U.S. Army and Army Air Force, as the latter then was, spread across the face of the land. There were jokes: "The Americans are overfed, overpaid, and oversexed." One heard, on trips to the countryside, the usual complaints about our people: their driving, their tipping, their freedom with women, their total disinterest in the British, and their way of life. All true and all, I believe, natural in young men who had been taken out of familiar surroundings and sent to a war only a few of them understood.

Some generals and some units handled the new responsibility with tact. That winter I visited Winchester, headquarters of the U.S. 9th Division, then commanded by that bluff, skillful, and intelligent soldier General Manton S. Eddy. His headquarters were in the regimental headquarters of the 60th Rifles, a very fine British regiment that had lost a battalion sent to hold Calais in 1940 against the German push toward Dunkirk. Eddy had the rare good sense to put the 9th's 60th Regiment in Winchester and to stand retreat each night on the parade ground where those soldiers of the Rifles, now dead in France or rotting in prisoner-of-war camps, had once stood retreat. Not all American commanders were as sensitive to the feelings of their hosts.

For all the friction it caused, this American invasion made some contribution to understanding between the two peoples. The English masses until then had had almost no contact with Americans and tended to think of them as a transplanted race of English. They now learned that many Americans had strange names of Italian or German or Polish origin and that two hundred years of immigration, intermarriage, and expansion had created a new breed which, if it spoke English, had little in common with the English.

The English spent a good deal of time deploring the average G.I.'s ignorance of what some of the former still thought of as "the Mother Country." Their ignorance was matched by British ignorance of America.

The United States military presence made the English aware of the race problem in America. The segregated army aroused the indignation of British liberals. Reports of scuffles between black and white troops, usually over women, produced excited protests in the livelier, leftish publications.

The blacks found themselves in a novel situation: unrestricted contact with a largely nonracial society. For the first time many found themselves admitted to white homes as friends and able to meet white girls. They had money to spend, more money than most had ever seen before, and they were generous. They were popular and enjoyed their popularity. They did not offend by boasting, they did not look down on the British.

Their popularity angered white soldiers, especially the southerners among them, who called the British "nigger lovers." They predicted "big trouble" when the Negro soldiers returned home. Real racial violence, however, didn't start until twenty years after the end of the war. The blacks didn't forget England. One family in Norfolk, England, receives every Christmas a long letter, usually accompanied by family photographs, from a Negro who ate his Christmas dinner with the family in 1943.

Since then a race problem has developed in Britain. Racism is most violent in the industrial working class and the lower middle class, which during the war were the most hospitable to the blacks. There is less criticism of America's handling of the race problem now that a similar problem has invaded Britain.

Londoners were tired. On September 3, 1943, they had been at war for four years, much of the time under bombing or the threat of bombing. Anticipation of victory, however, was very strong. It enabled people to accept stricter rationing and a more thorough mobilization of national resources than that in any other western allied nation or in Germany. Clothes, food, gas, and fuel were doled out in sharply reduced quantity. The "baby blitz," a series of night raids, made this grim and dreary period no easier to endure. But once again these unfathomable people drew on some hidden reserve of moral strength, and they endured.

When I returned to the London bureau in the autumn of 1943, I found myself writing most of the military news under James B. Reston, then well started on his remarkable career on *The New York Times*. During that winter I saw much of Scotty and of Sally, his pretty, intelligent wife.

I cannot say I knew Scotty well then or at any other time.

He is one of the most important figures in American journalism and, as such, the object of curiosity from gossips, in which the newspaper business abounds. But, as the English say, "he keeps himself to himself."

We worked closely together, discussing stories, offering and receiving criticism of each other's pieces, railing against the real or imaginary iniquities of the New York desk, sharing drinks in the small hours. We did all this, and we worked together after the war at international conferences. Yet I don't know Scotty. I doubt if anyone does except Sal.

Here are some keys to his character. Scotty is moral. He is no prude. But philandering, drunkenness, and indecency, all the moral deficiencies which our generation considered "loose living," offend him. He is eternally surprised when the Old Adam appears among friends and colleagues. He has the Scots Presbyterian's love of thrift, probity, and restraint, and he practices all three.

He was shocked at the outspoken lasciviousness of some American G.I.'s he encountered during a stay in a hospital that winter. When I suggested that soldiers normally thought of women, liquor, and dodging the next hard job that came their way, he was offended. My point, that all soldiers in all armies behaved this way, and that despite their earthy preoccupations the Americans had fought and would fight as well as any others, failed to comfort him. For Scotty is that brand of patriot which believes that Americans can and should be better than other men. Why? Because they are Americans. Iike anyone who believes this, he is often disappointed. He came to the United States from Scotland as a child; he never takes his own Americanism for granted. He feels he owes the country much.

Scotty is inspired by a desire to excel. I do not believe he ever thought that he, and he alone, had the answers or that as a columnist he was entitled to guide and reprove Presidents and chart the Republic's course. His great quality as a reporter and columnist is the presentation of complicated situations in words understandable to the average reader. The fullest exploitation of this talent has won him an unrivalled place in the newspaper world.

No journalist reaches his eminence without plenty of hard work. Scotty believes in the Anglo-Saxon Protestant ethic that hard work never hurt anyone (I say "Asp" for "Anglo-Saxon Protestant" instead of "Wasp" for "White Anglo-Saxon Protestant": I've never yet met one who was anything but white) .

If I have portrayed a humorless fellow, the portrait must be amended. Scotty has a fund of laughter, he likes the raffish chatter of the city room, he loves his profession, its legends, its heroes. He has won a great position in journalism, but he has never lost touch with the men in the ranks.

"Jesus," a young reporter said one day when I was visiting the New York office, "last night Mr. Reston, the Executive Editor, came and sat on my desk and talked about a story I was doing. And he knew as much about it as I did."

That winter of 1943–44 I handled military news, chiefly the air war then moving toward a climax, the Bomber Command of the R.A.F. hitting the enemy by night and the Eighth Air Force of the U.S. Army Air Force doing the job by day.

Any reporter trying to do an accurate, balanced job was at the mercy of the public-relations officers and of the censors, both German and Allied. The Germans were telling lies about the Allied offensive faster than a horse could trot. The Allies, basing their first reports on the eyewitness accounts of pilots, were providing an exaggerated impression in one important respect: the two Allied commands interpreted the results of the bombing offensive as a serious blow to Germany's ability to continue the war. Death and destruction there was, to a hideous degree, but not enough yet to turn any German's mind, certainly not Hitler's, toward surrender.

Both the American and British bomber commands were fighting a battle inside a battle. This was to establish, over the doubts and criticisms of the politicians, army generals, and admirals, the heavy bomber as a decisive weapon of war. The two commanders, General Carl A. Spaatz and Air Marshal Sir Arthur Harris, were bent on establishing what to them was this obvious fact of war.

I had known Spaatz since 1940. I had found him a genial character then, and his present eminence had not changed him. Men in command of great engines of destruction—and the Eighth Air Force was that—are seldom given to second thoughts, to personal recrimination, or to philosophical musing on the ethics of their tasks. "Tooey" (his nickname is an example of West Point humor) was in the familiar mold. A job had to be done, he had been given the weapon, and done it would be.

When the Eighth Air Force began to deepen its penetration of Germany in the winter of 1943–44, casualties mounted. I never saw in Spaatz or in his Chief of Staff, General Edward P. Curtis, that cold unconcern with casualties attributed to the air generals by liberal novelists of the postwar period. They had been fliers themselves in World War I, they had fought, Curtis as a civilian, for a stronger air force between the wars. The instrument now given them was part of themselves, and when the losses from Regensburg and other deep raids came it, Spaatz and Curtis died a little.

Casualties hurt. The air war was grim, was costly. No one sang about flying off into the wild, blue yonder. There was a gray, pinched look about Spaatz as he explained why this job or that had to be done, ball-bearings production knocked out, tank plants destroyed. He knew that every operational order meant death, maiming, or imprisonment for Americans. This was made no easier to bear by the knowledge that he would watch the battle on the maps at a safe headquarters, that he would sleep through nights untroubled by nagging fears of his next flight over Germany.

Spaatz and Curtis certainly had moments of doubt, especially when the casualty lists were high. Men who hold such commands in war learn to quell their doubts, to see the bright side of any picture, and to throw themselves completely into their daily duties. Perhaps it was this complete mental absorption and the physical energy required by the job that enabled the military leaders of World War II to escape any feeling of guilt that might arise from the daily dispatch of thousands, sometimes hundreds of thousands, of men into battle.

Planning and directing the air battle demanded the utmost concentration. The bombardment of Germany now was a far more complex business than the air forces had anticipated. Involved were the most delicate calculations of routes of approach to the target and return, of cooperation with the fighter escort, of diversionary attacks, and of secondary targets. Planners took a mass of information from intelligence sources, selected what was pertinent and, they hoped, accurate, and set themselves to out-think the German air commanders and antiaircraft gunners.

Actions were planned with the knowledge that error would mean more planes lost, more grieving families. Yet success would establish the validity of the Air Force's claim that, given the planes and the crews, it could do the job.

I never heard Spaatz or Harris claim the war could be won by air power alone. They did believe that air power, properly and continually applied, could so diminish the German ability to resist that the invasion, then being planned, would be much easier than it proved to be. The outcome, as might be expected, was indecisive. Clamant armies and navies and ambitious commanders, as sure as the air generals that they knew the right way to end the war, got their share of American and British resources for tanks, for guns, and landing craft.

Spaatz was an easy man, friendly, full of human juices, fond of a drink and poker. Harris was as genial as a trapped wolf. Spaatz seldom railed against the capricious powers in Washington; Harris was eternally at war with the meddlers of Whitehall.

"Some bloody fool is always coming in with a new target that is guaranteed to end the war," he said once in an unbuttoned conversation. "The MEW [Ministry of Economic Warfare] will send some chap to me with a cabinet directive to bomb some factory that makes all the boot laces for the German Army. If the German Army has no boot laces, he says, obviously it can't fight. So we blow the place to buggery and lose a lot of good chaps doing it. A week later the German Army is still fighting. So I call MEW and ask what happened. They tell me the German army is using string for boot laces. Bloody silly business."

As the year turned, the German army was much on people's minds. Hitler's army and air force might be dismissed as spent forces by the editorial writers in the United States and in Britain, but no one in authority was complacent.

I saw Eisenhower one winter afternoon at an exercise.

"I hope you're not telling people at home it'll be easy," he said abruptly. "It's going to be tough, very tough. Just look at Italy. And I'm sure the Russians are having a tougher time than they admit. We're going to have to drive our people to be ready."

Manton Eddy was equally realistic.

"This [the 9th] is a damned good division. We can get in and do our job. What worries me is the backup, these new divisions back home that will have to come over once we've landed. What did the old kraut say? 'Troops have to be shot over a little before they're any good.' Well, these divisions will be new to war. It doesn't matter how well trained they are. It's gonna be rough."

Gradually the idea of the invasion began to pervade men's minds. Despite the warnings about "Careless Talk," everyone talked about it, mostly in ignorance. A German spy, operating in, say, the Savoy bar or the Berkeley Buttery would have been driven crazy by the amount of uninformed chatter that filled the air.

The women were the worst. During one week in April I was informed by various ladies that the invasion was to take place in Biarritz, Schleswig-Holstein, Antwerp, and Brest. Most of these confidences were imparted in tones very audible across the Channel. The possession of such "inside information" conferred social prestige on the ladies involved. Indeed, the woman who bet on Brest boasted later that she had been almost right.

Everyone knew that the invasion would take place. Where and when were the questions. As spring wore on, tension rose. The British, already cruelly spent by the war, believed the landing could be made only at heavy cost. Happily, they exaggerated the casualties. The Americans, most of them untried, and recognizing it, fell back on the familiar and not misplaced American confidence that sheer mass of ships, tanks, and guns and cascades of bombs would do the job.

Confidence among the military varied from General Omar Bradley's calm assurance that "we have the men, the training, and the technical assistance to do the job" to Field Marshal Montgomery's exuberant "We're going to hit them for six."

I saw Monty in his private train near Southampton one cold spring day. There was more gray in his hair now, and he was thinner, but he was still the intense little fox terrier of a man I had seen in France four years earlier. He had a curious trick of repetition for emphasis. The battle, he said, would depend on the infantryman.

"When you have a well-trained infantryman, you have a pearl of great price, yes, yes, a pearl of great price. Tanks, bombers, support ships, will all do their job. But in the end it will depend on the infantryman. What did that French chap tell Napoleon? 'The British infantry are the best in the world, sire, fortunately there are not many of them.'

"We have enough this time. And," he added, with what he evidently thought was a handsome compliment, "your chaps are very good, very good, too. Of course I've had to alter the plans a bit. My good friend Ike understands that, certainly he understands that. It's going to be hard slogging, but we'll do it, we'll do it."

Montgomery even then was cordially disliked by many American general officers, and this dislike filtered down to various temporary officers at 12th Army Group, whose military acumen fitted them for shifting battle maps for their superiors at briefing sessions. Personally, I found Montgomery bombastic and egoistic. I thought Field Marshal Alexander the better soldier and the better man. But Monty must be given his due.

In the winter of 1946–47 I was sitting with General Walter Bedell Smith before his fire in Spaso House in Moscow. As Eisenhower's Chief of Staff, few had suffered more than Smith from Monty's antics. But the General, then Ambassador to the U.S.S.R., interrupted some strongly worded comments on the Field Marshal to say, "Yes, he was a trial at times. But, you know, no one but Monty could have got us across the Channel and fought that battle as well as he did."

In June of 1947 I was in Washington lunching with General Eisenhower. Montgomery was in the news with one of his shoot-from-the-hip comments about war and generalship. The General sighed and said, "Yes," Monty had been a problem, "but D-day was his sort of battle, he was the only man who could have got us ashore and done the job."

By "his sort of battle" Eisenhower meant that Montgomery excelled in the "set-piece battle," in which the lines are drawn and the positions established, rather than in an encounter battle. One of the odd things about Montgomery is that his reputation, among many, is that of a dashing, hell-for-leather general when, in fact, no one was more cautious in maneuvers, more hesitant to attack until he was sure that he had everything he needed.

My own job became progressively more demanding. Each day the number of sorties and the weight of bombs dropped on Germany, and now on France, mounted. Nightly I would gaze at the big map in the office and try to estimate just how much damage was being done to German communications with western France. All southern England was an armed camp. Vast piles of stores sprouted along railway branch lines, and tanks rumbled through obscure country villages.

One weekend ("It's quite safe for the next week," a friend in the War Office told me) I spent at Broadway in the Cotswolds. The nights were quiet. We spent the days in long walks. At the Lygon Arms we drank the last of the house's hock to that most poignant of all toasts, "Absent Friends." There were many absent then; there were to be more in a few months.

II

To many D-day was the climax of the war in Europe. In this they were wrong. The climax, the single, most important battle was the long, costly struggle of the Americans, British, and Canadians to break out of the bridgehead established in Normandy. In this the U.S. First Army played the most spectacular and successful role in the fighting of June, July, and August. This was the heaviest fighting in which an army of the United States had been engaged since the Civil War. The ultimate result of the First Army's success was the great sweep out of Normandy that liberated Paris and Brussels and brought the Allied armies to the borders of Germany by fall.

Normandy is a rich agricultural area. In the *bocage* country just inland the fields are enclosed by walls of earth heavily overgrown with bushes and grass and, at that time of year, by flowers. These walls, which the British called hedgerows, provided splendid cover for defending infantry and impeded the deployment of attacking infantry and tanks. For the Allied soldiers it was a war of stealth, of guesswork, of quick rushes across fields from hedgerow to hedgerow, of sudden explosive clashes between small groups. The *bocage* country was ideal for the Germans, who were inferior in tanks, planes, and guns but not in courage and skill.

To be in France again was an odd experience. I realized then how great an impact the events of 1940 had had upon me. I could not follow a French road without thinking of other roads and the German fighters strafing the refugees. I saw a British officer in a café in Bayeux and thought, hello, there's Charlie Wyatt—forgetting, for an instant, that Charlie was dead these four years gone and his bones somewhere along the Escaut. I saw the British armored troops, confident, even gay, as they went forward to attack south toward Vimont and break out of the Caen position. They made some progress but then were checked by 88s. I thought of others, no less confident and gay, who had swept into Belgium that May morning long ago. As in 1940, no one seemed to know just where the front was. The present and the past existed simultaneously in my mind.

One morning, driving toward the front in the First Army, a sergeant flagged us down.

"Get outta that jeep unless you want your ass shot off," he said. "There's a bunch of krauts up the road. We're trying to get at 'em through these fields."

Out of the hot sunshine came the tap-tap-tap of an enemy machine gun. The sergeant wondered where "that particular obnoxious son of a bitch is at?" The German machine-gunner had been holding them up for an hour and had killed a second lieutenant and two good men. Three soldiers had been sent to work their way through the fields and knock out the machine-gun position with grenades. The sergeant and the rest were to give covering fire. That is, he added wearily, if they could see anything to fire at. He wished to Christ he had a tank for support or that they could get away from these fucking hedgerows.

We waited, the sergeant looking frequently at his watch. Finally he nodded to three riflemen, and they clambered to the top of the heavy dirt wall enclosing the field. Their weapons sounded, and I scrambled up behind. Someone murmured that he, meaning the machine-gunner, "must" be over on the slight rise of ground. The tap-tap started. But before the gun found us we heard the explosion of two grenades. The machine-gun fire ended. Someone shouted "okay, sarge, we got him."

"Yes, you goddamn fool and you let them know we were here."

He looked at me. I had better get in a ditch, he said; before long there would be mortar fire. Before long was an exaggeration. It began almost instantly, the bombs falling in the field beside the road. Then, high above us, we heard the whine of an engine: a reconnaissance plane looking for the Germans. Now, the sergeant said, perhaps we'd have some artillery support. One of the privates thought it was high time. In his opinion the artillery spent its time on its ass reading comic books and chasing women.

I got out my notebook and began to write. One of the G.I.'s asked if I thought anyone at home would care a damn about this. I said I hoped so; this was the level at which battles were won or lost. He was from Queens and said that, no offense, he was a *Daily News* man himself. What had he done in civil life? Construction, and "if I had any sense I would a swore I was a fag and got out of the army, some of them guys are making five times what I make."

"You taking that down?" he asked. I said I was. He thought for a moment. "Won't make no difference. My mother sends me magazines. We're fighting for apple pie. Apple pie, my ass. I want to beat these bastards and go home. Do you think it will take long?"

The shelling started. A few at first whined over our road, and then more began to crash in the fields beyond and in a copse where the sergeant thought a German company was located. He got up slowly and told the rest it was time to be moving on. When would they get to St. Lô? How the hell did he know? He had lost an officer and two good men just getting one lousy machine gun.

At night the sky was alive with gun flashes and the flare of exploding bombs. By day the First Army pushed, fumbled, and then caught hold at St. Lô. The 29th Division took St. Lô, and on July 25 the army broke out and headed westward for Avranches. From that drive came the loosening of the German grip in the west, the encirclement of the German armies now gripped by the British Second Army on the left flank, and the wild dash across France and Belgium that ended on the frontiers of Germany.

When the hinge at St. Lô gave way, the Americans burst into rich, sunlit country, where the opposition consisted mainly of scattered groups of weary, shaken Germans. Pursuit was, for me, exhilarating and, for all, dangerous. Weary and shaken though they were, the Germans fought well. A company would turn and offer tenacious battle until overcome by fighters, tanks, and artillery. Once, on the road from St. Lô to Perriers, I saw five of our tanks stalk and finally destroy a huge Mark VI barring the advance.

The German tank commander, using farm buildings beside the road as cover, employed his 88-millimeter gun as a sniper would a rifle. Moving from one position to another, he disabled one American Sherman. Then he got another. But, doing so, he exposed his tank a second too long. Another Sherman stopped the Mark VI with its first shell, then hit the back of the turret with a second. The German began to burn.

When a jeep halted by the roadside, groups of Germans often would come out of the fields to surrender. Just as often Germans fought in twos and threes, from church steeples, farm buildings, clumps of trees.

By the standards of the German Army this was brave and honorable. The G.I. didn't see it that way. He couldn't see why the Germans didn't give up. He was not particularly moved by German inhumanity to the French, although there was abundant evidence of it. What enraged him were Germans who continued to fight when all was so obviously lost and, by so doing, prevented his escaping a life he loathed and returning home.

Mark Watson of the *Baltimore Sun,* one of the best correspondents ever to put key to ribbon, and I set out one morning to visit the Americans holding the flank facing south. This protected the spate of troops, tanks, and guns from pouring through Avranches to begin the sweep through France. Mark had a feeling that the Germans would do something on that flank, that, battered though they were, they could not retreat without one final crack at the Americans.

The trip forward had become stereotyped. There were always smiling French offering calvados, cheese and apples, and makeshift banners across village streets welcoming the American liberators, and bands of scruffy young men armed with odd weapons and wearing the white armbands of the French Forces of the Interior, the guerrilla army.

We soon saw something was wrong. The villages were empty. No peasants worked the fields. Then—an unbelievable sight in Normandy behind our lines—a column of refugees came down the road. Farm carts piled high with furniture, women pushing baby carriages, old men leading elderly horses. I thought of 1940.

"The boche are coming," an old man said, "they have broken through. They are heading for this road. What will they do to us? Only two days ago we were feasting the Americans." He made "Americans" sound like a dirty word.

We doubted that the directions given us at Corps headquarters were accurate. Mark said he would follow telephone wires which should lead to a forward headquarters, and I went back to a village where I had seen an aid station.

There they offered calvados but no information. Yeh, they'd heard heavy firing up the road. But that was normal. The phone? Out of order. A young medical-corps captain said he wished to God he was back in England in a nice, quiet hospital. I wandered into an empty house and sat in the sitting room—one that never, I suppose, was used by the family except on days of high ceremony—and rocked gently in a chair covered with green plush. Across from me on the wall was a hideous portrait photograph of a young man in the French Army uniform of 1914. I wondered idly if he had ever returned from that war. On the mantlepiece were things such as a French bourgeois family cherishes: the souvenir from Deauville, one of those gilt models of the Eiffel tower that are sold by the thousand to tourists on the rue Rivoli, a framed letter citing someone for services to the state in the local agricultural association, an elegant, crystal jar that seemed out of keeping with the rest of the room.

Then I heard the jeep driver shout and saw Mark's sturdy figure moving imperturbably down the road. He hadn't found any headquarters. I had no information. We paused, and I mentioned the advice of a British general: "When in doubt, bum on." We moved off down the road in the direction from which the refugees had come.

There was firing, all right. But it didn't sound ominous until we reached the top of a slight rise. The driver slammed the jeep off the road under some trees and beside a low stone wall. In the field to our left were three American antitank guns, well dug in. A dirty-faced lieutenant came over.

"If you guys don't want to get killed," he said, "you better take cover. The krauts have got through up ahead with tanks. We think they're coming through that wood there."

They were Mark VIs, and even at that range they looked enormous through my glasses. German infantrymen clung to them like lice. They moved slowly, ponderously. The barrels of their guns moved slowly, searching for us like the antennæ of some huge, obscene insect. I could hear the lieutenant saying "hold it, hold it" to the gun crews.

When they finally opened up, the American guns might as well have been blowing peas at the tanks. I could see the shells ricochet off the tanks' heavy armor as the infantry tumbled off and started up the slight incline toward the Americans.

Mark told the driver to turn the jeep around. There was a burst of rifle and automatic weapon fire off to our left. The lieutenant thought our infantry must be coming back. Suddenly every other sound was drowned in a high, piercing whine. Out of the west flying low came three Typhoons of the Royal Air Force. They loosed their rockets. One hit the lead tank in the belly: a great gout of flame and oily black smoke. Another rocket hit the second tank on the turret. American fire engaged the infantry. More British fighters blasted the Germans with machine gun and cannon fire. I could not see any Germans now. But their mortar shells were falling just ahead. Then more fighters, American P-47s, came in and bombed the tanks and the infantry. The mortar fire dwindled, stopped.

"Jesus," said the lieutenant, "who were those first guys?" Mark told him. "Limeys, eh? Well, thank Christ for the limeys today."

By chance we had stumbled onto the spearhead of a German counteroffensive mounted by bits of five Panzer divisions: the 116th, the 2nd, the 1st S.S., the 2nd S.S., and the 17th S.S. The *Shutz Staffel* divisions were the Nazi Party's military arm and of high quality. They had broken through between two American battalions. The Typhoons and Thunderbolts had checked the advance long enough for a colonel named Frankland to rally the Americans and restore the position. Reinforced that night, the line held.

When we returned through the villages, people were at the doors, belongings packed, looking anxiously toward the east. We told them the line would hold. A woman patiently coaxed a weary farm horse around and, mounting the cart, started back up the road.

In France I have read numerous accounts and heard interminable stories about how the French Forces of the Interior helped the Allied armies in Normandy. I don't doubt that those forces performed notable feats in certain areas. All I can say is that I didn't see any. I have often wondered whether Frenchmen were really gulled by the persistent Gaullist propaganda that France liberated herself. If the F.F.I. was doing so at that time, no one mentioned it.

Defeat often brings out the best in men. But more often the worst. There were Germans who fought honorably and well during that retreat, others who vented their humiliation upon the French.

There was a little bar in Granville that looked out upon the sea. I stopped one evening for a drink and talked to a short, fat, one-armed Frenchman.

He did not think it right that the French should be drinking and laughing.

"What has happened to us will not be repaired in fifty years of peace—if there is peace. They sing and laugh and forget the others. But not three kilometers from here are the bodies of a man, his wife, and their five children. The Germans killed them, shot them, you understand, because he resisted when they tried to take his last two horses for their guns. I knew him. An honest, peaceful man.

"So many good ones are gone. Not just the prisoners and the dead and those of the Resistance killed by the Germans. But others, like that man. What is left, you will see, will not be strong enough for the task."

He looked down at his cognac. "I tell you, sir, occupation pulls the entrails from a country." And he made a clutching motion at his belly.

Not long after I stopped the jeep at the top of the hill that stands above the village of St. Aubin d'Aubigne. The village lies eleven miles north of Rennes at the base of the Brittany peninsula. I had spent my last night in France there in 1940. We had told them we would be back. But they had looked politely at us and turned away, all but one or two. Their world was crumbling. The Marshal was asking the Germans for an armistice.

The jeep stopped by the schoolhouse. A policeman inquired politely whether we were lost. I told him No, I had been in St. Aubin once before. His leathery face broke into a grin when

I told him the date. We stood in the middle of the street, grinning, our hands clasped.

"So you have returned. I always said you would; that summer when the English fought, I was sure. Many of us are sorry for the things done and said in those last days. But we were a frightened people."

The church bell began to toll.

"Come, we are burying three boys of the Resistance," he said. "We had a Resistance here, not very great, but they did what they could. It was we older ones who really fooled the boche. Come."

Gathered around the church were two or three hundred people of St. Aubin d'Aubigne. The men wore Sunday blacks and, here and there, ancient cutaways and rusty silk hats. Firemen in their brass helmets were drawn up in a line. Half a dozen boys of the French Forces of the Interior holding a mixed assortment of weapons stood at attention. Out of the church came three coffins borne on the shoulders of other boys. The mayor and the council and the families of the dead boys followed the coffins to the graves. Then came the firemen sweating in their uniforms. Finally the people of St. Aubin. Many wept.

The mayor was a tall, gaunt man who had been mayor since 1924. He shook hands, when I told him my connection with the village, searching my face with his deep blue eyes. Finally, he said, he remembered the night.

"The curé thought we should take care of you, and we did. Two nights later some English soldiers came through, very hungry, and we cared for them, too. By then it was forbidden, and he and I did it together in the schoolhouse. One of the soldiers gave me this to remember him and in thanks. I looked at it many times in the bad times." He pulled out a half-crown piece.

I asked for the curé.

"He was the first to go. He said that the Germans' ways were not those of God and that those who broke God's laws would be punished. They took him away for three months for that.

"The next summer an English aviator came down near the village. It was in the night, and the curé brought him to his own house. The boy was not of the curé's faith, but he was badly burned. The Germans came searching for the boy and because of what the curé had said before and of this they took him away. He has not returned. We hope he is not dead."

We went back to the inn for a glass of wine with the town council. The members were in black and very solemn. One man had an enormous wen on his neck and a bright, merry eye. Another looked like a Spanish peasant with a square, flat face and sad eyes. Another was fat with a bristling mustache.

"Here is our Communist," said the mayor, "what fights he had with the curé!"

The fat man grinned. "The new man will not argue. He raises his hands and says that he will pray for me. Things have changed a bit, my friends, he had better pray for himself."

Some boys of the Resistance walked past singing a patriotic song. The man with the wen smiled. "They make a lot of noise, but they did well a few days ago. They did not attack the Germans, you understand. They shot at them from a distance. They made demolitions, little mines.

"But when your people drove the Germans out, they thought it was all over. There were some Germans on the hill behind the airfield, and the young ones tried to take them. They suffered two dead and three wounded. Then, when there were more Americans, three more were killed trying to help. These we buried today. They were impetuous. The Americans knew what they were doing."

I asked how long the Resistance had been organized in St. Aubin. The mayor said that it had not been long, not as a guerrilla force.

"Always, I think, from the start, some of us did what we could. Then as the war went on and the Germans became less correct and more as they truly are, others joined us. It was knowing that the war went on that decided many. They told us first that it was all over, that the English were defeated."

Early in 1941 they had seen planes, many British planes—it must have been one of the R.A.F. fighter sweeps over northern France—and their attitude toward the Germans altered. Yes, of course, they had heard of de Gaulle. But monsieur must remember that this was a German-occupied area, not the free zone in the south. Resistance had to take a different form.

"We always made things difficult for them," the mayor said.

"They would ask for things, figures on farm production, the number and location of automobiles and trucks and horses. We always gave them a great many papers. And every time they found some error. The Germans would come and say, 'You stupid people, give us a true report!'

"We would bow and take the papers back, but it would be a long time before they got their report, and by then—well, things were not where they had been before. You understand. And the information about the farms. They wanted the food. They would ask us where the best wheat was grown. So we would say at M. Latour's, where it is nothing extraordinary, and tell those who had good wheat to wear a long face and say their crop was bad. When they wanted a job done, you may be sure it took the longest possible time. When they came looking for people, French of the Resistance, English pilots, we had never heard of them."

He spread his old, mottled hands. "We did what we could."

The others began to leave. I asked the fat butcher to have a last glass. "What now for France?" I asked. "Why," he said, as though surprised at the question, "France must rebuild herself." I suggested Pétain had said just that in 1940. The butcher said Pétain and Laval should do unmentionable things to themselves. And de Gaulle, as well. He had no faith in generals; all fascists.

In the dining room lunch was ready. Lamb such as I had not tasted in four years. An apple tart. Everyone apologized for the wine. The boche had taken the best. But after the fourth or fifth bottle no one complained. The butcher went out and returned with a bottle of Marc de Bourgogne. I said I would have a drop in anticipation of snake bite on the way home. The remark taxed my powers of translation. The mayor said it was a good idea. It was well known that there were many snakes in Brittany.

After Normandy I went back to London to resume the job of writing what was called the "war lead." This was a daily story, running from one to two thousand words and rounding up the events on land, on sea, and in the air during the previous twenty-four hours. It was written in London because, even then, in July of 1944, London remained the main center of information on the war. It was not an exciting job, although the V-1s, then attacking London, provided noises off stage, but it was an exacting one.

Encouraged by the successes in Normandy, the American public was in one of its "all over by Christmas" moods. An important aspect of the daily job was focusing the reader's attention on the vital developments along the front. An advance of five miles in one sector, for example, often meant more than another advance of twenty-five miles in another area. I had to emphasize that German resistance would stiffen rather than weaken as the Allies approached the Rhine. To give news and balanced interpretation in the same story was a taxing job.

London became an endless round of maps, briefings, telephone calls, and the typewriter. We were blown out of our flat in Great Smith Street by a V-1 and moved to the Savoy Hotel, then the site of *The New York Times* office. I grew tired and irritable; this was a hell of a way to cover the war.

Suddenly the information section of Supreme Headquarters, Allied Forces Europe (SHAFE), announced it was moving to Paris. Happily I packed my bags and followed. My last visit had coincided with the opening of the German offensive of 1940. The city had lived through four years of occupation. I returned to it with breathless joy and, as I walked the boulevards or perched on the Pont Neuf and looked at the lovely sweep of the Seine, I wondered how the Germans could ever have believed, whatever their strength, that they could tame this wanton miracle of grace and light. Or subdue so perky and intransigent a people as the Parisians. I knew many French had returned to the Allied side at certain well-defined periods of the war: a few after the Battle of Britain, more after Stalingrad and Alamein, a great many after D-Day. But the working people of Paris had been with us from the start.

At first I sought people I had known in that gay, rootless winter of 1939–40, a melancholy, harrowing business. No, monsieur, the concierge would say, madame moved away two winters ago. She was ill, you understand, and could not stand the cold. No, monsieur, Lucien was seized by the Germans when he returned to see his family. At the flat in Passy: Madame Nicole was in the Resistance and had disappeared.

Nevertheless it was Paris. Little bars where one could drink at any hour still flourished. Charlie Collingwood and I found a particularly disreputable night club in Montmartre, so disreputable that the proprietor whispered that it was not the place for a well-raised young Englishwoman like my wife. In the mornings I walked beside the Seine. In the afternoons I trudged the corridors at Supreme Headquarters at Versailles searching for information that would amplify the briefings held at the Hôtel Scribe.

Harold Denny, covering the U.S. First Army, was to go on leave. I took his place. I had had enough of the "big picture" at Supreme Headquarters. I wanted to get back to "the sharp end" of the war. Besides, things were looking up all along the front. Hemingway, living in royal state at the Ritz, thought we just might make it this year. I packed my bedding roll, bought two bottles of whiskey at a staggering price, and arranged transportation. Friends in Paris told me I was a damned fool. I had been shot at often enough. Why forego the comforts of Paris and a good story for the uncertainties of the front? They had an argument, but I was glad to go. Ho, for the wars!

If there must be a war, an army and, therefore, a headquarters, Spa is highly recommended. The Germans used it as General Headquarters in the first, or inconclusive, world war. They were wise to do so. There are good hotels. The local streams provide tasty trout in war or peace.

I sought out Bill Stoneman when I arrived. He asked what they thought of this front at Supreme Headquarters. I told them they believed we would break through to the Rhine by October. The Doctor expressed his opinion of Headquarters in well-chosen words. He said we would be lucky to get to the Rhine by spring; the Germans were fighting hard and the terrain was murder.

The 1st Infantry Division had been assigned the task of taking Aachen, the first sizable German city to be assailed. The division had made itself comfortable. It was never one of those "live hard, fight hard" outfits. But it fought harder, and more successfully, than some that made a fetish of rough living.

We spent a day with a mortar battalion commanded by Lieutenant Colonel Jim Batt. The mortars were deployed to the southeast of Aachen in country that was half urban, half rural. This area was strongly held, because through it ran highways along which supplies moved to the German troops in the city. It was a crisp, September afternoon and very still.

A battery was firing at a building believed to be a battalion headquarters. In the silence between explosions you could hear men grunt as they lifted mortar shells. They stood poised for an instant and then dropped the shell into the round, black mouth of the tube. They moved with practised precision, like votaries sacrificing by ancient rite before some old, loud-bellowing priest.

The mortars were emplaced in the backyards of pleasant suburban villas. I entered one to write some notes and fell into conversation with two soldiers from Chicago. They commented freely on the German movie magazines they had found in the room.

"All the actors look like fags," said one. "They probably were, at that. They got a lot of them. A friend of mine, he was killed a while back, got three Germans down in Belgium. Two of them was fags.

"He says, 'Lootenant, I'm a son of a bitch if this guy ain't got women's clothes on under his uniform,' that's when they was searching them, you know, and the Lootenant like to eat his ass out until he comes over and sees for hisself. Honest to Christ. Women's clothes and a hairnet and powder on one guy. The other guy was just paint and powder and perfume. Stunk wors'n a whorehouse."

In the late afternoon the searching mortars found two trucks full of ammunition that had been parked in the open. The observation officer said they went up like a mine. We drove back passing one crossroads under German observation. An 88 shell had burst there since our outward trip. As we sped up the road to Brand we heard another fall.

Aachen lies in a hollow. The 1st Division had contained the city on the west, south, and east. The battle for the first German city was about to begin.

Either from a distance, equipped with maps and field glasses, or in the streets the battle had no form. From a distance Aachen was a sprawling mass of gray and brown buildings marked here and there by licking tongues of flame and pierced by church steeples and factory chimneys. A cloud of dust and smoke hung over the city. You could hear the guns slam in the hills behind us and then watch for the shell bursts. Once a 155 shell burst in a two-story building, and I watched the building collapse. At that distance the movement was slow, almost deliberate. As the shells burst, little sparks of flame ran through the gray and brown backdrop. There were no soldiers and no civilians visible. Sometimes the fighter bombers came and dove on the city. From that distance it was hard to realize that there were people in the cellars cringing under the impact of the bombs or shaking as the machine-gun bullets whined and spattered on the streets. The Germans were experiencing what the people of a hundred cities in Europe had known at their hands since 1939.

The division fought many fine actions. Aachen must be reckoned with the best. The attack was systematic, sure, not wasteful. While the division attacked, it held off attempts to reinforce the city by very good German divisions sent south from Arnheim. On October 10 General Clarence L. Huebner, commanding the 1st Division, sent an ultimatum demanding Aachen's surrender. There was no reply. So the division went in to take Aachen. It was the last battle I was to see.

On the third day the division was well into Aachen. The fighter bombers and the artillery would soften German strong points, and then the infantry would advance. I left the jeep and walked past a row of empty apartment houses. They looked substantial enough. Behind their brown or gray fronts there was nothing but rubble. It was raining hard. The streets and sidewalks were littered with debris. On one wall was the slogan "For this we thank our Fuehrer." Underneath an American had scrawled "fuck you, Joe."

A captain named Gilbert Fuller took me to his command post in the house of a doctor. It was just such a house as one sometimes saw in New York, what was called a brownstone, solid, comfortable, exuding smug prosperity. The furniture was heavy and elaborate. The curtains were of a heavy red material. Outside there was the rattle of machine-gun fire and occasionally the crash of a shell.

The fire lifted, and I ran down the street toward a house to which Fuller had directed me. The cellar had the dank, musty smell I associated with those New York brownstones long ago. By some trick of memory I recalled my mother's helping me up the cellar stairs on 93rd Street with my new sled. I went down a passageway, across a backyard, and into another house. I went through it and dashed across the street and into another house. This was the front line; a parlor looking out on an ordinary street in an ordinary town, three American soldiers.

Each had a heavy growth of beard and smelt strongly. Their eyes were very bright. The corporal said, "Keep away from the window, bud, there's a jerry trying to get us." I asked him how long he'd been there.

"Day," he said.

Machine-gun fire swept the street. I rolled on my stomach and listened. The corporal explained there was a German at the corner covering the street and that "a guy upstairs was watching for him" and would get him.

I went downstairs and into the next house through a gap torn in the cellar wall. There were more soldiers there. Our mortars had been shelling the houses opposite, and when they had finished they were going to make a rush. A corporal and a private flung themselves across the street. There was no fire. Other men followed. A shell burst. A voice cried "Jesus, Joe! Oh, shit! Oh, my fucking back! Oh! Oh, baby! Mother! Oh-h-h Christ!"

I wanted to be anywhere but in that room. The corporal said he thought the street was clear. The wounded man was sobbing in pain. I started across the street. Something slammed into one of the houses, and I was flat on my face, winded but otherwise all right.

Upstairs two G.I.'s were firing from the window of a back bed-room across backyards. There were sheets on the beds and heavy eiderdowns covered in red silk.

"Who are these guys?" I asked, "S.S.?"

"Just kraut soldiers," said one, "They fight like S.S. but they're just kraut soldiers. They can't shoot worth a shit, but they keep on firing. We took a guy back to Captain Fuller yesterday. He looked like old man Stein in the bakery back home."

I asked if the Germans surrendered easily.

"He didn't have nothing left to shoot with when we got him," said the other soldier. "All them guys are alike, all fucking, tough bastards. Jesus, I'd like to shoot them all! All of them, from that Hitler on down, all of them!"

"The sons of bitching bastards, the fucking, fucking bastards!"

he yelled. He got to his feet and emptied his rifle across the yards. Bullets hit the walls of our house and whispered as they ricocheted.

This was hard, blind fighting in narrow backyards or on steep staircases where men met unexpectedly, threw a grenade, or lunged with a bayonet. House by house, foot by foot, the Germans were driven out of the city. Their dead lay in the streets or in dim rooms in shattered homes. One by one the German strongpoints were eliminated. On Saturday, October 21, Colonel Gerhard Wilck surrendered to the 26th Infantry of the 1st Division. The city was silent, and in the afternoon when the sun came out, our men, dirty and weary, emerged and stretched. They were old soldiers. They didn't think the war had been won. They only knew another battle was over.

That afternoon I stood above Brand and looked down the road into the city. German refugees, the first I had seen, trudged up the hill. The war had come full circle. These haggard men and women, pushing wheelbarrows, pulling small carts, were the end of that caravan of misery I had seen nearly four and a half years before on the Belgian roads.

One should be compassionate. Compassion is difficult when you think of the roads of France and Belgium black with frightened, tired people, the gray faces of Londoners leaving their shelters to start another day's work, the Arab woman holding her dead baby outside Medjez-el-Bab after the German fighters had been over.

The Germans stopped at the hilltop and looked back at Aachen. They had left because they knew that, once the surrender was known to the German army, the city would be shelled unmercifully. So they were hurrying to the protection of the Americans, to sleep in the army barracks at Brand. They knew they would get food and shelter from the Americans. And they did.

By the barracks gate a well-dressed woman of forty or so was searching the faces of the arrivals. She told me in French she was looking for her mother who had been delayed because she wanted to pack heavy clothes. The mother arrived, a tall, arrogant woman in a fur coat. She said something rapidly to her daughter.

"She says Hitler is a devil for having brought such sorrow

on the German people. The war is insane. The church she has gone to for thirty years is burning."

I said that other churches had burned, other people had been driven from their homes in a dozen countries.

It was as good a time as any to leave the front. A German city had been taken. The war was returning to its origin. Aachen lay silent, and the wind brought the faint smell of corruption and death. The final victory was still months away. I knew it was inevitable.

III

The plane lumbered down out of the cloud, and there beneath us lay Berlin—dead. It was June 1945. I had had five and a half years of war. Nothing I had seen before gave an impression of such utter hopelessness, of devastation so extensive and so thorough. A carpet of gray and black lay below; the gray was the ash and rubble of homes and buildings, the black was burned timbers or scorched stone. There was no movement in the streets. No chimney smoked. When we got out of the plane, we caught, I hoped for the last time, the sweetly sickening smell of many bodies decomposing.

A number of correspondents had been flown from Frankfort for the proclamation of four-power rule in a conquered Germany. This could be considered the final act of the drama of the Third Reich. Or the first act of Germany's new history.

I favored the latter. I had seen what I considered the last act ten days before at Flensburg in Schleswig-Holstein near the Danish frontier: bored British troops rounding up the last government of the Third Reich, that led by Admiral Doenitz. It had been done as swiftly and as completely as the dismissal of an unsatisfactory servant. The only German to come out of it with a touch of grace was Albert Speer, who had been Hitler's master builder. When the British took him, he made no protest. He said only, "So, the comedy is over!"

In Berlin the Russians ruled. We drove through empty avenues. The exits from the side streets were barricaded and guarded by sentries. But a block or so down from the streets' intersections with the avenues little groups of Germans peered timidly at the cavalcade of big black cars. They had been told the Allies were coming. The Russians, protesting the security of the Allied commanders, kept the Germans out of sight. The looting and the raping were still going on. It was a bright, hot June day.

The meeting was in a villa carefully selected by our hosts. There was, there always is, a delay in anything the Soviets arrange. We stood around in the sun and talked. Eisenhower, grumpy at the delay; Montgomery, talkative, full of himself; de Lattre de Tassigny, gorgeously uniformed, very military. Then Marshal Zhukov entered: a short man, very broad and powerful across the shoulders and chest.

"Looks like a wrestler," said Eisenhower. "Well, let's get this thing over with."

The big, resounding words rolled out. They represented a death sentence on Germany. Eisenhower and Zhukov represented the new masters of Europe. Within four years, in that same city, I was to see the start of the great duel between the Soviet Union and the United States that was to last well into the 'sixties. But at that time nothing seemed as final as the end of Germany, the dawn of peace. Men thought, and not without reason, that with the defeat of Germany and Italy and the coming victory over Japan that a new era had opened. There would be problems but none to match those of the past ten years. The peoples deserved peace, they wanted peace. In its true sense it was to elude them.

Even then there were those in the U.S. Army and the British Army who were apprehensive about the great wave of Russian soldiery that swept across eastern Europe. They wondered where it would stop. They had a sharp memory of Russian double-dealing in the past, and they wondered. Whatever the people of the United States, Britain, and France felt about the Russians, these men were sure that as far as the Soviet leadership was concerned we, the West, were its enemies. Events were to prove them right.

A week later Charlie Wertenbaker of *Time* and I were talking with Bedell Smith. What would have happened, we asked, if the Russians had continued on, if they had attacked the western armies to drive them out of Germany. In the uncertain atmosphere of June 1945 this was not a frivolous question. The General thought for a bit.

"All things considered and given our superiority in the air, we would have taken them. But tough, tough all the way."

The war had started for me in the confident, comfortable London of 1939. It ended in the ruined Berlin of 1945. In the years between I had been taught cruel lessons, assumed a harshness and cynicism ill-suited for the piping times of peace. Why this should have happened to me, I do not know. It did not happen to others who saw far more fighting. In the tumultuous quarter of a century since I have done my best to exorcise these demons. I have been unsuccessful. I can never forget the war.

CHAPTER 7

RUSSIA AND THE START OF THE COLD WAR

1946-47

> I sit on a man's back, choking him and making him
> carry me, and yet assure myself and others that I am
> very sorry for him and wish to ease his lot by all possible
> means—except by getting off his back.
>
> Tolstoy

One May afternoon in 1946 I picked my way along a shabby street in Moscow. I paused to check my bearings. As I did, the sun broke through, touching the golden domes of the Kremlin so I saw them, serene, infinitely graceful against a patch of blue sky and framed by decaying old buildings at the far end of the street. I stood transfixed. Then the sun disappeared, and I was back in the shabby street with its rancid smell and broken pavements.

Those few moments, early in my stay in the Soviet Union, have since symbolized my essential feeling about Russia and the Russians: the tantalizing, promised vision that fades in a moment into shabby, sordid reality.

My assignment to Russia had been given me over a year earlier in the closing months of the European war. It was a plum. It was evident then that the Soviet Union would end the war as the strongest power in the Eurasian land mass and that what happened in Russia would be of the utmost consequence to the United States and to the people of Europe.

I was profoundly grateful for the assignment. I had hoped to get the Paris job. But, I told myself, Russia was new, a greater challenge. I was replacing that gentlest of men, Brooks Atkinson, whom I found weary and cynical; I could not understand it then. I did later.

I do not remember having any fears about my ability to do the Moscow job. My self-confidence had grown during the war. I felt *The Times* had recognized my ability by giving me the assignment and, perhaps too credulous, I thought that good work on one assignment would invariably lead to a better. Things did not always follow that pattern. In time I learned to appreciate the wisdom of Malcolm Muggeridge's fundamental rule for correspondents: get a good expense account and stay as far as possible from the home office.

The year between the surrender in May 1945 and my arrival in Moscow on May 19, 1946, was spent in Germany. I worked in Frankfurt, in Berlin, and at the Nürnberg war crimes trials. I did not find Germany, devastated and occupied, particularly interesting. Allied military government—in the American Zone of Occupation an odd mixture of revival meeting fervor and military authoritarianism—was superimposed upon the great mass of Germans still mentally numb from the experiences of the past six years.

My work enabled me to talk to enough Germans to get some idea of how they felt on the morning of defeat. My diaries show three overriding impressions.

The first was that, desperate though the Germans' situation might be, the war and defeat had not drained them of all vitality. On the contrary, I encountered among the young signs of a deep desire to restore the country, if not to the glories of the Third Reich, at least to a viable, economic entity. Even then, when the widening breach between Moscow and the Allied capitals had not been exposed to public view, many Germans were confident a split would come and that they would benefit. In this they showed unusual prescience.

"You've defeated us and you hold the country," a student said at Erlangen. "But we Germans can work. The coal is still there. We'll build another sort of country. And you'll need us. Oh, yes, you'll need us. You think you can get along with Ivan? Nonsense!"

My second impression was that the traumatic experience of the war had eliminated, for the time being, the Germans' old belief in themselves as a decisive world force. They had flown so high from 1939 to 1942, then had fallen so low in the three short years. Their confidence had evaporated. I did not believe that the Germans yet understood the danger of authoritarianism or were ripe for democracy. I did believe the Germans had learned that the immense military strength deployed by the United States, the Soviet Union, and Britain made nonsense of their pretensions to hegemony in Europe, let alone the world. This lesson, I believe, sank in. Today one can meet arrogant Germans, boastful Germans, but never one who dreams the old dreams of world leadership.

Indelibly stamped on my memory is one last impression, that of Berlin as it was in the winter of 1945–46: a combination of garrison town, wide-open mining camp, espionage center sprawled across acre after acre of dark and frozen desolation. The soldiers of four nations brawled in the streets. Shots sounded in the night. Dives catering to raw sex, and, for those so inclined, every perversion flourished. Occupation currency rolled off the printing presses, and the United States garrison sent home hundreds of thousands of dollars from the sale of watches, lighters, and other Post Exchange goods to Russian troops.

There were German women everywhere, and the soldiers of four armies made free of them. A young reporter from a news agency asked a very senior general if he could bring his wife to Berlin.

"Wife? You must be nuts!" said the general. "You're bringing a sandwich to a banquet."

Moscow, on the other hand, offered the prospect of reporting on a revolutionary society that had proved its strength and that now might be willing to show the world what lay behind that strength.

Except for the very few who are willing to stay in Russia forever, six years, I would say, is about the minimal dose for an adult. Few correspondents learn a great deal about the Soviet Union no matter how perceptive, intelligent, and aggressive they may be. They should not be faulted. There is too much to learn. Even if the Soviet Union were to allow a foreign correspondent the freedom a British or a French correspondent enjoys in the United States, there is too much of Russia, there are too many different nationalities, too many different problems local as well as national, and too many nuances.

Beyond the complexity and extent of the country is the refusal of the Soviet government to open their country to the inquiring reporter, friendly or otherwise.

Over the years Russian writers and diplomats have bewailed the West's ignorance of their country. The solution is in the hands of their government. Open up. Let the correspondents loose. End censorship. This has never been done or, as far as I know, even contemplated, although there was a brief easing of the censorship rules under Nikita Khrushchev. Communism is usually blamed. But Russian xenophobia and the intense secrecy are much older than Communism. By stretching the imagination it is possible to conceive of a Soviet government eliminating censorship and giving foreign reporters access to the government statistics that are available in free countries and the right to travel. But by no stretch of the imagination is it possible to believe that the people in government departments would willingly implement the order. It would go against the grain of five hundred years of Russian history.

In my time the censorship was harsh and capricious. For a period it was "blind." That is, the correspondent submitted his dispatch to the censor, and two or three days later it was returned to him as it had been sent. One dispatch of eight hundred words was returned to me with one sentence of eight words remaining.

I found it was possible to play on the censors' ignorance to make points. I once wrote that the series written by Ilya Ehrenburg about his tour of the United States had no rival in travel literature since the works of Charles Lutwidge Dodgson. The literary will recognize the latter as Lewis Carroll. This was a petty trick. But it relieved a harassed reporter and had notable antecedents. During the war Philip Jordan of the London *News-Chronicle,* enraged by the constant lying of the Soviet spokesman about the Red Army's position in 1941, had written "Dr. Josef Goebbels is the most accomplished liar in the world. Abraham Zoslovsky, the Soviet spokesman, is not." The censor let it through.

The Soviet government not only exercised an iron censorship.

It also forbade contact between correspondents and all but a few Soviet news sources. The head of the news department was Constantine Zinchenko, an amiable enough fellow whom I had known in London. Zinchenko would accept with every sign of good will my requests to see this minister or that official and would promise to do his best. I'm sure he did. But I never saw the ministers. For source material a reporter fell back on friendly embassies and the newspapers and magazines.

I was lucky in one respect. The American Embassy was headed by General Bedell Smith assisted by an able staff including John Paton Davies and Elbridge C. Durbrow. They knew the country, Marxism, and American policy, and they were willing to talk. The minister at the British Embassy was Frank Roberts, an acute observer, who later returned to Moscow as ambassador.

Reporting, consequently, was almost invariably second-hand. The newspapers and magazines were read thoroughly. Friends in the embassies were asked for their views on the reasons behind the news and for information on what Soviet diplomats were saying. They said very little. Stalin still ruled in the Kremlin, and the purge was an occupational hazard for anyone in the governmental machine. The Russians, by nature open and talkative, had been cowed into silence.

Life for westerners was incestuous. The same people exchanged the same ideas at luncheons, cocktails, dinners, and after-dinner parties. Conversations begun over a prelunch drink could be continued through three other meetings. It was rather like an ocean voyage except that the ship never arrived.

A trip out of Moscow was a rare prize. I had been there less than a week when Brooks Atkinson told me that a trip had been organized by the Foreign Ministry to Byelorussia and that I was to go. On it I made my first acquaintance with that other Russia beyond Moscow, with the people, so cruelly ill-used, so magnificent in their courage and endurance, so worthy of greatness and fated by their own political system never to obtain it.

My diary records the impact of the other Russia.

May 28, 1946. We travelled on what Farny [Farnsworth Fowle of CBS] assured me were "soft," i.e. first-class, coaches. The train was very long and very slow. Found several flea bites on my legs in the morning. As we passed through a country station, I noticed people sleeping in the waiting rooms. Waiting for trains. Also brass faucets dispensing hot water for those who wanted to make tea.

We approached Minsk around a long curve on an embankment. Looking forward I saw tens, scores, of people jumping off the train and rolling down the embankment to the fields. We asked an affable Russian officer about it. They were peasants, he said, probably from the nearest village, and they took this method of getting off the train instead of going into Minsk and walking home. I said something about baggage. When this was translated, someone farther down the corridor laughed and said, "Baggage, who has baggage, today?"

May 29, 1946. Minsk is in ruins. Worse than any town I saw in Germany and comparable only to those towns and cities fought over in Normandy. We were told with pride that the only building saved intact from destruction was Party Headquarters. The partisans [the Russians' name for their guerrillas] had entered town on the heels of the retreating Germans and cut the wires leading to the demolition charges. Part of the damage is the result of shelling, the rest from methodical German demolition as they prepared to withdraw.

German prisoners of war were clearing the debris in the center of the city. They wore old uniforms, stained and dirty. But they were tanned and they looked healthy. "Wie Gehts?" I asked one. "Gehts gut," he said and winked. He was from Berlin and started to ask me to take a message, when the Russian guard snarled and he went back to work.

Alec [Alexander Werth, the author, then correspondent for *The Manchester Guardian*] said that it was "exactly right" that the Germans, who are responsible for the mess, should clean it up. Perhaps he's right. But "responsible." Now there's a word. Who is responsible? Some farm boy from Bavaria shoved into the Wehrmacht? The Nazi leaders? Or the German generals the Russians are babying in captivity with an eye to the future?

Later we were shown a kindergarten, and I was shocked. I don't think I shock easily. Here were a dozen shaven-headed little boys going through military drills with wooden rifles. The teacher told us they must learn to defend their country. God! Now, after no one knows how many million dead.

Two thoughts before I turn in. You see Russia and its limitless space and enormous population, you remember the weight that the United States and Britain brought to bear in Europe, and you must consider the Germans, no matter who led them, very considerable people. You also note in Russia the appalling lack of machines, the primitive organization, the absence of modern technology, and you conclude that American and British help, especially in advanced weapons, may have been more important to the Soviet Union in the war than the Russians will ever admit.

Fear permeated life in Moscow. The war and the appalling inefficiency of the Soviet production and distribution had created shortages in food, household goods, housing. Yet no one complained. The propaganda machine had embarked on the long and, up to a point, successful campaign to impress the Russian people that victory did not mean an end to their sacrifices. They were now menaced, they were told, by the capitalist West. Everyone must work to avert this new danger although, in a contradiction the perspicacious must have noted, the glorious Red Army, Navy, and Air Force were able to defeat all enemies if the need arose.

The editorials in *Pravda,* which then and now set the tone, had a certain monotony. From the titles I could guess the content. "Speed the harvest" appeared above a call to harder work in the fields. "Speed the Production of Footwear" meant an attack on those laggards not fulfilling their normal production quotas. The editorials were a poor instructor to anyone learning Russian. Cliché tumbled after cliché. The words "Wall Street," for example, invariably were followed by "capitalist imperialist." Dull stuff.

There were ideas abroad that may have caused some uneasy nights in the Kremlin. When the first troops returned from Germany and eastern Europe they bore with them not only everything they had been able to loot but strange tales of life in the occupied countries: individual houses for workers, white bread, good clothes. The Russians, a naturally avaricious people, thought these material benefits wonderful. I doubt whether they were moved by propaganda to the effect that the Europeans had lived under an odious tyranny from which the Red Army had freed them. As experts on tyranny, the Russians said nothing in public.

I was walking one evening in Moscow's Park of Culture and Rest. There is damned little culture there and, in those days, because of the constant blaring of the loud-speaker system, even less rest.

A small girl, just learning to walk, toddled a few steps toward me and fell. My daughter, back in Wales, would be taking her first steps. I picked the child up, set her on her feet, and said a few words in Russian. Suddenly she was snatched away by her mother who hustled her out of the park. Mike Handler explained that the mother didn't want to be seen talking with a foreigner.

Shafts of bitter disillusionment often pierced the gray atmosphere. I heard a grandmother shout at a food queue, "The guns are firing for victory, but where is the food?" An old man in a crowded train in southern Russia harangued the other passengers about the iniquities of Communist rule. A worn woman of faded prettiness, once a member of the Party elite, said quietly in the midst of an otherwise banal conversation, "We thought we were building a palace; we built a jail."

I have never encountered a more hospitable people. In those years they had very little. But the single bottle of "store" vodka was always brought out for the visitor (after that you drank *samogon,* literally "self lightning," with disastrous results).

One winter's day I journeyed to a collective farm outside Moscow. We left the car on the road and boarded rude sleighs. There was a crust on the snow, and we swept across the fields in bitter cold. Inside farm headquarters there was lunch and vodka. The accompanying Foreign Ministry official was a tolerant type, and we were soon deep in comparisons of the American and Soviet ways of life. This, remember, was in Stalin's time, when Americans were daily portrayed as enemies and American reporters as spies. But among our hosts there was nothing but warm kindness and a devouring curiosity. Because they had no standards for comparison, they clearly doubted my descriptions of life in America. Thinking of these decent, friendly people as the sleigh took me back to the car, I considered, not for the first time, how fine it would be if peoples could talk to peoples.

A dream; it won't happen. The most we can expect is a desire for understanding.

The harvest of 1946 was the worst since that of 1894. Cavalry had to be brought into Kiev to put down a bread riot that winter. In the spring of 1947 perhaps two or three times a week we would hear a faint knocking at our door in the hotel: outside, a peasant woman, often accompanied by a gaunt, wide-eyed child. She would hold out one claw and say, "Bread, please." When the Foreign Ministers of the United States, Britain, and France came to Moscow for a conference in March 1947, the government set up roadblocks on the highways leading into the capital to prevent peasants' begging in the city and exposing Russia's plight to the foreigners.

That was Moscow in Good King Joe's day. That was the Russia that a generation of addle-headed academics in the 'thirties had painted as the society of the future. A stay in Russia has one advantage: you learn what *not* to believe.

By what magic did Communists succeed in convincing otherwise sane men that they had the answer, that theirs was the road of the future? I recall a professor at Syracuse who told us—it was in the midst of the Great Depression—that none of the frightful problems then confronting the United States existed in the Soviet Union, where there was food and work for all. He was a nice man, a well-meaning man, an educated man, usually difficult to deceive. He had made one carefully supervised trip to Russia.

To fear and to occasional reflections of disillusionment there was added that special hopelessness that Communism has implanted in the Russian ethos. No one said things would get better. They only hoped they would grow no worse.

Bedell Smith said one night, "These could be a great people. But you let this system continue for another couple of generations and they'll be cattle, just cattle."

In the late summer of 1946 a group of other correspondents and I visited the Ukraine and Byelorussia. This, by far, was the most stimulating experience of my tour of duty in Russia. The Soviet government arranged the trip, not because they wanted us to go to the two republics, but because the bills in Congress and the House of Commons that allocated funds for United Nations Relief and Rehabilitation Administration said that newspapermen should be allowed to see the distribution of the goods sent to the Soviet Union.

My diary for that trip is too long to quote in full. But I hope the few extracts below will give the flavor of life in Soviet hinterland.

Kiev. This city has been renamed the capital of the Ukraine. We halted, briefly, at the prewar capital, Kharkhov, en route, and I am sure the Russians regret the stop. As we emerged from the plane and started for the lounge, we heard faint piping cries of *"Xleb, xleb,"* bread, bread. They came, not, as I first thought, from German prisoners, but from a group of emaciated *Russian* prisoners digging on some construction project. Their guards were fat and truculent. When the shouting reached us and we turned, the guards prodded the prisoners with rifle butts.

We have been shown a collective farm. Not a model, of course, we were told, just an average collective farm. The head of the farm rode up to us on a magnificent young stallion. The head's name was Gordon, or so we were introduced. The farm machinery, which he showed us, was a mixture of Russian and German machines. The Germans were welcomed as liberators in many parts of the Ukraine. The capital was changed from Kharkhov to Kiev because of the high number of collaborators in the former. The jerries did their best to introduce modern agriculture to the Ukraine and to some extent succeeded. Mike says that they would have done even better had the S.S. not followed the Wehrmacht and instituted its usual persecutions and shipments of slave labor. Gordon said the harvest was in, it had been "medium good" and, with the addition of new machines to the Machine Tractor Station, which provides them for the farm, they looked forward to an even better year in 1947.

By chance I was able to see this farm again in 1959, when I accompanied Prime Minister Harold Macmillan on his trip to Moscow. It was, of course, a "show" farm, probably the best in the neighborhood. Thirteen years after my first visit the only improvements I noticed were that there was more Russian-made farm equipment and that some of the houses had been whitewashed. I said as much to Randolph Churchill. He said that they were not the only things being whitewashed: "Look at your colleagues, lapping it up."

This city strikes me as one that has a certain intrinsic grandeur. We were taken to an old monastery and a new department store. People here have a prouder look than those in Moscow. We spoke to a couple in the street, and they didn't break off the conversation at once, as they would have done in Moscow. There is one grand, wide street filled with people strolling in the September sun. You feel here that you are in something more than an administrative capital, that Kiev has seen a lot—famine, bloodshed, and terror—and will see a lot more but will continue somehow vigorous, friendly, even serene.

Stalino. We are quartered in Stalino in a worker's guest house. It is very hot, and the windows are screened with cheesecloth to keep out the flies. Stalino is the industrial capital of the Donbas, western Russia's Ruhr. A long day going from steel plant to factory to coal mine. The steel plant was in operation but still in dreadful condition. It was built before World War I by a British company, and it looks like the old plants you see in the Midlands. Everything makeshift but the steel workers. They draw a high category of ration card and are stalwart and nimble. Our guides were thorough. Like all Russians, they seem to think that there was nothing like this plant in the world. Natural enough. They have no standards of comparison. So they went on and on about how the plant used electric power for some operations, as though this happened nowhere else in the world.

Moscow newspaper editorials rejoice that the Donbas is again producing coal and steel. No production figures, of course. We were taken through a coal mine to prove it. Why, I don't know. It seemed to be running at about ten per cent of capacity. Mike Handler asked an engineer if the coal fields had been restored. The engineer said they had, to the extent that the water had been pumped out. The Germans flooded the mines when they retreated three years ago.

Odessa. The city was planned by French royalist emigrés and has, despite the appalling modern buildings and the ruins, a faint breath of a French provincial city. It looks out on a bay and reminds me a little of Algiers.

Two odd incidents. After lunch our party trooped out of the hotel into the brilliant sunshine. As we waited for our cars, a man came by carrying in his hands what looked like a box covered with old newspapers. When he was dead in front of us he stopped. We all saw the lens of a camera peeping through the newspaper in the center of the box and heard the click as the man snapped his picture. We shouted with laughter. Even Simonov, the Foreign Ministry guide, was embarrassed. Again, why? The NKVD must have dozens of pictures of all of us in Moscow.

When we returned to our hotel in the evening, a big Russian car drew up, and a stocky, purposeful-looking general got out. Zhukov. We knew that the papers said he had been transferred to the southern command. Some in Moscow believe he has been exiled. But here he was, as bouncy and assertive as ever. He waved us away and walked into the hotel. He is one of the legitimate military heroes of the Russian war. So much so that I guess Stalin feels he cannot eliminate him. Of course, he's eliminated marshals before this, Tukachevsky for example.

Zaporozhe. It seems incredible in this security-sick country, but we flew over the Donbas today at a height of what I judged to be five thousand feet. Here we are, correspondents, considered spies by the Russians for the simple reason that their correspondents *are* spies, and we are flown over the most important industrial area in the Soviet Union.

We arrived at the Odessa airfield early this morning to find that the flight to Rostov and Zaporozhe had been discontinued. An air-force colonel listened to Simonov's anguished complaints and told him that he could supply three planes and pilots to fly us to Zaporozhe.

The planes were single-engined monoplanes, the pilots young air-force officers. We flew over the Donbas, and it was clear that, despite what the Moscow papers say, the area is far from being rehabilitated. Some smoke from a few factory chimneys. But very little traffic on the railroad spurs leading into the industrial plants. Not as bad as the Ruhr in '45 but the resemblance was there. There were two others in my plane and none of us had a camera. I wondered what the pictures would be worth in London or Washington.

Stopped once for gas at an airfield, and that's what it was, a field, on the edge of the Donbas. The pilots were friendly enough. They knew the names of Allied planes and they were interested in American and British jets. They kept a careful eye on the airfield mechanics. One of them explained to Mike that it was impossible to trust them. He considered the mechanics lazy and inefficient hicks.

We are at Zaporozhe because it is near the great dam on the Dnepr river, first built with American engineering help and some American equipment. I can remember how English editorial writers anguished over its destruction by the Russians in the face of the German advance. Such destruction of one of Russia's proudest achievements, they said, showed how rigorously the scorched-earth policy was being carried out.

But the "destruction" was only partial. The chief engineer, a big, heavy-set man named Loginov, showed us the pictures the Germans had taken when they arrived. The retreating Russians had blown out about fifty meters of the top of the dam to prevent the Germans' using it as a bridge. The real destruction was done by the German engineers in *their* retreat. Explosives blew generators out of the plant and into the river and snapped the turbine drive shafts. One whole side of the dam, that nearest the canal, was blown in. Thousands of workers on the site; Russian men and women and German prisoners. We are lodged in a quiet house with apricot trees blooming in the garden.

Minsk. The end of the trip. Minsk, as I noted on my earlier visit, is in terrible shape. But we've seen so many other cities in ruins that one grows hardened to it. All I have seen leaves the impression that what the Russians are now doing, largely with manual labor and the help we are sending through UNRRA, has no more effect on the essential damage than sweeping the floor in a bombed building.

How strangely this grim and massive destruction, these shortages of machinery and equipment, contrast with the bellicose statements about the United States and the other "imperialist powers." From the editorials in *Pravda* one would imagine Russia is ready for another war. Yet cities are in ruins, the farms are fighting for every grain of wheat. There is an immense, an inescapable, falsity about the whole business. Does the Kremlin think people will work harder if they are told that the Americans will get them if they don't watch out? Or are these warnings about the American militarists and their desire to use the atom bomb on the U.S.S.R. only an unconscious reflection of what Stalin and his gang would do if they had the bomb and we were helpless?

After each trip I would discuss what I had seen and heard with Bedell Smith and others at the embassy, particularly John Davies. I was fortunate to have two such wise men at hand. John Davies, later hounded from the State Department by men not fit to sharpen his pencils, was and is one of the most intelligent of men. He brought to international affairs a trained and skeptical mind, great powers of application, and political insight. That he was driven from the State Department is one of the blots on our national record.

Bedell Smith I had known since Algiers. As years pass, many men whom I considered giants of their time have diminished in stature. This is not true of Bedell. In him was the combination, more rare than most believe, of the man of action and the man of reflection. His mind was penetrating, quick, and powerful. Without pretensions to expertise, I believe he grasped the essential nature of the Russian people and the Truman administration's problem with their rulers more rapidly than many who had spent their professional lives studying the subjects.

The General (I always thought of him more as that than as Ambassador) had risen to Chief of Staff of the Allied Expeditionary Force by sheer ability, overcoming formidable obstacles. Bedell had entered the army from civilian life in the first war. He was thus outside the "trade school club," as the irreverent called the West Pointers. There were no old classmates around to give Bedell a helping hand or to cover his mistakes. He made it on his own.

"Do you know why everyone likes Ike?" Jock Whitely, a British general, asked me at one point in the European campaign. "It's because he has Bedell as his son of a bitch. Ike wants to tear a stripe off some general. Bedell does it. Ike wants to remove a corps commander. Bedell does it. And Ike writes nice letters and is great at slapping backs. In the circumstances, who the hell wouldn't like Ike?"

Bedell took the criticisms, the venomous gossip of the army, as he took praise, without outward show of emotion. He was a hard, sometimes a ruthless, man, But he did what had to be done with efficiency and skill. If only a handful of his peers recognized the great part he played in the direction of the war—well, he could live with that. His job was to win the war, not to win popularity. He could not understand those who evaded hard duty.

A year or so after I left Moscow I met him in Berlin, then under Russian blockade. He had just been to see General Lucius D. Clay, another notable soldier but of a very different type.

"What the hell's the matter with Lucius?" he began. "He's worried because he has to confirm a death penalty on some soldier. Hell, I used to confirm ten or twelve such sentences a day. It's tough, sure. But it has to be done. You protect the army that way. And you protect society. My God, boy, no one guarantees us an easy time, no one promises any easy options. This is a damned hard world."

So he found it. But he had all the same an appealing self-deprecation, a guileless vanity.

There was a party one winter's night at Spaso House, and Bedell, who had been to a diplomatic reception, arrived late, in tails, top hat, and his officer's cloak, which had been lined with white satin. He stood at the top of the stairs. My wife and I, who had been dancing, were at the bottom. My wife called up that he looked wonderful.

With a grin Bedell pirouetted, and the cloak swirled out around him. He raised his silk hat above his head.

"Yes," he said, "I'm a vain son of a bitch. And I love it."

Bedell's progress in the old army had been accelerated by General George C. Marshall's confidence in him. When, in March of 1947, Marshall, now Secretary of State, came to Moscow for the Foreign Ministers' Conference, Bedell assumed his old position at Marshall's right hand. This, incidentally, irritated John Foster Dulles, who was present as the Republican Party's representative.

I never saw in Dulles those intellectual and moral gifts which others, particularly President Eisenhower, discerned. He was not entirely unattractive, however. When he was in the company of people who lived outside his closed circle, there was a wistful desire to be accepted, like that of the rich kid who wants to be friends with the gang from the next block.

Dulles's policies are now derided and his character harshly judged. I had no use for some of his policies, seeing in them personal attitudes of John Foster Dulles rather than well-conceived plans for the conduct of our foreign policy. I believe, for example, that he made a grave mistake in rejecting out of hand Polish Foreign Minister Adam Rapacki's proposals for a military détente in central Europe. Quite possibly nothing would have come of a positive American response. But it is always possible that there would have been a hopeful reaction from the other side. We shall never know.

Contemporary critics of Dulles misunderstand the atmosphere in which he labored. Indeed, critics of the New Left argue that the cold war was largely the product of over-heated American imaginations and that Dulles, misled by his almost fanatical anti-Communism, was the most destructive of cold warriors.

Facts, as Molotov used to intone at every opportunity, are stubborn things. The United States *did* propose a loan to the Soviet Union after the war. The Russians and her satellites *were* invited to participate in the Marshall Plan. There *was* a Baruch plan for atomic sharing, which the Soviets rejected. Czechoslovakia *was* taken over by the Communists. Western Europe, her economy shattered, her governments feeble, her defenses negligible, *did* invite Soviet aggression, political or military.

Like Truman and Acheson before him, Dulles reacted to an existing, serious challenge and responded to a national consensus that Communism must be contained. Certainly he sometimes overreacted. At one moment he would be irritatingly sanctimonious, at the next, bombastic, using phrases like "massive retaliation." He was, however, a man of pragmatic turn of mind, and I am sure that he was able to convince himself that he was right and that what he did was right for the United States, when he double-crossed the British and French over Suez in 1956.

If he saw the Communist danger in more than life size, he

still was able to communicate to his countrymen some of the realities of the world around them. If his lessons were distorted by succeeding administrations, Dulles cannot be blamed.

The Foreign Ministers' Conference was expected to solve the German problem. It failed disastrously. By its end the divisions between the Soviet Union and its wartime allies, the United States, Britain, and France, were deeper than they had been at the start.

Those interested in the conference can follow its torturous course in the many volumes written about international diplomacy of the immediate postwar era. It is sufficient here to say that this was the first and most strident example of Soviet diplomatic intransigence and of the vilification and abuse of the West and its leaders.

The conference involved some of the hardest work I have ever done. Cyrus L. Sulzberger, then the Chief Foreign Correspondent of *The New York Times,* and I handled the conference alone. Were the conference to be held today, or had it been held then in any western city, there would have been a staff of at least six *New York Times* correspondents on hand. Between us we covered the three main sources of news, the American, British, and French delegations, besides the Yugoslav delegation and the Moscow embassies of minor powers interested in the work of the conference.

Censorship had been lifted for the duration of the meeting. This was one of the western ministers' conditions to their agreement to assemble in Moscow. Each night Cy and I returned to the mean little room in the Hotel Métropole that was *The New York Times* office, and set to work. There were always two stories a night, sometimes three or four. In most cases they were complicated and long.

Looking the stories over now, I do not feel that either of us has anything of which we should be ashamed in that record. When I think of those nights and the work we did, I am irritated at the laymen who see the foreign correspondent's job as one long joy ride. We finished each morning at about two o'clock, and at eight we were up and at work. We anguished over rumors that, on investigation, proved false. We waited hours for a few words from some great man who had condescended to see reporters. We ate terrible meals at odd hours and drank too much. It was tiring and infinitely exciting.

One night, very late, I found myself seated with General Marshall listening to him talk about generalship in our Civil War. His knowledge was encyclopædic, his insight impressive. I learned nothing about the present conference; no questions or allusion from me brought any information. But I think I learned a good deal about the quality of that great American's mind: a mind at once flexible and powerful, informed by wide reading and by mature consideration of what had been read. He said one thing I noted down: Success can have a bad effect on generals; only a general of very strong character, a Lee or a Wellington, can withstand the enticement of battlefield success that asks him to plunge when he should wait and regroup.

The lessons a correspondent learns about a country are not always directly connected with the length of time he spends there. I have often regretted that I was unable to remain longer in Moscow and that the Russians refused to grant me a visa when I applied to return. But my stay sufficed to provide some insight into the Soviet Union and its policies and, more important, its people. I left with two impressions that have not been altered essentially by time. The Russian people, despite half a century of Communist rule, are warm, hospitable folk, basically peaceful in their outlook on the world, and wishing no more than a quiet life. They are ruled by a corrupt, inefficient, and xenophobic system that is steadily eroding the essential decency of the average Soviet citizen. The leaders of Communist Russia have never, even during the worst days of World War II, when they desperately needed American help and friendship, regarded the United States and the Americans as anything but enemies.

In the United States we are going through one of those spasms of national introspection in which the beliefs of the past are turned inside out and shaken and, by the vocal minority always anxious for change for change's sake, found wrong. Should this lead the American people to disregard the facts about the Soviet government and the Communist Party, we are in for trouble, and we shall deserve all we get.

The Russian people, on the other hand, are not our sworn enemies. The past influences all peoples. Few have been so cruelly used by history; many Russian attitudes, the addiction to secrecy, for example, can be traced to that past. What other European past compares with Russia's? The long, virtually unbroken night of absolutism, repeated invasions from east and west, recurrent famine, the ignorance of the West, have bred a fatalistic acceptance of authoritarian rule that is the Kremlin's greatest political advantage.

The historical experience has made so great an impression on the Russians that it is reasonable to accept that many national characteristics which the West finds most baffling and, indeed, repulsive, such as governmental secrecy—itself reflecting a widespread xenophobia—would remain prominent if, tomorrow, the Kremlin, the Communist party, and all their works were to vanish into limbo.

The problem, then, is not simply the continuation of Communist rule. It is the survival among the Russian people of dark, archaic concepts that have no place in a modern, free society. Only after these are overcome can the world expect a Russian government to develop toward its version of a free society.

CHAPTER 8

THE BLOCKADE OF BERLIN AND A NEW GERMANY

1948-53

High deeds, O Germans, are to come from you.

Wordsworth

I

Fear is an easily communicated emotion. You could taste fear in West Berlin in the spring of 1948. Americans and British talked lightly, but with an undercurrent of uneasiness, about "a trip to the salt mines in Siberia." West Berliners, their memories of Russian occupation, looting, rape, and murder still painfully vivid after three years, prepared for flight or suicide.

"You're bringing your family here, to Berlin?" a German woman asked.

As they do in war, people looked no further ahead than the next day. Since late winter the Russians had been threatening. Now they turned to harassment. The Communist *Putsch* in Czechoslovakia was in men's minds. Stalin ruled in the Kremlin, and Western Europe, with its thriving Communist parties, lay almost defenseless beyond the Elbe.

Berlin was granted a lovely spring. Flowers blossomed in backyards, and grass appeared in the rubble. But it was a silent city. The nascent recovery in the western zones of occupation had no counterpart in West Berlin. The streets at night were quiet, almost empty. The mining-camp atmosphere of 1945 was gone, replaced by an air of patient submission. Isolated in the Soviet zone, one hundred miles from West Germany, the West

Berliners seemed condemned to float in a never-never land, the pawns of the great game of nations. History was waiting just around the corner. A dramatic crisis would catapult these people into the world's spotlight and give them the opportunity to show they were not pawns but free men.

I took over in Germany as Chief Correspondent in the middle of May. *The Times* had three other correspondents in Germany: Ed Morrow in Berlin, Jack Raymond in Frankfurt, and Kathleen McLaughlin in Munich. My directive from Edwin L. James was "pull the god-damned thing together, will ya, fella?" Mr. James did not waste words.

My notebook held a long list of suggestions for stories and of plans for improving the bureau. These had to be put aside. From my arrival I was deeply involved in one of the most important postwar stories, the blockade of Berlin. In retrospect this was only one battle in the struggle between the Soviet Union and the United States for western Europe. Yet time cannot diminish the importance of that battle. Had the west abandoned Berlin, the whole of western Europe would have been at hazard. Don't think of western Europe then as it is now. Think of the western Europe of 1948: industry just beginning to recover from the war, agriculture suffering from a shortage of manpower and equipment, ruined cities, ruined lives, vigorous Communist parties. The chance was there. The Russians missed their chance.

The second Foreign Ministers' Conference on Germany broke up in London in the autumn of 1947 after Soviet Foreign Minister Molotov had made a particularly malignant attack on American and British policy in Germany. The policy that so upset Molotov was an attempt by the two western governments to improve economic conditions in their zones of occupation, an attempt that would include a reform of the currency. By spring the Russians were ready to move against West Berlin and its people. To the Kremlin the target must have seemed eminently suitable and highly vulnerable; two and a half million people in the western sectors depending for fuel, food, and hundreds of other items, including medicine supplies, on railroads, canals, and highways that ran through the Soviet zone of occupation.

General Vassily Sokolovsky, the Soviet Military Governor and Commander in Chief, began to turn the screw on March 20 when he walked out of the Allied Control Council. On June 24 all railroad traffic between West Berlin and the three western zones was halted due to what the Russians called "technical difficulties." By August 4 the canals and highways were closed. The blockade was complete.

Berlin was saved. And Berlin helped save itself. The elements of salvation were General Lucius Clay, United States Military Governor in Germany, a people, those of West Berlin, and the American and British airlift. A major share of the credit must be given General Clay.

Whenever I hear people talking of the limitations of the military mind, I think of Clay. Ostensibly he was not cut out for the role he now assumed. He was an engineer officer, a logistics expert, one of those sharp-featured, sharp-tongued men who gets things done. However, he saw more clearly than many diplomats and politicians the essentials of the Soviet challenge in Berlin and, now cajoling, now goading, his British and French colleagues General Sir Brian Robertson and General Pierre Koenig, he rallied the city to meet the challenge.

Clay, during that hectic summer of 1948, gave the impression of making snap decisions. The impression was false. The man pondered each step, weighing every consideration. Once he had made up his mind, however, the decision was implemented with dispatch.

The fainthearts, who always give tongue in times of crisis, thought Clay too bold. They were upset at his proposal to send an armed convoy to Berlin from the United States zone. The convoy would carry equipment that would enable the Russians to overcome the "technical difficulties" that had halted traffic. President Truman's administration vetoed the idea. Clay believed the convoy would have reached Berlin. So do I. The Russians, for all their bluff and bluster, were in no position to risk war with the world's only atomic power.

Long years of discussion with senators and congressmen over appropriations in Washington had given Clay command of the art of public explanation. But rubbing shoulders with politicians had not robbed his character of steel. For example, he learned early in April that some officers of the Berlin garrison and some officials connected with the U.S. administration had applied for permission to move their families to the United States. Clay's response was that such conduct would be "unbecoming" to Americans. And, if any officer or official wanted to send his family away, he had better go with them. Nothing more was heard of the matter.

The people of Berlin, led by the Socialist Ernst Reuter, were the second element in the city's salvation.

The war had left me with a strong antipathy toward Germans, an attitude strengthened rather than diminished by what I saw and heard in Germany in 1945. When the blockade began, I did not doubt that under Clay the American garrison and the civilian officials would meet the challenge. And although the Labor government in London sometimes took a weak-kneed approach, I was sure that the British in Berlin would be all right. The French in my estimate didn't count. This proved to be true. The Americans and the British were the prime movers on the West's side in the cold-war battle for Berlin.

My doubts were reserved for the Germans. They were, I believed, a people who, although viciously cruel and insanely ambitious in power, were boot-lickers when someone else held the power. In Berlin the Russians had the power. I was unprepared for the Germans' reaction.

The West Berliners had every reason to temporize, to stay out of the struggle among their conquerors. The western sector's material resources were slim. On June 24 there was food for thirty-six days and coal for forty-five days in the three sectors. Hundreds of thousands were unemployed or underemployed. Psychologically they were unprepared for any test of will. The suddenness of complete defeat, coming so soon after the *"Sieg Heil"* years, the fury and duration of the Allied bombing, the well-remembered holocaust of the Soviet siege and its terrible aftermath, should have drained the Berliners of any resiliency of spirit, any spark of morale that would enable them to endure new dangers, any political motivation for resistance.

What was the conflict between Communism and democracy to them? What did a citizen of the city the Nazis had ruled for twelve years know of democracy? All he might be expected to know and want were the elementals: food, warmth, shelter.

My opinion of the West Berliners began to change on September 9, 1948. I had heard that the people of the three western sectors planned a demonstration against the blockade in the

Reichstag Platz near the Brandenberger Tor in the British sector. Before I was within a mile of the Platz the car was engulfed by people.

I have seen and been moved by many crowds. But none, not even the people of London bidding goodbye to Winston Churchill, has moved me as much as that vast throng. They were from every part of the western city and from every walk of life: fierce old men in carefully brushed suits, workmen from the few industrial plants still operating, housewives a little timid at this desertion of the home, young wives with babies in their arms, students. Slowly they trudged toward the Reichstag, and when the figure of Ernst Reuter, the Socialist leader appeared, a tremendous roar, half defiance and half stubborn, corporate pride, arose.

You did not have to listen to the speeches. All that was necessary was the comments of the listeners. They meant to stand by the Allies, there must be no surrender, no appeasement.

These were brave words then. But they were repeated later that year when the cold and the long nights of northern Europe came. There was almost no coal for domestic fuel. Electricity was rationed to a few hours a day; some districts had only two hours. There was no hint of appeasement, and when the West Berliners decided to elect a new city assembly to replace that wrecked by the Russians, 86.4% of West Berlin went to the polls.

I talked to a housewife in the Tempelhof district. Her apartment had electricity from two to four each morning. During this period she did her washing and ironing and her cooking for the next day.

"So it is bad," she shrugged. "But better than to have electricity *and* the Russians. No, there's not much complaining about the dehydrated foods. Of course, we're not used to dehydrated potatoes. But my old man and I, we tell people to shut up when they complain. We ask them if they want the Russians back."

During the election campaign the politicians of every party showed unexpected moral courage. They knew their activities were known to the Russians and to the East Germans, and they were convinced that, if West Berlin were abandoned by the Allies, they and their families would not live long. But in speech after speech they attacked the Soviets and lashed their puppets in the eastern sector and zone.

The West Berliners did not turn into town-meeting democrats. The Social Democratic Party, which assumed control in the government of the western sectors after the elections, was well stocked with convinced Marxists. What the blockade did was introduce the mass of West Berliners to resistance to political tyranny and to make them realize the value of the freedom they enjoyed.

Reuter, the new Lord Mayor, had only one lesson for them: "Hold on."

He was a plump, balding man with an oval, melancholy face. A Communist in his youth—he had been "the young Reuter" to Lenin—he discerned earlier than most that the Russians were baffled by the Allies' ability to beat the blockade.

"It's all over," he said at a luncheon on January 31, 1948. "The Russians know they cannot get Berlin by blockade. Soon they will start to find a way out. Face is very important. Give them some chance to save face. We have only to remain firm, and they are beaten."

The Allied airlift was the instrument that beat the blockade and the third element of Berlin's salvation. The U.S. Air Force and the Royal Air Force were soon delivering food and coal to the city—but not enough. The minimum required was four thousand tons a day, and this figure was not bettered until December, when the daily average rose to four and a half thousand.

Operation Vittles, as it was called, was the kind of military operation in which the Americans and British excel. A high degree of organization both at the bases in the western zones and at the two principal airports in Berlin—Tempelhof in the United States sector and Gatow in the British sector—was essential. So was a high degree of ability on the part of pilots and navigators. Finally, courage.

Everyone knew that the air approaches to Gatow and Tempelhof lay over areas controlled by the Russians. Every pilot knew that if the Russians decided to raise barrage balloons over those approaches, planes would crash, air crews would die, and the operation might have to be abandoned. The young men went on flying.

Coming in one night from Frankfurt a pilot remarked that he got "quite a belt" out of each flight.

"It's a test, see. Watch, you can look right into some of the windows in the Soviet sector."

We landed and taxied to the unloading ramp.

"What I mean is, we're doing something. Those poor slobs over in the Russian sector, they can see us. We thumb our nose at Joe Stalin every flight. And these krauts on our side. Well, maybe they'll realize that it *is* their side."

Week by week the tonnage delivered rose. C-54s with a capacity of eight tons were summoned from Alaska, from Panama, from Hawaii. The British brought in York transports, the civilian version of the Lancaster bomber. By the spring of 1949 the planes were carrying an average of eight thousand tons of supplies to Berlin each day. This was more than had been brought to Berlin by railroad or canal before the blockade. As a strategy for throttling Berlin into submission, the blockade had failed. The Russians were beaten. After another conference of foreign ministers had been arranged, this time in Paris, the Soviet authorities lifted the blockade at midnight of May 11–12, 1949.

The victory had one lasting effect. The demeanor of the West Berliners in a time of great pressure was such that they won for themselves and, indirectly, for the Germans of the western zones a new respect. I did not believe that public opinion in the United States, Britain, and western Europe would have accepted so readily the establishment of the Federal Republic of Germany in the autumn of 1949 had not the Berliners demonstrated such steadiness in the blockade. They had won Germany's passport into Europe only four years after the death of Hitler and the Third Reich.

II

The stage had been set for the birth of a new Germany, the Federal Republic. The blockade lifted, the Berlin situation was of secondary importance, although the Russians and their East German clients continued to harass the western sectors in minor ways. The discussions between the western occupation powers and the West Germans on the new government and the first elections to its Bundestag, or parliament, assumed paramount importance. Late in 1949 I moved to Frankfurt and established bureau headquarters there.

In one respect I was lucky in Germany. My colleagues in *The New York Times* bureau not only were most competent reporters, which, of course, was to be expected, but were also exceptionally decent men and women. In Berlin I had the help of the late Ed Morrow, a reporter of energy and enthusiasm with an eye for the problems of ordinary folk caught in the struggle between the two giants. In Frankfurt I worked with Jack Raymond, able, experienced, and dedicated.

I disliked leaving Berlin. The game the Russians were playing in East Germany fascinated me. I admired the West Berliners, and I had come to like the city. After the end of the blockade West Berlin's economy began to revive. The western sectors had a purposeful, confident air. Psychologically, economic recovery was an extension of the blockade. West Berlin had thumbed its nose at the Russians during the blockade. It did so with equal effectiveness by achieving a prosperity that was the envy of the East Germans and the despair of the Russians.

There had been occasions during the war in London when my dispatches had irritated the British government. The Russian press had given me a going over more than once, but this, of course, was an occupational hazard in Moscow. Generally, however, I had maintained fairly good relations with the politicians, military figures, and diplomats who provided the bulk of my material. I was not so naïve as to believe that these gentlemen either liked or trusted reporters in the mass. They might form friendships with individual reporters, but despite the latters' trade, not because of it.

Consequently, I was ill prepared for what awaited me in Frankfurt and Bonn during the next three and a half years. My reporting on neo-Nazism in West Germany, on the western powers' denazification program, and on the past histories of some of the respected figures of the new republic brought upon me the abuse of the West German authorities and the sharp criticism of the U.S. High Commission. At one point officials of the exasperated High Commission complained forcefully to Arthur Hayes Sulzberger, the publisher of *The New York Times*. My subsequent discussion about the complaint with him explains why reporters trusted that sensible gentleman.

Seated in his office after I had left Germany and was headed for London as Chief Correspondent, Arthur asked me what about it. I went over the ground carefully and in detail. I cited the High Commission reports that had been the factual basis for my stories. I quoted from the statements of German politicians and editorials. I argued that giving attention to neo-Naziism in West Germany was an important part of a reporter's job in Germany and that the tendency toward fascism was there, we could not blind ourselves or our readers to it. He thought for a minute, knocked out his pipe, and said we'd better go down to lunch. I never heard anything more about it.

My stories challenged the powerful desire of the Truman Administration to establish a West German republic as a viable European state as soon as possible. Because of the memories of Naziism and the war this policy aroused considerable distrust in the United States. It was exploited by the Soviet Union, its allies, and the Communists and fellow-travellers in western countries by a massive propaganda campaign seeking to prove that the Americans, British, and French were reviving a National Socialist Germany.

In this situation stories that showed that there *were* unrepentant Nazis in the Federal Republic, that a tendency toward National Socialist thinking had *not* been eradicated, and that many officials with whom the Allies dealt daily were ex-Nazis were regarded as mischievous innuendos damaging to the program of the administration and the High Commission in Germany. I was writing such stories when I had reliable information.

A great part of the information was given to me either orally or in the form of written reports by members of the High Commission who were critical of the manner in which they believed the German political scene was being whitewashed. The stories caused the High Commission considerable anguish.

One of its senior members told me, "You're not playing for the team." "What team?" I asked. "Why, the High Commission team, of course." This, I fear, is the way a great many people in any administration see the reporter's function, that of a sort of cheerleader for government efforts.

I was able to take the criticisms of the High Commission and the hostility, expressed in articles, of the German newspapers and magazines. What I found most difficult was the breach that my reporting opened between me and John J. McCloy, the High Commissioner.

McCloy is an admirable man, a distinguished servant of the Republic, who brought to his post in Germany great knowledge, unstinted energy, and an enthusiastic view of the future of Germany.

McCloy must have been convinced that the Germans had changed to the extent that they could be allowed their own government and a considerable measure of freedom. I say "must" because, as an honorable man, he would not have implemented the policy, which he had helped formulate, had he not been so convinced. A factor in his conviction was the characters of Konrad Adenauer, the first Chancellor of the Federal Republic, and of other West Germans, notably the commercial and industrial nabobs then presiding over the country's economic miracle, the recovery that gradually pushed West Germany to economic primacy in western Europe.

Holding such views, the High Commissioner naturally felt a strong distaste for my stories reporting that all was not well in West Germany. He was unsympathetic to the idea, which a good many others held, as I did, that it might be well to wait until the democracy the western Allies had planted flowered.

The criticisms and pressures of the High Commission and the sniggerings of other correspondents played on my nerves. As most people do, I liked to be liked. If anything, my position made me more careful in checking facts, more restrained in my writing. But, whatever the pressures, a reporter has only one course open in such a situation. He must write what he learns. His allegiance is not to any High Commission, to any government or ideology, but to the truth as he sees it.

So I continued. If I obtained intelligence reports that detailed the manner in which the Soviet Union was building up the strength of the armed forces in the satellite states, I wrote the story. If I discovered or was given data about the revival of Naziism in Hanover or Bavaria or of the attitude of the West Germans toward democracy, I wrote that story, too.

In such situations a reporter depends greatly on the support of his organization. In my case that was never in question. E. R. "Manny" Freedman, then Foreign News Editor, and Edwin L. James the Managing Editor, backed me to the hilt. Shortly before he died, Mr. James wrote me that there was nothing in *The New York Times,* from the weather report in one of the "ears" on page 1 to the last paragraph of the last column of the last page, that did not cause complaint. I could almost hear his familiar growl in his last sentence: "You appear to have the stuff; write it; I can take care of your critics."

McCloy had brought to the High Commission a mixed group of civilians. Some, Benjamin Shute, Benjamin J. Buttenwieser, and the late Chauncey Parker, were men of high ability. They were experienced enough not to expect too much of the Germans. Others of the High Commission were very much members of the McCloy "team" and resented anything, including my stories, that marred its record.

The High Commission also included some extremely able State Department officials: Sam Reber, Jimmy Riddelberger, and John Davies. They treated me with courtesy and honesty. None of the information about the High Commission's reports on the political state of mind of the Germans, whose appearance in *The New York Times* so infuriated McCloy's toadies, came from them. They were not surprised by it, however. Experience had bred a healthy skepticism. They did not expect the German nation to be reborn in pristine purity overnight.

In thirty-odd years of foreign reporting I have had a lot to do with the professionals of the State Department. I have a very high opinion of their probity and skill. Often I have been on the other side of the fence on important issues. But I have never ceased to admire the devotion they bring to their work. Some criticisms of them are hard to understand. For example, why does the United States maintain the curious practice of appointing nonprofessionals to key embassies? Some are amiable nonentities. Others are so puffed by their temporary importance that they make mistake after mistake and thus give the professionals the added task of cleaning up after them. Of the appointed ambassadors with whom I have worked closely only one, John Hay Whitney, our Ambassador to the Court of St. James in Eisenhower's time, compared favorably with the professionals.

The ineptitude of the nonprofessionals led to some ludicrous situations. One American ambassador was so muddle-headed that the government to which he was accredited devised the following scheme to insure that its views were accurately reported to Washington. After the ambassador and the government's foreign minister had held their weekly talk, the latter would delay the American's departure for the embassy. There were pictures to be shown. Or there were amiable conversations about nothing. Meanwhile the foreign minister's private secretary would telephone the ambassador's deputy to tell him all that had passed between the two principals. When the ambassador wrote his dispatch, the deputy could correct the misinterpretations and supply the facts the ambassador had forgotten. By that time the ambassador would have turned to the more congenial business of patting the bottoms of lovely ladies at cocktail parties.

I have never been able to fathom the attacks on State Department personnel, at home or abroad, by members of Congress. Continual sniping against decent, honorable men doing a complex, difficult job, often in the most trying circumstances, hurts the man by lessening his influence with the foreigners with whom he deals, and it demeans the country.

Konrad Adenauer was the central figure of Germany's political rehabilitation. He was an impressive figure, easy to respect, hard to like.

Adenauer saw early in the game that the Americans were to have the decisive voice in arranging Germany's future. Consequently, he was willing to placate McCloy and the High Commission but not at the price of abandoning any important point in Germany's interest which he thought could be obtained by intransigence. Understandably he was upset by my stories and wasted a good deal of valuable time lecturing me on my errors. He could not understand why I did not see that the "true Germany, the Germany of Goethe and Schiller and the men of 1848" was now emerging. Once I answered that I, at least, could not be sure that this was the true Germany. Was it not possible that the true Germany was represented by Buchenwald and Malmedy? The interpreter, shaken by the question, drew in his breath with a sharp hiss; the Chancellor did not lose his temper. No, he thought that such things were aberrations of the German people brought on by evil, un-Christian influences.

Adenauer distrusted and feared the Russians. In his views on the Soviet Union, as in much else, he was strangely ill informed.

I, too, feared and distrusted the Russians, but Adenauer's ignorance of Soviet society was, at the outset anyway, abysmal. Adenauer had spent most of his public life immersed in the politics of the city of Cologne. His patriotism was strong, but in his first term as Chancellor it was that of the Rhinelander, not the German. He disliked and distrusted the Berliners. They were not only largely Socialists, whose creed he came close to equating with Communism, but city slickers always ready to do down the honest Rhinelanders. Sometimes he became so involved in the parochial problems of his beloved Rhinelanders that one might think the German Empire and the Third Reich had never happened.

His unworldliness was no help in his great task. Once in the course of another lecture he asked me why I disliked the Germans. I explained that it was National Socialism and the things Germans did under it that I detested. No one could forget things like the massacre at Oradour sur Glaine. It was evident from his expression that he hadn't the slightest idea what I was talking about.

Later I related the incident to André François-Poncet, the urbane and sophisticated French High Commissioner. François-Poncet promised me that he would inform Adenauer about this massacre of French civilians. He did and later recalled, "You know, the old man really couldn't believe it. I had to repeat the story again and again." Finally Adenauer had shaken his head and said, "Unbelievable, that such things could be done by Germans."

In the first years of his chancellorship Adenauer was not accorded the almost universal esteem that he later enjoyed in the West. He was simply the best, which meant the safest, of a mediocre lot of Christian Democratic politicians, honest, capable, and never a Nazi. The National Socialists had jailed him briefly, and this, of course, strengthened his credentials. Had events not conspired otherwise, Adenauer might have served his term and departed to be remembered as a skillful bridge-builder between the new Germany and the victorious Allies.

He had been chancellor less than a year, however, when North Korean forces, armed and instigated by the Soviet Union, invaded South Korea. This transformed the situation in central Europe. What the Russians had done in divided Korea they might do in divided Germany. In the eyes of military and political leaders in Washington, West German rearmament developed from a distant possibility to a necessity. Field Marshal Montgomery and other soldiers, viewing the disparity between western Europe's military strength and that of the Soviet Union, had cast longing eyes on German manpower since early in the occupation. But the question was, as British Foreign Secretary Ernest Bevin told me in 1948, "the political dynamite 'ere and in Europe." Stalin and the North Koreans made west German rearmament in some form inevitable. It was another instance of how, between 1945 and Stalin's death, his actions helped to build a strong, stable Europe.

The North Atlantic Treaty Organization (NATO) had been set up in the spring of 1949. Progress toward western Europe's military revival was slow, however, until June 1950, when the Korean war began. Then there were frenzied stirrings in defense ministries. General Eisenhower was persuaded, with no visible signs of anguish on his part, to shed the robes of academe at Columbia and assume the role of Supreme Allied Commander, Europe. The West chose wisely. Eisenhower, with his towering military prestige and his immense popularity in Europe, was the only soldier who could have jolted the European governments and peoples out of their lethargy and started them on the road to effective defense.

Moreover, by clearly expressing his conviction that the West Germans could and should play a role in European defense Eisenhower facilitated the creation and expansion of the Federal Republic's army, navy, and air force. He respected and trusted Adenauer. He also believed that, if Europe was to be defended east of the Rhine, the Germans must be part of that defense.

The Eisenhower who returned to Europe was quite a different man from the one who had left on wings of glory in 1945. I do not know how much he contributed to Columbia University, but the years there did a great deal for him. In World War II he approached problems with a mind largely conditioned by military training and experience. At Columbia he entered, somewhat gingerly, the civilian world and, because he had great ability to absorb, he became better rounded, more aware of the complexity of problems at home and abroad. I found him thinking more like a statesman and less like a soldier.

Talking in his familiar staccato fashion, he said one day in Paris, "We have quality and efficiency in production at home. We have to strengthen quantity and continuity. You can't be strong unless you have economic strength. We all know that. But morale is terribly important. And morale is going up. The greatest change I see in Europe is the steady rise in morale. And morale means confidence and willingness to work and sacrifice now to save the West."

I did not consider Eisenhower a phrase-making politician. When he talked about "saving the West," I was more inclined to take European rearmament more seriously than I had. We talked a long time that day about Russia and Communism's grip on the country.

"If we get into the position of two ideologies fighting for men's minds, we'll win. Our moral, intellectual, and economic concepts appeal more to men than any others. We'll win, all right."

The General acknowledged wryly that his prestige was being used to galvanize Europe into rearmament. He said he was quite willing "to use up my credit, if we can make rearmament work."

By that time the king-makers in Washington were talking about Eisenhower as a Presidential nominee in 1952. Those who didn't like Ike, for President at any rate, accused him of playing politics by filling a highly publicized position, one that would aid his quest for the presidency without getting him involved and committed on American internal problems.

"That makes me sore," he said. "I get damned angry when anything I do is criticized as politics. Of course, lots of things in my job here touch on politics. But what I am trying to do is more important than politics. It's to prepare Europe to save itself."

Leadership was more important than dollars in Europe, he thought.

"Let's get the young men persuaded that it is important for them to go out and get interested in persuading Europe to stand together. Let's get them to understand that they have to forget about watching other nations. Make them think in European terms rather than in French or German or Dutch terms."

He paced the floor. He picked up a putter, swung at an imaginary ball, put the club back in a corner, and resumed his promenade. He picked up a paper, glanced at it, and dropped it back on the desk. He poured a glass of water and drank thirstily. He looked out of the window onto the quiet Paris street. Supreme Headquarters then was still in the city.

"Hope we can get the new headquarters ready soon," he said. "I don't like cities. Just a country boy. Now what was I saying?

"We have to give the people a chance everywhere. If there's one thing I believe in, it's the dignity of the individual. We ought to expect some changes in Europe, give the individual a chance.

"Those Russians. That's a totalitarian state. Everyone knows that, but they don't think of what it means. It means that if Europe is given freedom, freedom to let the individual develop, they can never stop us."

Eisenhower's reasonable, unexcited approach to his enemies was one of his most notable characteristics as a general. I saw him excited often. But never when he discussed the other side.

"They come and tell me that the Russians have this and the Russians have that. But the Russian problem is always presented to me as though the Russians were one hundred per cent. Don't believe it.

"They have the same difficulties as everyone else. When someone tells me they have a thousand tanks at this point or that, I always wonder whether that means a thousand tanks all in good shape with all the gas and all the shells and all the mechanics they need.

"Of course in war it's a good thing to think that the other fellow has everything he needs. That's the way to plan operations. But let's not get too worried about it. He has his problems. And, after all, we're pretty strong, too."

He saw his job simply.

"What we're trying to do is to develop a mechanism that can preserve peace, that can make it possible for free countries to develop themselves in their social and political objectives for the betterment of all the people living in those countries.

"Europe, the United States, and the free world have sufficient force, sufficient power, and sufficient resources to take care of ourselves and make sure we are not attacked as long as we are peaceable, don't become aggressive, and as long as we are animated by a basic desire for security for a common purpose."

The General glanced at the big map of Europe on the wall.

"If we can unite in a common understanding, this thing can be done; if our hearts are in this thing, it can be done."

He did not think negotiations with the Soviets out of the question, although this conversation took place at the nadir of East-West relations.

"When we can defend Europe, we can talk reasonably and, possibly, profitably with the Russians. Drew, none of this is easy. It takes time. It takes money. It means sacrifice for a lot of people. But it's a lot better than fighting a global war. Don't make any mistake about that."

"Suppose," I said, "the Russians don't want to talk."

"Then we've got to retain and strengthen our military forces. Now we're raising the troops, getting the materiel, that's the expensive part. You've got to keep the materiel in good shape, train troops and reserves. Europe must have trained, effective reserves. In time we'll balance the Russians in military strength, and we'll be far stronger in economics and ideology."

Eisenhower thought then that it might be possible to consider the withdrawal of some American forces by 1954; in 1973 there are still approximately three hundred thousand Americans in Europe. By 1954 or so, he predicted, Europe would have a sound economy and would be able to maintain its collective and individual defense programs without inflation. These programs, he emphasized, would rely largely on "reserve forces, because democracies are defended by reserves."

I said we hadn't talked much about strategy and tactics.

"Pretty hard to do that until we have the troops," he said with a grin. "Oh, you can guess pretty well what the Russians would do. They'd come down through the Fulda gap at us, and they'd send a lot of armor across the north German plain at the British. Probably looks easy to them. If we get the time, we'll fix it so it won't be."

This was the Europe of the troubled early 'fifties. German rearmament became more important, as Eisenhower sought higher defense budgets from balky governments in other countries and as Soviet strength grew. The High Commissioners McCloy, François-Poncet, and Kirkpatrick of Britain considered methods of arming the Germans. Would the Germans enter the European Defense Community in which their units would be restricted to six thousand men and be brigaded with troops from other nations? Would the Petersburg plan, evolved by the Germans themselves, for an army of twelve divisions be acceptable to the rest of western Europe? Would western Europe stomach a new German General Staff?

Adenauer, with considerable political insight, showed himself cool, in public at least, to German rearmament. This did not hurt him with German youth, which showed a strong disinclination to enter a German army or, indeed, any army. Hopes rose and fell.

Meanwhile, frivolous young men of the High Commissions sang to the tune of "Hark! The Herald Angels Sing":

Hark! The High Commissioners sing
German army in the spring.
Just in case the *Ubermensch*
Want to go and fight the French,
We will keep divisions small,
Give them no tanks at all.

The Germans got their army. In 1954, after the European Defense Community had been defeated in the French National Assembly, Anthony Eden, again British Foreign Secretary, suggested that the Germans be rearmed under Western European Union, a then almost defunct predecessor of the North Atlantic Treaty Organization. They were and, by committing all their forces to the western alliance, became the most militarily powerful of the western European states.

I asked Eden once how he had come up with the idea. Oh, he said airily, he had thought of it in his bath one morning.

By the end of the fifties Adenauer had become Germany's father figure. Admiring foreigners who didn't know much about Bismarck or Adenauer often compared the two. One wonders what the Iron Chancellor would have thought of the comparison.

In his last years in office Adenauer's uncompromising hostility toward Communism and the Soviet Union, which had been understandable and, indeed, necessary during the late forties and early fifties, was a handicap. He did not, he could not, see in the death of Stalin and the eventual transfer of power to Khrushchev any opportunities for diplomacy. Every western movement toward the Russians, the Summit Conference of 1955,

the Foreign Ministers' Conference of 1959, was stubbornly resisted by the Chancellor. Under his guidance the Hallstein doctrine, which withheld Bonn's recognition from any state that
established diplomatic relations with East Germany, was promul-
gated.

Such an attitude was well and good in the years after the
Berlin blockade and before NATO became a credible deterrent
to Soviet aggression. From the death of Stalin onward it was
wrong. Adenauer's intransigence, when he had grown very influ-
ential in western affairs, solaced those in the West who saw the
cold war as a crusade: his policy appeared a barrier to those
Germans who wished to sound the Russians anew on the future
of Germany.

When I left Germany for London in 1953, my last call was
upon Adenauer. I had developed a healthy respect for his mind
and his character. He regarded me, I think, as an intelligent
irritant who, since he could not be crushed, had to be instructed.
At any rate at our last meeting he told me, "Whenever you write
anything approving about Germany, Mr. Middleton, people believe it. I told my ambassador in Washington"—note the royal
pronoun—"that you were a skeptic, but a just skeptic."

When I left Germany in 1953, the prospects for the reunification of the country were a prime issue, not only in the Federal
Republic but among its new allies in NATO. Many west Europeans paid lip service to the objective, while their foreign ministries quietly sabotaged any substantive movement toward its
attainment. Twenty years later reunification no longer troubles
Germany's neighbors. But the issue cannot be buried. Potentially
it is the most dangerous question in central Europe.

West Germany in the intervening years has become the primary economic power in Europe. Bonn has begun to use that
power in the last five years to alter the old view of the Federal
Republic as an economic giant and political pygmy. West Germany's status as the Soviet Union's most important trading
partner helped Chancellor Willy Brandt implement his *Ost
Politik,* the policy of normalizing his country's relations with the
Soviet Union and its allies in eastern Europe.

Peace of a sort has been made with the Democratic Republic
of East Germany. Berlin's position has been regularized to the

satisfaction of both Germanies and of the four powers occupying in 1945: the United States, Britain, France, and the Soviet Union. The Hallstein doctrine has been junked.

For Bonn this has meant a stabilization of the political situation on the eastern frontier. For NATO it has meant that her most powerful European member has recognized the status quo in eastern Europe—that is, a system of Communist states dominated militarily, politically, and economically by the Soviet Union and assured of ideological purity by the threat of the Brezhnev Doctrine.

Will west Germany stop now?

To patriotic Germans their country includes both East and West Germany. For most of the last twenty years prospects of bringing these two Germanies together into one state appeared to be receding. Europe was frozen into the molds set by the cold war. Those molds are cracking now. This is a different Europe from that of Konrad Adenauer. The 'seventies are likely to see a revival of efforts to reunite the country.

Reunification, if it comes about, will be a long and difficult process that will depend to a great extent on progress toward a real détente between the NATO and Warsaw Pact governments. East Germany is the keystone of the Soviet military position in central Europe. Only tangible evidence of a reduction of western forces is likely to induce Moscow even to consider reunification. The Russians probably would not surrender their hold on East Germany without assurance of the neutrality of a united Germany. This would be a death blow to NATO as a viable military alliance.

Will this matter to the Germans seeing in the future a united country? In my time in Germany I feared that movement toward unity would awaken those dark passions in the German soul that twice in this century have contributed to the making of two European civil wars. My fears are less today on this score. For I believe there has been a fundamental change in the German national attitude. The old German conviction that their race is destined to hegemony in Europe no longer is a serious problem.

The Germans have learned two lessons. First, and this may be the more important, they have learned that Germany can win respect without vast armies and bellowing leaders. West Germany leads western Europe. But there are no German colonies as evidence of her importance. German chancellors inspire confidence, not fear. German soldiers, sailors, and airmen are loyal and willing allies. The second lesson is that Germans realize that nations of their size, no matter how virile, industrious, and inventive their people may be, cannot aspire to hegemony, political or military, in a world dominated by superpowers.

The conditions under which the two German states were born are changing rapidly. To many the great diplomatic and military edifices constructed during the cold war are increasingly irrelevant. NATO, the greatest and most powerful of these, was not divinely ordained to exist indefinitely. We are in a time of change in Europe, and the greatest of these changes will occur in the two Germanies. I believe that we can leave to the West Germans, a people now aware of their limitations and confident they can reach their goals by means other than war, the burden of rationalizing the situation in central Europe. This must be done.

CHAPTER 9

BRITAIN IN THE SOFT TWILIGHT OF EMPIRE

1953-63

The people of England are never so happy
as when you tell them they are ruined.

Arthur Murphy

The years in London were the happiest of my life abroad. One can ask no more than to live in a place he knows and loves, among people he understands, respects, and likes. Much of my best work as a reporter was done in London.

Why has London, of all places I have lived, exerted this attraction? My experience in the war helped. London was in the front line almost until the end, and a people's superficialities are stripped away by war. London, and much of Britain, discarded pretense from 1939 to 1945. People were easier to know. It was difficult not to admire them. When I returned in September 1953, I did not find the national character much altered by the experiences of the immediate postwar years, a period in some ways as testing as the war itself. There were the same tolerance, the same friendliness, the same decency, I have never found the British cold or taciturn. On the contrary, I have met more real warmth among them than among any in Europe, and I reckon them a talkative, even garrulous, people.

And there was the city: a comfortable grandmother of cities, old, wise, friendly. I never reckoned London, even in the last moments of imperial splendor before the war, a symbol of power. For me there was a familiarity, a reassuring coziness. Moving back to London was like discarding a tailcoat and putting on an old, well-worn tweed jacket.

Naturally some of this showed in my writing, and I was criticized by some as an Anglophile. This was a familiar criticism twenty years ago of any writer who approached the British sympathetically. The folk notion that Britain was eternally bent on fooling honest old Uncle Sam was stronger in America then.

Such a view of Britain was ludicrous then and is even more so now. The boot was on the other foot. The fifties even more than the forties saw an amazing growth of American military, diplomatic, and economic power in every part of the world. In the forties the United States to some extent had shared the leadership of the West with Britain. In the fifties we took over. The British were not trying to tell us what to do, although many of them thought they would have done better in our position, but they were trying desperately to hold on to such independence from America as the economic consequences of the war and the progressive dismemberment of the Empire had left them.

The stuffed-shirt popes of journalism consider Anglophilia a much more heinous crime than Francophilia. Is this because they have sour memories of the days, not so long ago, when Britain was *the* world power and her outlook on international affairs influenced such aspiring imperialists as Senator Lodge and Theodore Roosevelt? Is it a residue of the strong Anglophobia of Irish-Americans? Or is it that we have always, unfairly, considered the French a light-hearted light-headed lot unworthy of our envy, while we saw in the British, not only the things we professed to despise, such as titled aristocracy and a class society, but the characteristics of stability, continuity, and homogeneity that we lacked?

I was both happy and unhappy in my work. Ambition is good in measured doses. In some circumstances it can be a curse, as it was to me. I was on a good assignment. London at that time was the best foreign assignment *The Times* could offer. But I thought more about what the job could lead to than about the job itself. I do not mean that I did not apply myself. I worked longer and harder in London and with better results than I had since the war. It did not seem like work. To sit in the House of Commons and listen to Churchill speak, to explore the intricacies of Irish politics in a Dublin pub, to listen to Ivone Kirkpatrick's swift, accurate, and pitiless analysis of Soviet policy in the Middle East—was this work?

Still, there were black periods of depression. Odd. For not only was I Chief of Bureau in the most interesting and attractive foreign assignment, but I was sent repeatedly to Geneva, Paris, and other cities to help cover international conferences. At these I customarily did the overall lead, the main story on the conference. I could not honestly believe that my work was not valued. But I could not rid myself of the nagging question: where will this lead, what will I do next?

To some extent the years have answered the question. I am more content nowadays to concern myself with the job at hand. Possibly this is because the job I always wanted, writing a column on international affairs, appears permanently out of reach. Possibly it is because the character of *The New York Times* has changed. The trend toward interpretative, explanatory writing has helped, because it has given me the opportunity to use to a fuller measure what I have learned in thirty years as a correspondent.

The experienced reporter must fight a natural tendency to say "Yes, this is quite a political campaign, but you should have seen the one Macmillan fought in '59." But he is a fool who overlooks the lessons of the past in writing about the present. Much hysterical tripe was written about the Vietnam war by reporters who had never seen a war before and had no standard of comparison. A reporter can live too much in the past. He ignores it at his peril.

The past was very much with us in the London of 1953. Churchill was at Downing Street and Eden at the Foreign Office. The austerity of the postwar years was slowly disappearing. London had a prosperous air. The easy formalities of life reappeared.

To the middle class this was proper. They had had enough of war. And enough of socialism under the Attlee governments. Their incomes had been reduced, their servants had disappeared, the verities of their old way of life had been under continuous attack. Now, however briefly, the outward symbols of the life they had loved returned. But only the outward symbols.

One night at a gala performance at Covent Garden, Field

Marshal Lord Wavell, surveying the bright uniforms, jewels, and evening gowns, said to Air Marshal Lord Tedder, "Just like the old days, isn't it, Arthur?"

Tedder's reply was to the point.

"The difference is that tomorrow night we'll all be doing our own dishes."

Aneurin Bevan, the leader of the left-wing Labor M.P.'s in the Commons, viewed the current euphoria with distaste.

"Complacency, that's the enemy," he said over a drink soon after my return. "This country's troubles aren't over, they're just beginning. If we're to survive, we've got to build a new economy, we've got to have a new approach to politics."

He didn't think it would be easy for the Labor Party to regain power. With singular prescience he said he expected the Tories to be "in for ten years."

"The Old Man [Churchill] has the voters mesmerized. Lots of them, our people as well, think that, as long as he's in Downing Street, everything will be all right, they don't have to worry. And they don't want any new challenges, they just want to enjoy their football and their beer and their racing.

"The Tories have got a lot of young ministers that are clever as monkeys—Macleod, Maudling, that lot. You'd better meet them. They're smarter than the old prewar crowd. And they work harder."

Reporting on a highly political country like Britain has its problems. About three quarters of the important political and diplomatic news, the staple of day-to-day reporting, originates with the party in power, that is, the Government, which takes decisions and announces policies. These must be reported and interpreted in relation to the condition of the country and its relations with foreign states. An estimate must be made of their effect at home and abroad. To maintain balance, the speeches and comments of the opposition must be reported too. But the opposition cannot act for the country. Inevitably, the reporter is more concerned with what the government does than with what the opposition says about what it is doing. Just as inevitably, he is accused of bias, usually by lightweights of the opposition.

Hugh Gaitskell and Bevan, my best friends in the Labor Party, were intelligent men. They understood the job I had to do. Instead of criticism, they gave me and other members of *The New York Times* bureau every facility for reporting on the making of Labor policy and on the involved and often comic feuds within the party.

I was fortunate in my associates. For nearly ten years Tom Ronan was my deputy, "second man" in *Times* lingo, and I could not have had a better. He arrived in 1953 with no experience as a foreign correspondent and remarkably quickly became one of the best men in our foreign service, accurate and fast and as reliable as the tides that alternately flooded and drained the Thames outside our office window. We worked in the most intimate association, and there was never a cross word.

The list of those who also served in the London bureau in my time contains the names of men who went on to become bureau chiefs elsewhere and to establish themselves as outstanding correspondents: Ben Welles, Kennet Love, Tom Brady, Seth King. The bureau had, and still has, at its heart two remarkably able English deskmen, Joe Frayman and Joe Collins. I felt that we could handle any story, an international crisis, a general election, a massive strike, as long as we were assured of the calm, skillful activity on the desk of one or both of the two Joe's.

We tried, all of us, to venture into a new dimension of international reporting—new, that is, to *The Times*. Politics and diplomacy continued to be the basis of the nightly report, but our correspondents also covered weird folk ceremonies in Suffolk, hydroelectric schemes in the Scottish Highlands, the search for a sunken Spanish galleon in Tobermory Bay, and parliamentary by-elections in obscure districts, blending social and political reporting. It was a good bureau.

On 'Nye Bevan's advice I sought out the young Conservative ministers. I found them easy to deal with. We were of the same age. We had been to the wars. Heath, Macleod, and Maudling were a new element, remolding traditional Conservativism. They did not represent old, landed interests nor great industrial companies. Their constituency was the middle-class conservatism of lawyers, doctors, accountants, and proprietors of small companies. They knew what these people wanted from life, and they knew exactly how to talk to them. Unlike their predecessors in prewar Tory governments, they approached the trade unions without fear or distaste. They were, perhaps, too confident that they could deal with the unions on a practical basis and that the unions would understand and respond to their down-to-earth approach to Britain's economic problems. They underestimated two factors: the powerful vein of class solidarity in the rank and file of the unions, which encourages opposition to any change that can be described by union leaders as infringing on the "rights of labor," and the character of many of these leaders, who were men of narrow vision and petty accomplishment and were often animated by misunderstood Marxism or by devotion to Soviet Communism.

A great deal of noise was being made then about John Osborne's first hit, *Look Back in Anger*, which was applauded by the very people he attacked and by the Angry Young Men. The Bright Young Men of the Tory Party, who shared some of Osborne's views, however, had more impact on Britain of the fifties. Perhaps this was because they were led by a wise old man.

The Old Man, as almost everyone called him, was well into his seventies. The pretentious called him Winston, although not to his face. Age had only slightly dimmed his gifts. He retained the political virtue that had so impressed me during the war, that uncanny sense of what the people—with whom ostensibly he had very little in common—wanted and needed from government. He never held a press conference in Britain, but no one considered this at all outrageous. The only way a correspondent saw him was through a personal invitation. I was lucky enough to get one.

We sat in the cabinet room at Downing Street on an autumn afternoon. He was in good humor after a successful speech in the House. He was then the most famous and revered statesman in the western world. But he never forgot that he was a statesman because of being a successful politician. He talked for a bit about "the sense of the House," how difficult it was for a newcomer to catch the nuances of parliament feeling, how fair the Commons was to those who made mistakes as long as it recognized sincerity.

We sipped long whiskies. He was smoking a Monte Christo No. 1. When he offered me one, I took it, saying I had always regarded it as the best cigar. Sir Winston agreed, adding that all cigars nowadays were better than they had been. He was not, he added, one of those who thought the old days were always best.

"The people have a stronger voice today. The rise of the trade unions to their present position is one of the great changes. I rejoice that this is so, even though we have our differences."

We talked for a moment about the Labor Party, then involved in one of its internal wars.

"Interesting to observe," Sir Winston said, "but, of course, if our foot should slip, they'd be on us like tigers."

He went on about the Soviet Union, using several phrases he had employed in speeches and writings. One was "They fear our friendship more than our enmity." At that time—it was in Nikita Khrushchev's early years, when he was still paired with Nikolai Bulganin—there was strong hope for liberalization in Russia. He didn't believe in it.

"They do not believe they can relax their grip on their people. They have, all those I have dealt with—Stalin, Molotov—an odious contempt for the people. We say, 'trust the people.'"

British prime ministers in office, the authors of novels of espionage to the contrary, do not disclose the inner secrets of government to reporters, however friendly. Their first responsibility is to the House of Commons. This responsibility, incidentally, is one reason that prime ministers do not give news conferences in the United Kingdom and, if they can be induced to give one while abroad, limit their remarks to platitudes.

Inevitably our talk slipped back to the war. We got around to the Casablanca conference and President Roosevelt's unexpected announcement of the doctrine of "unconditional surrender."

"Did I look surprised?" Mr. Churchill asked. "I certainly felt surprised. He's been criticized for it since. And I, too, for agreeing. I fear some critics do not take into account the atmosphere of the time, the dangers of our position, the Russians' suspicion. Well, all came right in the end."

I ventured that it had not come as right as all that: Europe was divided, and East and West lived in hostility.

"That could have been averted," he said. "I wished at the time that your great president—he meant Roosevelt—"would see the Russians more in terms of their ancient ambitions and hatreds. But he did not. Why this was so, I do not know. I have been told that men of ill will convinced him that we were plotting a return to the old anti-Russian position of the twenties. Nonsense, any anti-Russian bias has been forced upon us by the Russians themselves.

"He was a man of sublime confidence and faith. Perhaps the two led him to the belief that he could reverse the whole tide of Russian thinking. I believe, you know, that we must think of them as Russians and of Communism as only the latest manifestation of old stirrings and desires.

"Why should they not, this great mass of Russians, have peace and security? But why should their leaders, who care nothing for their people, attempt to win it at the expense of others?"

Discussion of the war led us to his advocacy of a thrust from Italy into the "soft underbelly" of Europe.

"It could have been done," he said. "Not easily. Nothing was easy. The stake was high: a foothold in eastern Europe. But the President and his military chiefs felt otherwise. So did some of ours. But it did come right, Mr. Middleton, we destroyed an odious tyranny and an evil man."

When, during the war, had he been most concerned? He pulled at his cigar, looked reflectively at an inch or so of ash at its end, and sipped his whiskey.

"The summer of 1940 undoubtedly was a period of the greatest danger. But I believe now, as, indeed, I believed then, that in the face of our command of the narrow seas the Germans would have suffered most grievous losses in invasion. The Royal Air Force prevented them from obtaining the conditions which their military lore regarded as necessary for an invasion. Thus we were saved to fight on.

"But I was most gravely concerned about the shipping losses in the period before the United States entered the war. Despite all the precautions, which we had not taken in the first war, the number of ships sunk rose week by week. This country, indeed all free men, owe a debt to those men of the escort forces and of the merchant navy who withstood this terrible attack."

When had the tide turned?

"At several points. Stalingrad certainly. After Alamein we

never looked back in the Mediterranean. The foothold in Normandy. But all, all goes back to those days of 1940."

He paused and thought a space.

"It would be well, however, if we British recalled that all done then was not done without unity and great exertion. And it will go ill with us, should we believe that the world still owes us for that stand. We must move forward, there is much to be done."

He had a charming, old-fashioned courtesy. When I rose to go he said, "They tell me you are alive to the importance of good relations between our countries. In this uncertain world there is nothing more important."

And, as I neared the door, "Pray give my warm good wishes to Mr. Arthur Sulzberger."

He had drunk perhaps a quarter of his whiskey by the time I left. I have always discounted the stories of his excessive drinking. Of course, by the standards of, say, the Temperance Union of Hutchinson, Kansas, he did drink a lot, but in the society in which he lived he was not considered a heavy drinker. He liked the fellowship of a shared drink, he found spirits a stimulant when he was physically tired. If he ever drank as a solace for his troubles, there is no record of it, although he complained often enough about depression, "the black dog" that seized him at times. Ernest Hemingway called his moods of depression "black ass."

Such a phrase would not have come easily to Churchill. He disliked dirty stories and coarse language. His conversation customarily dealt with international affairs and politics, but on occasion he would talk of India as he had known it as a young cavalry subaltern or of the social changes he had seen in his long life.

I recall his saying once that in his youth gentlemen had drunk brandy and soda but that in the years before the First World War sportsmen shooting in Scotland had become "strongly attracted to the wine of that country, and we are drinking it still."

Sir Winston's retirement from the premiership was the occasion of a legitimate scoop. Five weeks before the event one of the Prime Minister's secretaries told me over luncheon at the Garrick Club that the Old Man would resign on April 5 and that Anthony Eden would succeed him. If I attributed the story to him, he said, he would make my life uncomfortable.

My story, providing the date and other details of the resignation, raised a furor. Everyone had speculated about the Prime Minister's retirement; here was a definite forecast in the most prestigious of American newspapers. Randolph Churchill, an old friend and a good one, gave me a hard time. But I refused, even in those long, verbose, and slightly alcoholic, telephone conversations to which Randolph was addicted, to divulge my source.

What was much worse was the period of waiting before the event took place. I had gone very far out on a limb. Fleet Street pundits hot from Downing Street said I was wrong, that the Old Man had decided to stay on another six months because of the international situation or because the newspaper strike would deny him the full attention he craved. They were wrong. I was right. When the day came, I wrote the story with satisfaction.

It must be difficult for a new generation to understand how large a shadow Churchill cast in the 'forties and 'fifties. It was not simply a matter of great speeches and brave actions. These were part of the history of his times. But he conveyed a sense of security, memories of great dangers faced and overcome, confidence that right does triumph, that evil men are defeated and weak leaders confounded. He did bestride this narrow earth like a colossus, and I count myself fortunate to have seen him at the apex of his extraordinary powers.

With Anthony Eden, his successor, I was on friendly terms, which have developed over the years into intimacy. Critics of his short, tragic premiership have forgotten the appalling psychological handicap that faced him when he took over office from the greatest man of his time. Eden was popular. But his popularity, earned as Foreign Secretary and as an antiappeasement Conservative M.P., was nothing compared with the international esteem and domestic affection for "good old Winnie."

Eden's best-known role was that of a diplomat. He had twice served as Foreign Secretary, holding that office for more years than any other modern politician. His gifts as a parliamentarian and as a politician have been overlooked. After all, no man remains an M.P. for a third of a century without a large share of political nous. Until then I had always dealt with Eden the diplomat. His first months in office were to display a different man, Eden the politician.

At that time international affairs were moving toward the first Summit Conference, in 1955. There had been a more or less successful Foreign Ministers' Conference in Berlin the preceding winter and in 1954 the famous, or infamous, Geneva Conference at Geneva, which supposedly settled the future of what had been French Indo-China. In these conferences Eden had played a dominant role, to the ill-disguised jealousy of John Foster Dulles, and had been instrumental in winning American agreement to a meeting with Khrushchev. He realized that this was the moment to go to the country to win support for his foreign policy and for the Conservative government's domestic program.

I met him in Leeds midway through the election campaign. He displayed an unexpectedly hard-headed grasp of internal issues. Productivity, transportation ("My God, our roads are terrible") exports, housing—he went down the list. I said I was surprised, I'd always thought of him as a Foreign Secretary.

"I know people do," he said. "It's true, but rather unfair. No one can be a cabinet minister and not know about other problems. You have to think of the whole of policy, not simply your bit."

Monarchies, no less than republics, are ungrateful. Almost from the start the Eden government labored under severe criticism, much of it centered on the Prime Minister. The political serenity of Sir Winston's last months in office was replaced by a storm of abusive fault-finding, attacking not only the Conservative government but what now came to be called, in an echo of the eighteenth century, the Establishment.

The Labor Party, defeated for the second consecutive time in the general election of 1955, naturally led the critics. But there were plenty of others with less reason. Eden, handsome, intelligent, debonair, was almost too good to be true. His presence, his manner, his overwhelming charm, affronted many Conservative supporters. Their criticism was vindictive and personal. Academics, avid for Fleet Street checks and advertisement, joined the attacks. They found Eden's prewar record open to criticism; they doubted his abilities in the present.

All this fell on a man by nature highly strung, one who coupled a high degree of civilized intelligence with a violent temper. He was—and his critics did not know this nor would it have affected them had they known it—beginning to suffer from the recurrent internal illnesses that attacked him at moments of tension. These were the result of an operation two years before and not, as was whispered at the time, of cancer. The tragedy of Anthony Eden's premiership was that when he finally achieved the goal to which he had aspired, he was driven from office, not by Egypt's Nasser, not by the duplicities of Dulles's policy—at his best he could have handled these—but by an illness which, though not mortal, left him incapable of the arduous work of his office.

He was unfortunate in being at the top of the political tree when Britain's wave of self-criticism gathered volume and velocity. This has been one of the most disturbing developments in post-Empire Britain. Its origins are obscure. Perhaps it expresses the inner uncertainty of a people who have seen their importance in the world decline with startling rapidity. Possibly it is the long-delayed revolt of an industrial society stifled by the monotony of existence. Whatever its cause, it is potentially dangerous.

There is an almost gleeful willingness to denigrate, not simply the government of the day, but the entire society. A new Left, far more anarchistic and iconoclastic than the old, assails laws, customs, and institutions on which democratic society has been built. This group is urged to new excesses by men and women of high professional attainment in the universities and the literary world.

Feelings of doubt and even guilt have been encouraged among ordinary folk. Foreigners, viewing this orgy of national self-abasement, are likely to take the British at their own valuation. There has been a loss of the national self-confidence that enabled the British to overcome so many trials in the past.

If you believe in democracy, you believe in criticism and dissent. But criticism and dissent carried to the perilous lengths of the last fifteen years in Britain can be dangerous. Nations that lose their self-respect, as the French did in the early 'fifties, are easy prey to political adventurers with authoritarian tendencies. The masochism of the British may yet clear the road for a British dictator with more sinister intentions than those of Charles de Gaulle. Powerful undercurrents of nationalism lie just beneath the surface of British politics. We may see in the future a Britain striking out along the road of nationalist self-assertion regardless of her economic position and strategic vulnerability.

The Summit Conference of 1955, attended by the leaders of the United States, Britain, France, and the Soviet Union, was one of the most preposterous of international gatherings. At the time the high priests of journalism, before an incivility had been exchanged, accorded it an importance akin to that of the Second Coming. All this on no better grounds than its being the first meeting between leaders of East and West since Potsdam ten years earlier.

Factual reporting is the law of *The New York Times*. My colleagues and I had to report the proceedings on a factual basis. Only Scotty Reston, in his interpretative pieces, was able to inform the reader of the essential fustian of those proceedings.

The conference marked the apogee of the huckstering of the American presidency in international relations. James C. Hagerty then held the role of Eisenhower's Chief of Public Relations. In some areas he did an excellent job. He could make the President's lightest remark sound like the Sermon on the Mount. He was assiduous in telling hundreds of reporters, avid for significant news, what the President had had for dinner.

When news conferences got down to cases, Jim was not as adept. Although he knew to the second when news should be released to make the maximal impact, he knew beans about the problems confronting the conferences. He took serious, but basically unacceptable proposals—the American Open Skies idea was one—and blew them up out of all proportion. He floundered on the German question. He was ignorant of large sections of the United States' basic negotiating position. The consequence, of course, was that the more serious American correspondents sought out the British and French public-relations chiefs, professional diplomats, to find out what was going on. Hagerty resented this.

The inclination on the part of presidents and their aides is to see international relations as an adjunct, sometimes unwelcome, to domestic politics. John F. Kennedy did so. But he was a wily fellow, smart enough to hide his politicking in orotund pronunciamentos on global matters, which entranced his admirers, impressed the voters, and made good copy. In his first eighteen months in office Richard Nixon showed in this field a shrewdness that his enemies found unbelievable and unforgivable.

Without any obvious gesture toward political gain in the United States Nixon expanded his administration's horizons. The windows of the White House no longer looked out only on Viet Nam, as they did in President Johnson's day, but now also on China, the Middle East, and Europe. Much of the malaise that overtook Europe from 1965 to 1969, expressed in wavering support for the North Atlantic Treaty Organization and in some acceptance of de Gaulle as spokesman of Europe, resulted from Johnson's apparent indifference to Europe. Nixon, by visiting Europe soon after his inauguration, made friends for America in Europe.

The question whether Europeans "like" Nixon or any other American president is irrelevant. International politics are not a popularity contest. Eisenhower was popular abroad during the war, unpopular as a "do nothing" president. To Europeans the essential question is whether an American president is interested in Europe and shows his interest by consultation and cooperation. You could put what Harry Truman knew about Europe in your eye, but he was interested in Europe, and his interest paid off in constructive, beneficial relations between the old continent and the United States.

A lack of understanding of Europe, particularly of Britain and France, contributed heavily to the making of American policy at the time of the Suez adventure in 1956. During that summer I was in the United States on vacation. The Suez situation was coming to the boil late in September when I visited Washington and talked with President Eisenhower. I found him, as always, affable and courteous. Harold Macmillan, then Chancellor of the Exchequer and in the Capitol for a meeting of the International Monetary Fund, had just been in, the President said, and he was a little puzzled by Macmillan.

"Harold said," the President reported, "that, if it came to the worst, they'd go down with the bands playing, the guns firing, and the flags flying. What do you think he meant by that?"

I said I'd been away from London for two and a half months but that it sounded very much as though the British were prepared to fight, if they got no action from the Suez Canal

Users' Association, the United Nations, or American pressure on Nasser.

The President's eyebrows went up. He didn't think it possible. Why should they fight? I told him that most of the leaders of the Eden cabinet had lived through appeasement in the thirties. Rightly or wrongly, they were against appeasement of Nasser.

"Well, where are the troop movements then?" he asked. It was September 26. I said I didn't know, but I'd try to find out when I returned.

"You do that," he said, and we drifted to other topics.

As a footnote: in mid-October I was able to file from London detailed dispatches identifying the British army, navy, and air force units that were moving or had moved to Cyprus and other concentration points in the Middle East. Like others who had done the same, I was surprised when the administration, with its enormous intelligence resources, later gave the impression it was caught unawares by the Anglo-French action.

The British and French invasion of Egypt provoked the bitterest debates in the House of Commons I had ever heard. Eden, a very able parliamentarian, held his own in the House, but Selwyn Lloyd, his Foreign Secretary, was roughly handled.

The criticism in the Commons by the Labor Party, supported by some Conservatives like Anthony Nutting (a Minister of State in the Foreign Office, who resigned), the outcry in the opposition newspapers and among the Communists and their allies, and the disavowals of British policy by some Commonwealth governments, notably India's, opened divisions unparalleled in British life since the war.

Criticism of Eden, which, as we have seen, had been building almost from the moment he took office, redoubled and was expressed by Tory and Socialist alike. I was invited to a luncheon given by a group of High Tories, people who twenty years before would have belonged to the Cliveden set, to be asked how I thought America would take Eden's replacement by R. A. Butler, then Home Secretary.

At *The New York Times* office we set out to find whether the British people were as hostile to the Middle East adventure as the Labor opposition and the intellectual Left claimed. Our findings were to the contrary.

These findings were confirmed later in talks with all manner of people. Whatever was being said by the opposition, by the indignant writers of letters to the *Manchester Guardian* and the *Daily Herald,* there was in Britain a powerful swell of support for Eden and his ministers. This had little to do with a careful weighing of the issues involved. It was due, rather, to the fact that some hundreds of thousands of Britons had found themselves in the Middle East in two world wars and retained a strong distaste for the Egyptians, or "wogs." They did not like to see Nasser closing the Suez Canal, thumbing his nose at Britain, and strutting the international stage. Not, perhaps, a very high-minded rationale, but those who look for high-mindedness in public opinion should stay away from politics.

British withdrawal from the canal was largely the consequence of American financial pressure. Eden put the best face he could on the measure when it was announced. But it was a defeat for his policies. The strain of the crisis had weakened his physical condition. It was time for him to go, and his enemies rejoiced. I have always considered his departure from public life a sad blow for Britain.

The Labor Party, understandably, clamored for a general election. The Tories kept their heads and after a few days of consultation chose a new Prime Minister. It was not Butler, the darling of the party's left wing, but Harold Macmillan. When the Queen consulted the party elders, Lord Salisbury among them, they plumped for the Chancellor of the Exchequer.

On the day Macmillan was summoned to the palace I was lunching in the Garrick Club at a side table where I could count on talking with Dan Macmillan (Harold's older brother), Bill Casey (former editor of *The Times*), Stanley Morison (the great typographer), Jake Carter, and others. I was called to the telephone.

When I returned, I told Dan that his brother had been summoned to Buckingham Palace by the Queen, which could mean only that he was to form the new government.

"Mother always said Harold would do well," was Dan's comment.

Harold Macmillan was the most adept politician I have ever watched in action at close range. Stoutly defending Eden's course on Suez, he set about, almost from the moment he took office, to tiptoe gracefully out of the Middle East mess and to restore relations with the United States. In the latter task he was helped by his longstanding friendship with Eisenhower. Macmillan had been the British government's political representative in the Mediterranean when Eisenhower had been Supreme Allied Commander, and the two had become friends. They made a strange pair then, Macmillan politically sophisticated and articulate and Eisenhower still feeling his way in the rarefied air of international politics and, on everything but the business of war, stumbling in his speech.

Macmillan's first gesture toward the United States was to arrange a meeting with Eisenhower in Bermuda early in 1957. There he did much to end the quarrel that had developed between the two countries, soothed the irritated Dulles, who seemed to take the entire Suez affair as a personal insult, and impressed, as he set out to do, the American reporters present. They, incidentally, had often been put off by Eden's polished charm. Macmillan, who had just as much polish, gave them the tough, pragmatic politician. They loved it.

A strange man. The favorite adjective applied to him when he was at the height of his power was "unflappable." He was that, all right. He seldom showed anger. He always seemed to have enough time; he would sit drinking whiskey and talking at Pratt's or the Beefsteak for hours. He had a highly cultivated taste in literature; his admiration for Trollope was well advertised, but he also liked diaries and collections of letters.

"After a time you conclude that you've read enough biographies and autobiographies and histories," he said once. "Then you turn to diaries and letters to get the real flavor of the time and the motive behind the actions the histories describe. Creevey's really much better reading on Wellington than any other."

Macmillan was an anachronism in London of the swinging 'sixties, with his rather shaggy look, his rumpled clothes, his grouse-shooting, and his love of clubs and club gossip. Was this the man to govern a Britain beset by economic difficulties at home and by the problem of disengagement in Africa and elsewhere? What did this wealthy publisher, married to a duke's daughter, have in common with the new men of the Conservative party, the technicians of Britain's new industries, the nascent middle class of industrial managers?

Oddly enough, he was successful. Beneath that Edwardian exterior lay a nicely balanced mind fed by a voracious reading of state papers. Long before some liberals had understood the situation Macmillan was aware of the winds of change blowing through Africa and of what de Gaulle called the "third world." In the Commons he could handle with aplomb a debate on almost any issue, speaking with grace and cogency.

During the Macmillan years the Campaign for Nuclear Disarmament became a factor in British life. As the campaign progressed, its ranks were swollen by sober, adult members of the middle class, respected dons and, naturally, ambitious politicians on the make.

Macmillan often chided me on the attention I devoted to the campaign. He was far too wise to attempt to exert pressure; his method was to repeat at every opportunity that "this is just froth, it doesn't matter, in ten years it'll be forgotten." He was right.

Macmillan believed in letting his cabinet colleagues "get on with it."

"We decide in cabinet what's to be done, and he leaves us alone," Iain Macleod told me. Iain was then Colonial Secretary. "He and I are at one on colonial policy, and he gives me a great deal of latitude in carrying it out."

I heard the same from other ministers. It was an indirect criticism of Eden who, as prime minister, had too often involved himself in the work of government departments rather than allow the respective ministers to do it.

In 1958 the spurious détente that was fatuously called the Spirit of Geneva was fading. Khrushchev, now the sole ruler of the Soviet state, was talking tough about Berlin. The alarm bells rang in western capitals. Macmillan decided that the simplest thing to do was to visit Moscow and talk to Khrushchev. With some difficulty, he sold the idea to the Eisenhower administration.

The Russians had agreed to let British and foreign correspondents in London accompany the Prime Minister, and in February 1959 I set out on my first visit to the Soviet Union since 1947. It is my purpose, not to offer detailed accounts of this crisis or that meeting, but to recall how the event impressed me and, when possible, to add information not generally known.

At the time the prevailing impression of the Moscow meeting was that Khrushchev had bullied Macmillan in their private meetings and insulted him by cancelling one meeting on the supposedly trumped-up excuse of a visit to the dentist. I never understood why this should be taken as a prima-facie insult. Most Russians I have met, including Khrushchev, look as though they should visit a dentist, if not that day, the next.

Khrushchev, of course, did not bully Macmillan. What happened was this. The Soviet premier began their private conversation with the usual threats about Berlin and what would happen to that city and to its supporters in the West if the Russians didn't get their way. This bombast surprised and worried Macmillan. He said later that he had always considered that the Soviets, in contrast to the Hitlerite Germans, had a highly developed sense of the possible. At this juncture Macmillan's celebrated unflappability came into play.

He was, he told Khrushchev, sorry to learn of the Soviet attitude. Drumming his fingers on the table and looking out the Kremlin window on the swirling snow, he said that in this case he must inform the Queen that reserves would have to be called to the colors and that arrangements would have to be made to evacuate children and nonessential persons from Britain. There was, he said gently, no question of Britain's abandoning her assurances to the people of Berlin or to her allies. Perhaps they could have another talk. They did, and Khrushchev's tone was markedly milder.

Khrushchev made himself available to the western reporters at a reception in the British Embassy. As usual, he was talkative about things he wanted to talk about and short with those who interrupted him. Malcolm Muggeridge, then Editor of *Punch* and an old Moscow hand, wanted to get the Premier's ideas on British and Russian humor. He phrased his question for the interpreter in those rich, pear-shaped tones that have been the delight of British television audiences for more than a decade. Khrushchev grunted and said something inappropriate.

As we went downstairs Khrushchev grabbed my lapel, not, as I hoped, to whisper some confidence, but to feel the cloth. It was cheviot. Where had I bought that, he asked through the interpreter. London. Fine material, he said, too fine for mass production. But, he added vigorously, the people of Russia would have all that and much more besides.

I recalled that we had met at Marshal Macduffie's rooms in Kiev in 1946. "Had the reclamation of the Don Bas gone according to his great plans of those years?" "Wonderful, wonderful," he said, "you should go there. Everyone here should go there. The Foreign Ministry will arrange it." And so it did for those who wanted to go.

Khrushchev, like all Stalin's toadies and associates, was stained with the blood of innocents. Even knowing this, it was difficult not to feel his attraction, much of it springing from his abundant vitality.

Two years before I had followed him when, in company with Bulganin, he had toured Finland. On one occasion he halted the cavalcade of cars at a farmhouse, bounced out, and invaded the house. Immediately he was involved in a highly technical discussion about wheat strains with the astonished farmer. The Americans, Khrushchev told him, were good, but the Russians were catching up. Meanwhile, his congratulations on such a fine house, such a pretty wife. He caught sight of a picture of Marshal Mannerheim, Finland's leader in the two wars with the Russians. "A great man," he said, "thank God, *slava Boga,* Russia and Finland are friends, and we don't have to fight any longer.

"Imagine Eisenhower's doing that," sniffed a British colleague. But that was just what I could imagine Eisenhower doing, and doing it just as well as the Russian.

The 1959 general election was Macmillan's political masterpiece. A long, hot summer and a perceptible but transient economic improvement set the stage. Macmillan walked home with a majority of one hundred in the House of Commons.

Macmillan then commanded a majority greater than any Conservative prime minister had known since Stanley Baldwin. One of the mysteries of British politics in this century is why he did not use it more vigorously. Macmillan was aware that the country's two besetting problems were the trade unions, with their continuing wage claims and their reactionary attitude toward new industrial techniques, and the tax system. He had a position from which he could attack either problem. He did nothing.

Another missed opportunity was the European Common Market. In 1959 this was just developing and did not have the cohesion and strength of later years. This was the time to make clear Britain's interest in joining Europe. Macmillan did nothing.

From later conversations with him and members of his cabinet I believe that the Prime Minister still thought of foreign policy largely in terms of the special relationship with the United States. This was entirely natural. His mother was American. He revered and admired Winston Churchill, who had laid down as a primary rule of foreign policy that the American connection came first and must be preserved, whatever difficulties British ministers might have in dealing with their opposite numbers in Washington.

Moreover, Macmillan did not see, as he might have been expected to, in view of his perception in other fields, the importance, to a stumbling British economy, of membership in the Common Market. He did eventually seek entrance to it. But that was in 1962, when the Market had coalesced and when de Gaulle, with his deep suspicion of the United Kingdom as America's spokesman in the Common Market, was on his way to leadership in western Europe.

Macmillan had been one of de Gaulle's supporters in Algiers in 1943. But he was mystified and alarmed by the changes in the man during the intervening years.

"He talks like a king," he said one night over a drink. "There really isn't any way of explaining anything to him in terms of practical politics, he's above that. What he needs is a couple of question periods in the House of Commons. But no one questions *him*."

That was late in 1962. Macmillan's premiership and the Tories' years of power were hastening toward their end. So was Britain's role as a great, independent power. No longer the center of an empire, clinging to the Commonwealth as a symbol of her importance, Britain was moving rapidly away from individual significance to a new status as part of Europe.

The Tory governments led by Churchill, Eden, and Macmillan were able to maintain, despite decreases in trade balances and foreign markets and falling industrial production and strikes, a prestige in the world that did not accord with the true position of the country. Britain's economic and military power had declined, but when her leaders spoke, others listened. In retrospect this maintenance of the country's world prestige in such unfavorable circumstances appears one of the great political feats of our century.

I had been in London for nearly ten years. Although, as always, I was subject to fits of restlessness and depression, I loved the job, the city, and the life. Old-timers talk nostalgically of Berlin between the wars before Hitler came. I have a similar nostalgia for London of the 'fifties: a stimulating, beguiling city, gay and serious by turns, majestic even in that decade of decaying power, naughty but never vulgar.

Life had such variety. A dinner party might be enlivened by a member of Parliament, a junior minister, an author, a movie producer. In any great capital—except Washington, which is a company town, the company being the United States of America —there are many circles: political, diplomatic, military, theatrical, literary. London is the only one in which all the circles touch, so that you might meet Peggy Ashcroft at a dinner given by a general and Cecil Woodham Smith at Hugh Gaitskell's house.

A friendly city. The Londoner always has time. He does not, like the New Yorker, continually look at his watch. He likes talk. And the talk in any one of a number of my favorite pubs is as good as the talk in the smoking room of the House of Commons. A cutter at Kilgore, French and Stanbury will retail his adventures with the French Resistance. A Covent Garden fruit merchant will discuss the philosophy of the Labor movement.

There was a policeman, a Scot, whose post was outside the House of Commons. Many a night I stopped to smoke a pipe and chat as Big Ben tolled the hours. He had intelligent ideas, well ahead of his time, on the effect of television on the young.

And, always, there is politics, for London is a political city.

Through friends and through my clubs, the Garrick and the Beefsteak, I met people from the literary world and the theater. The charmingly astringent Cecil Woodham Smith, author of *The Reason Why,* is one of the most intelligent women I have ever met. She had been a Fitzgerald, a "Geraldine," as the Irish call the family, and Woodham, her husband, called her "Fitz."

Once I was questioned about the contemporary United States by T. S. Eliot. Tall, stooped, reserved, the years in London had not robbed him of a certain essential Americanism. I said so, one night, and he seemed pleased.

I was buffeted on the outer shores of C. P. Snow. One of his novels, *The Masters*, had recently been made into a play, a very good one with John Clements, and it was amusing to hear Snow telling acquaintances that they must not miss it. I asked Dan Macmillan, head of the house that published Snow, what he thought of him.

"Can't stand his books," he said, "but we had to publish him to get her [Snow's wife, Pamela Hansford Johnson]. She's the real writer."

Convivial hours were spent with Osbert Lancaster, Alan Moorehead, Sir Laurence Dunne, the Chief Metropolitan Magistrate, and Sir Melford Stevenson, now a learned judge and a most uninhibited one. We sat late at the Garrick or the Beefsteak. Bill Casey and Dan Macmillan would recall the inside of stories like the Tranby Croft case, which had rocked London society. Sir Harold Nicholson would dissect the peace-making at Versailles and regret the dear, dead days when diplomacy had been a gentleman's profession; a snob, but a rather likeable one.

The theater was a delight: Peggy Ashcroft in Ibsen, Laurence Olivier and Vivian Leigh in "Macbeth," the Old Vic, Margot Fonteyn at her sublime best at a gala for de Gaulle.

Vivian Leigh was as handsome a woman as I have seen and one of the toughest. One night while I was talking to her at a party, I saw her face harden. "Let's go into the other room," she said. "Here comes that shit ——." He was, too.

A full life. I rose early four or five times a week to play tennis at Queen's Club. I learned the game late, played it indifferently, but liked it amazingly. There were the job and the unending fascination of politics, diplomacy, a whole society in flux, lunches and dinner where the talk was stimulating, and the quiet evenings at home reading or working on a book with Westminster outside as quiet as a country village.

I had seen much of the harsh and seamy side of British life. Now I enjoyed its gentle pleasures: Wimbledon in June, the Derby, long walks in the Lake district. I went to a Royal Garden Party, something one should do once for the experience. I lunched with the Queen at Buckingham Palace and found the conversation more informed and amusing than that at many directors' meetings.

I left London for an assignment in Ceylon. I went to Kenya, Rhodesia, and what is now Zambia. I spent happy, busy weeks in Geneva at the Laos conference in 1961.

The climax of Britain's first attempt to enter the European Common Market came in 1962. The British application was doomed from the start. General de Gaulle's suspicion that the British government would act as America's agent in the Common Market and his preposterous belief that France, under him, was destined to be the leader of Europe foreclosed any prospect of admission for the United Kingdom. To these basic reasons events added others. The Anglo-American nuclear agreement, concluded between President Kennedy and Prime Minister Macmillan late in 1962, was one. To de Gaulle it was additional proof that *les Anglo-Saxons* were in league.

Home on leave in the summer of 1962 I was told that it had been decided to send me to Paris as Bureau Chief. It was a blow.

Curiously, despite my anger, I never thought of looking elsewhere for a job. Several were offered; one of them would have allowed me to remain in London. Part of this was loyalty, if not to the newspaper as such, to Arthur Sulzberger, whom I esteemed as a man and a friend. But, I told myself bitterly, *The Times* was the only paper that would give me the opportunity I wanted to write about international affairs, if not as a columnist, at least as a bureau chief. I recognized then, as I do now, that *The Times,* for all it many faults, has great virtues. As Christopher Morley wrote years ago, it sometimes loses its head, but it has a head to lose. Nonetheless I prepared for my new assignment in a mood of bitter cynicism; not the best preparation.

January 14, 1963, was my last day in London. It was the day on which General de Gaulle vetoed Britain's entry into the Common Market. I knew the British people too well to think that this would appear an irretrievable disaster to them. Nor did I believe, as some gloomy people at the Foreign Office appeared to, that this marked the end of a "European Policy."

But the rebuff for Britain did not make departure any easier. I left London in a mood of discouragement. Driving through London in the cold light of a January morning was a torment.

My head and heart were full of thoughts of friends and places I had known and loved. I would come back many times, but the sense of belonging to a city, the feel of the place was gone. I had been a fool ever to be tired of London and of my job there. For, as Dr. Johnson remarked, he who is tired of London is tired of life itself.

CHAPTER 10

FRANCE UNDER GOOD KING CHARLES DE GAULLE

1963-65

French ignorance is often more amusing
than the wisdom of other people.

Henry Cabot Lodge

Looking back to London was profitless. It only fed my discontent. Nor was I so unhappy at my transfer that I could not recognize in France a situation as interesting as that in Britain. I encountered the French in perhaps the last of those epidemics of arrant nationalism to which they have been subject through history. Their normal view of themselves, compounded of esteem, rationality, and cynicism, had been replaced by a ridiculous chauvinism. In that state they are tedious and, occasionally, dangerous.

In January 1963 Paris was proud of Charles de Gaulle. His veto on British membership in the European Common Market had enhanced his prestige in the capital and the country. His followers saw him as the arbiter of Europe and France as the leading power on the continent, and their enthusiasm infected otherwise intelligent folk. They, along with the Gaullists, enjoyed Britain's discomfiture and applauded the General's rather theatrical defiance of the United States.

It was a strange political atmosphere, almost divorced from reality. Listening to French politicians, officials, and journalists, with their absurd estimates of France's position in the world and their unbalanced analyses of her influence in Washington and London, was like listening to children playing at being grown up.

I had seen enough of France in the 'forties and 'fifties to believe it was necessary for the health of France and Europe that the seedy irresponsibility of the Fourth Republic be replaced by something more vigorous and stable. I had not expected that progress made by France after de Gaulle's return to power in 1958 would mesmerize the French into delusions of grandeur.

I had watched the German phoenix rise from the ashes of 1945. There was much in the West Germany of Konrad Adenauer that I did not like, but the Germans had not indulged in the almost hysterical chauvinism that now appeared to have overtaken the French. Why, I wondered, were the French different?

The achievement of economic stability was only a partial answer. Steady finances, rising wages, a sound balance of payments, rapid technical advances in modern industries, which were perilously few but thriving, had enhanced the position of the middle class and increased both its self-satisfaction, always great, and its loyalty to de Gaulle.

A larger answer was the foreign policy conceived and directed by de Gaulle. In one respect this foreign policy was a tribute to the force of the General's personality and prestige. By words far more than deeds he was able to convince the French that they were indeed the great nation, the leaders of Europe, the admired leaders and teachers of the "third world" in Africa, Asia, and Latin America.

In relations with Britain and the United States de Gaulle touched one chord that brought instant, approving response. There were then in France—they are fewer today—many Frenchmen who had never recovered psychologically from the shock of defeat and surrender in 1940. This shock was made worse by Britain's decision to fight on and her eventual position at the war's end as one of the great victors, both moral and military. Had the British followed France's example in 1940 and surrendered, the French submission to Hitler would have been easier for the nation to swallow.

France's amour-propre was hurt again in 1944 when these same British accompanied by the Americans, *les Anglo-Saxons*, invaded France and drove the Germans out. There was under de Gaulle a ceaseless, insistent campaign to convince the French that they, rather than their allies, were responsible for their own liberation. I do not believe that, even at the height of Gaullist chauvinism, this campaign fooled those who had lived through 1944.

At any rate one effect of the war was to leave the French with a smoldering resentment toward the British, a state of mind in which Dunkirk was a term of reproach and the less glorious incidents of Britain's single-handed resistance ("They sank our ships at Mers-el-Kebir") were remembered by the French to the exclusion of more significant events. Antagonism toward the United States, in the French mind a country powerful but uncultured, by turns amiable and dictatorial, grew out of the overwhelming military power deployed by the United States in Europe in the last year of the war and by the powerful political and diplomatic pressures exerted upon French governments, often with the minimum of tact, by successive administrations in Washington.

The French should not be condemned for their feelings. No one, American or British, who has not seen his armed forces disgraced, his government shamed, is in a position to condemn. The remarkable thing is that these feelings persisted for so long and that a people outspokenly proud of their rationality should give way to them so easily when the master manipulator took power in the Elysée Palace.

For de Gaulle did play on these sentiments. Of course he, having endured rebuffs from Churchill and discourtesies from Roosevelt, had personal scores to settle. But as the sallies against the British multiplied, as the Olympian disdain for Washington and its policies became more pronounced, I could not avoid contrasting him with Churchill in 1940. Then Churchill, coming to power—supreme power—in a government that included ministers who had ridiculed and criticized his warnings of approaching disaster, refused to encourage public revenge against the men of Munich. If we opened a quarrel with the past, he said, we might lose the future. This was the path of statesmanship. De Gaulle, meanly stoking the fires of anti-Americanism and anglophobia, was the lesser man.

These tactics had to be supplemented by something more

tangible than vetoes and Delphic pronouncements, if the de Gaulle mystique was to catch on. The means were at hand. During the last days of the Fourth Republic successive governments had begun the development of atomic power for military purposes. De Gaulle took up the development, presenting it as his own idea—tactics he followed in several other fields—and the *force de frappe* was born. Here was an independent atomic bombing force. Ruffles and flourishes! Beat the big drum of national independence, summon the shades of Louis XIV, Napoleon, and Foch! France was a great power again!

Any government with military atomic power at its disposal enters a new dimension of power politics. I doubt whether any officer on the Soviet general staff lost a minute's sleep over France's infant atomic organization. Its real effect was upon France's allies and upon the French nation.

Like the possession of a revolver, the possession by a country of atomic weapons is what Damon Runyon called "the old equalizer." Whether the country is France, with the beginnings, in 1965, of nuclear power, or whether the country is the United States, both are members of the club. The nuclear powers sit at the top table. To the French, who had been discounted, scorned, ridiculed since 1945, this was heady stuff.

The politicians, the press, the radio, and the television—the last almost entirely controlled by the Gaullist government—failed to keep France's nuclear power in perspective. This power, it was believed, gave France a freedom in international affairs she did not in fact have. It led her to assume positions that, in a period of closer financial and economic relationships between industrial nations, were foolhardy. France not only emphasized her own individuality, she defied critics, exaggerated her strength and influence, and lost good sense in a welter of self-glorification.

A powerful, and underestimated, element in de Gaulle's choice of an independent course was his earlier failure to win acceptance as one of the leaders of the West. After his return to power in 1968 he wrote President Eisenhower and Prime Minister Macmillan, suggesting that he and they together should assume direction of the North Atlantic Treaty Organization.

The proposal was rejected. The American and British governments pointed out that NATO was an alliance of equals in which, theoretically, the United States was no more powerful politically than the Netherlands. The business seems to have been handled tactfully enough to suit anyone but de Gaulle. The rejection angered him. He considered that his old tormentors *les Anglo-Saxons* were freezing him out of a rightful share in the leadership of the West. Very well, he would show them that France, the great nation, could and would go her own way and, in the process, frustrate the policies of Washington and London.

Attitudes toward the United States, as much as toward Britain, developed a new sharpness. Diplomats in the Foreign Ministry said that it was high time France embarked on an independent course, that the country was strong enough to think for herself and stand on her own feet.

"We have been listening to Washington for years," Claude Lebel of the Foreign Ministry said one day over lunch. "You must understand that we feel it is time that we listened to our own interests. How can one say that all the international interests of countries as different as France and the United States can be identical? We can differ on things and yet remain good friends."

The last, of course, was perfectly true. It might have been possible to remain good friends had the French government been led by anyone but Charles de Gaulle. It was not only what he did, which was plenty, but how he did it.

Did the United States prize NATO as an instrument of collective security that discouraged Soviet ambitions in western Europe? De Gaulle would scoff at the idea and take France out of military integration in NATO. Was the United States worried about Communist China's present animosity, future ambitions, and military potential? Very well, France would court China and arrange diplomatic recognition. The United States favored Britain's entry into the Common Market. France vetoed that entry.

These were only the high points of the sorry story of relations between the two countries from 1963 until 1969. Their effect was exacerbated by the arrogance of the French government. Maurice Couve de Murville, Foreign Minister and later Premier, at the best of times a coldly arrogant person, gave the impression of being the final repository of all diplomatic wisdom. President Johnson, Secretary of State Rusk, Macmillan, Adenauer, all the others, were children playing at international affairs. It was the French with their long tradition of diplomacy, their expertise, who knew it all.

The condescension with which the French viewed their partners within the Common Market, particularly Germany, who was the strongest of those partners, was startling. Early in 1963 de Gaulle and Adenauer signed an agreement binding the two governments to the closest cooperation: periodic meetings of heads of government and foreign ministers and close consultation on defense and foreign policy. French diplomats explained candidly that France, through this agreement, hoped to draw Germany away from the United States and to replace American with French influence in Bonn.

The French were unsuccessful largely because the mutual interests of Bonn and Washington, economic, financial, military and political, were too numerous and too strong. But in concluding the agreement with Germany the French, perhaps unwittingly, did Germany a service, which was only dimly understood in Paris. By embracing the Federal Republic de Gaulle gave the Germans a standing in Europe that they could have achieved on their own only after a long period of preparation. The French were Germany's sponsors; here was France, after nearly a century of German aggression, arm in arm with the old enemy. If France could bury the past, why could not the Netherlands or Britain or Norway?

For a usually perspicacious people the French displayed singular short-sightedness in their attitude toward the pact with Germany and its consequences. First, they underestimated Germany's enormous and growing economic strength and its influence on power relationships in Europe. Second, they appeared to believe that Bonn's foreign policy would always follow the lines laid down by Adenauer.

Nor were they particularly wise in their dealing with the Germans. In the middle 'sixties German ministers were fully aware of the political power that could be deployed from their country's unassailable economic position. Yet the French attitude toward them ranged from condescension to arrogance. After one meeting between the heads of government late in the decade a German minister said that the French delegation to Bonn had treated the Germans "like pigs."

Gaullism went to France's head. Always self-centered, many French seemed to believe that by a simple wave of the wand they had become once more the center of the world. Phrases like "France's civilizing mission" and "France, the leader of Europe" were used by ordinarily intelligent men. No one asked whether the Emperor really had any clothes.

Was de Gaulle a dictator? The question was much discussed during his rule. If he is compared with Hitler or Mussolini or Stalin, the answer must be "no." The General wielded enormous power. He determined French military, diplomatic, and economic policy. The National Assembly was a rubber stamp. His appointments and policies encountered no significant political opposition. If not a dictator, he was, as a cynical French friend remarked, "the next worst thing."

Yet even at the high noon of de Gaulle's power, lively, open criticism and opposition existed in France. They were not stifled or liquidated as they had been in Hitler's Germany, Mussolini's Italy, and Stalin's Russia. The opposition was not effective but, given the atmosphere of France, it was surprisingly vital and outspoken.

De Gaulle's greatest enemy was France's tendency to become bored with her rulers. Louis Napoleon, whose methods of rule, particularly the plebiscite, were often used by de Gaulle, worried about national ennui. So did de Gaulle. The French, he said on one occasion, have a way of exhausting their emotional support for any man and becoming bored. Many explanations have been advanced for de Gaulle's retirement from power in April 1969. My view is that he knew the French were bored with him, his policies, and his style, and that it was time to go.

Such views of de Gaulle, which I held when he was in power, did not make for popularity either with his government or, surprisingly, with my colleagues. I say "surprisingly" because I had expected, when I came to Paris, that American reporters there would be searching for chinks in the armor. Not at all. Many of them took the General at his own valuation. Perhaps this was because many had worked in Paris under the Fourth Republic, when the country and its people were discounted and guyed by colleagues in other capitals. Whatever the reason, they went about now proclaiming the wisdom and justice of de Gaulle and all his works. They persistently underrated the strength of

Germany. They gibed at American policy. Objectivity took a beating. Odd!

The Paris of 1963 was serene and beautiful as ever. The shops and restaurants of tourist Paris were prosperous. The tourists, not yet antagonized by rising prices and Parisian rudeness, flocked to the city. Paris seemed the epitome of the middle-class virtues, the middle-class complacency. It was in tune with the General.

Charles de Gaulle was a man of the nineteenth century. This is reflected in his writings and his speeches. I noticed it in casual conversations over the years, the first in London in 1940. He lacked Churchill's full-blooded enjoyment of the present. Often in reading de Gaulle's memoirs one gets the impression of some great personage from an earlier time who has strayed into our century and who does not like it at all. The man yearned for the unshakeable verities of *la belle époque,* for the time when Europe was a tight, ordered society, before the first war, when the world revolved around the nations of Europe, when there were no superpowers. He saw the world in national, not international, terms. To him the European nation-state was the ultimate form of political organization.

Europe, consequently, was to be judged by that yardstick. The French, of course, were a very old nation that had maintained a national individuality since the Dark Ages. The Germans, he once explained to an astonished ambassador, were not. They had not become a nation until 1870. What were eighty years of unity compared with France's ten centuries? The Belgians, the Italians, too, were not nations but conglomerates of peoples. The Dutch, the Spanish and, grudgingly, the British, qualified as nation-states. These were solid, lasting entities. They would endure when Communism, Fascism, the United Nations, NATO, the Common Market, had all passed into limbo.

De Gaulle knew that he could not, alone, eliminate those international organizations that he believed threatened France's sovereignty. He sought either a measure of control, as in NATO, or, if this failed, to force them to be more amenable to French ambition.

He was, for example, willing to live with the Common Market as long as France's membership benefitted her economy and as long as France, in the person of Charles de Gaulle, was powerful enough in the Market to scotch progress toward the agreed goal of European political unity.

As we have seen, de Gaulle tried in 1958 to install himself as a member of a triumvirate directing NATO. When he failed, he soured on the alliance. France abandoned military integration in NATO in 1966, and the French General Staff proclaimed that the motherland was to be defended against attack from "all azimuths"; that is, the French would be as ready to repel an American invasion as one from Russia. It was stirring stuff for the mob but nonsense.

De Gaulle's ambitions for France, however, were wider than Europe. With great panache and little common sense he sought to extend French influence in the "third world," the have-not countries of Asia, Africa, and Latin America.

De Gaulle's visit to Mexico and the French possessions in the Caribbean in the autumn of 1964 was what Graham Greene would call "an entertainment." It had little to do with the realities of power. But the old charlatan played his part to the hilt. He stood on a balcony in Mexico City's Plaza Major and delivered a long, thoughtful speech on Mexico's independence— independence of the United States, naturally—to massed thousands. He concluded his remarks with a few words of Spanish. These evoked no great response from the Mexicans.

Puzzled by this seeming indifference to the General's essay into the native tongue, I asked the reason of a motorcycle cop, a hard-visaged character who had learned his trade in Los Angeles.

"Oh, Christ," he said, "these jokers are all Indians brought in from the country. They didn't know whether he spoke Spanish or German. They're here for the ride."

The visit to Mexico, Martinique, and French Guiana was preposterous. But it was sad, too. Here was this elderly statesman appealing to something long dead. He was, although he did not appear to know it, fighting the enormous United States economic influence in Latin America and all the political end products that flowed from it. This was true, too, of his journey to Quebec, where he fanned the flames of local nationalism. He knew, his associates told me, that in both Latin America and Canada he was opposing American prestige. But he did not understand, there or elsewhere, the solid basis on which this was built. He was a Don Quixote running a course against windmills of steel and concrete.

"What has France to offer us?" a Mexican congressman asked me one night. "Chicken feed!"

The longer de Gaulle remained in power, the more preposterous he seemed. The rabbits drawn from the hat at news conferences were altered by time and circumstances into skeletons. Recognition of China, a great disarmament conference, and other headline suggestions made a stir in the newspapers but never were transformed into benefits for France.

The student riots in Paris in the spring of 1968 were the revelation. They showed that, contrary to all de Gaulle said, Paris and France were not happy and stable, that opposition could not be smothered by grand phrases, that there were forces in France uncowed by the Gaullist majority. In the midst of the uproar he ran off to Germany to consult the army chiefs about their support if the crisis worsened. The Emperor had no clothes.

De Gaulle seriously retarded two of the most hopeful developments in Europe in the second half of this century: the move in Europe toward greater political cooperation and the maintenance through NATO of a strong European deterrent to Soviet ambitions. History will accord him the honors due a great man, but I doubt whether she will forgive him for that.

De Gaulle, like Churchill, had an ear for history. The Anglo-American rejection of his suggestion of a triumvirate to run NATO would have silenced a lesser man. But the General sensed, as time went on, a growing dissatisfaction in western Europe with United States domination of NATO. He also perceived that with the growth of Soviet nuclear power any American president would have second thoughts about implementing the basic clause of the transatlantic contract that is the basis of NATO. This is that, in the event of Soviet aggression against a NATO member, the United States is bound to support the European members, if necessary, with nuclear strikes against the aggressor. De Gaulle saw that this contract, however viable it may have been at the organization of NATO in 1949, was challenged by the development of Soviet nuclear power. Bluntly put, the new problem presented to the White House was: Are you going to use nuclear strikes to prevent the loss of Hamburg or Frankfurt or Lyons or Amsterdam, if such use invites a nuclear strike on New York? The question, in de Gaulle's mind, answered itself.

Consequently, he began the moves that ultimately took France out of military integration in NATO. By so doing he raised a standard around which all those in Europe who were dissatisfied with United States leadership could rally. Fortunately for NATO, these dissidents, although numerous, were not powerful. They did not control governments. Even if they had controlled them, they would have been forced to offer something in place of American nuclear protection. De Gaulle had his *force de frappe*. They had nothing.

De Gaulle may have been good for the fair land of France. He said he was, and there were many who agreed. Driving around the country in the summer of 1964, one got the impression that much was amiss behind the glittering facade. Off the recognized tourist routes a visitor was treated to diatribes against a government that thought of little but *la gloire* and left rural slums to fester. Unless the area is one benefitting from a remunerative crop, rural France is a wasteland of decayed villages and marginal agriculture. The improvements that have come to rural areas in the United States, West Germany, and Britain have missed France. The visitor finds villages lovely to the eye and stinking to the nose, where sanitation is primitive, the water dangerous, and education rudimentary.

To say that similar conditions exist in stricken areas in America and western Europe is not the full answer. For no one in Washington or Bonn or London at that time was consciously turning away from rural problems and proclaiming the country's strength and greatness. The gap between these French, worrying about the weather and the hole in the roof, sitting in smoky cafés wondering how long the mines would remain open, and doing two jobs to feed the family, accentuated the phony quality of *le grandeur* and *la gloire*. There was an arrogant irrelevance about a government that refused to face such problems.

France and Europe are better off without de Gaulle. He tried to return both to another century, to fasten upon his countrymen and their neighbors nationalist ideas that have been destroyed by two great wars. Rejecting internationalism for Europe, he chose, instead, a sterile nationalism that could not hope to match the growing power of the Soviet Union and the United States.

The realities of power in Europe are now clear to everyone, including the French. Germany, France's former protégé, is now the first power on the continent, clearly the leader of the Common Market, and due to become the leading military member of NATO. It is amusing to watch those French, who cheered on de Gaulle when he was harrying the British, now discreetly courting the United Kingdom.

De Gaulle faded rapidly from the national consciousness. One evening in the winter of 1970 I asked the proprietor of Le Sportsman if anyone ever thought of de Gaulle's return. The question surprised him.

"What is he doing now?" he asked. "Writing more books? No, I do not want him back. He had nothing to give but a certain ideal, and that is not enough for this situation."

Yet de Gaulle cast an enormous shadow. Years after his great moment of power I sit in New York, devoting almost the whole of a chapter to him.

For a correspondent in Paris de Gaulle was not only the major source of news but almost the only one. But it was news of an unsatisfactory sort: semiroyal visits, news conferences. One saw the old entertainer at the Elysée pulling his rabbits from his hat. But I never had the feeling, as I had in Germany under Adenauer or in England under Churchill and Attlee, that fundamental national problems were being tackled. The stately charade meant nothing. The more de Gaulle sought to emphasize the importance of France, the less really important she became.

No one can cavil at three years in France: to walk old, quiet streets in Paris on a Sunday evening . . . to sit in Fouquet's and watch the snow swirl through bars of light onto the Champs Elysées . . . to turn off the main road to Normandy into a half-remembered village and drink and gossip in the café . . . to see the brown knuckles of the Pyrénnées rise to the south and glimpse across a valley the towers of Carcassonne . . . to talk half the night away with old friends in Lille or Arras . . . to eat and drink at one of the great provincial restaurants (great French cooking is now found almost exclusively outside the capital) . . . to lounge at a window on a spring evening and watch the great barges on the Seine . . . to smell the fresh breath of Paris on a summer's morning on the way to tennis . . . to leave the Gare du Nord on a winter's night and see the lights of shops and bars.

Whatever you come to think about a country's politics, there are sights and sounds and smells that become part of your life.

In 1965 it was time to move. I was assigned to the United Nations. I was promised travel when the General Assembly was not in session. In Paris that spring there was little news. I was glad to go.

CHAPTER 11

THE UNITED NATIONS' THIRD WORLD

1965-67

A mad world, my masters.

Nicholas Breton

One summer afternoon in 1965 Adlai Stevenson asked me my first impression of the United Nations. My snap judgment was that there seemed to be a tendency to dodge real issues and an inordinate amount of attention to trivia.

He laughed. "You've learned Lesson 1," he said. "I spend a lot of time worrying about the proper way to refer to some new nation and listening to speeches that are completely irrelevant. Sometimes I fear the place has creeping paralysis. Let's hope we don't discover *rigor mortis* before it's too late."

I had approached the job without preconceived ideas. I did not regard the United Nations as man's last hope, but I was not as cynical as some of my friends in diplomacy. I may have had some slight professional bias. None of the major international stories on which I had worked since World War II—and they included almost every important story in Europe in twenty years —had involved the United Nations. I felt, too, that *The Times* was devoting far too much space to that organization and that certainly *The Times* would benefit from shorter, sharper coverage.

Any newcomer to the United Nations finds himself the subject of a sales campaign designed to convince him that the United Nations is of transcendent importance, that the world listens to every word spoken at Turtle Bay. To make their point, the permanent officials and bemused reporters, who have no other home or world, magnify U.N. events out of all proportion. Perfectly ordinary folk become, by virtue of some piddling job, august personages whose every word should be treasured. Dropouts from obscure Indian state governments are exalted into heavy-duty thinkers to whose words great governments should attend (but, fortunately, do not).

The continuous exaggeration of trivia, the boring wordiness, the alarming pomposity, the constant flight from reality, all are part of the myth that the United Nations, as it is today, really is an important organization.

This myth is propagated to a great degree by the permanent officials of the organization. Some diplomats, sentenced to serve at Turtle Bay, help. In most cases, however, since they are sophisticated fellows, they adopt a more or less admiring attitude toward the U.N. in public while laughing at it in private.

Our Communist friends are not immune. I once heard a Russian and a Czech talking in a corridor after a particularly stormy session of a committee on anticolonialism. The Czech said that some of the African and Arab delegates had talked like children.

"I know, I know," the Russian said soothingly. "But you're not supposed to say so."

The permanent staff can be pardoned their dreams. They are a strange lot. Some are easily recognized as international lay-abouts, the kind who infest any large organization. Some are office politicians, grafters and drifters, incompetents and ninnies. But the majority have a special quality that, if weak as a weapon against the ills of this world, is at least different. They are dedicated and sensitive. They work very hard, often at tasks that a sharper intelligence would convince them are silly if not counterproductive. They believe, oh, so deeply, in the United Nations. Their favorite defense of the organization is that, if it did not exist, it would have to be invented.

Their isolation from reality is a grave defect. They do not understand that, to the manipulators of real power in Washington or Moscow or Tokyo or London, or in Lagos or Cairo or Pretoria, what happens in the United Nations is of minor importance. Clearly, an adverse vote in the Security Council may be embarrassing, and a censorious speech of which, God knows, there is no lack, may be used by an opposition party against a government. My experience with governments around the world, however, is that what the United Nations does or says has little effect on their decisions and actions. The permanent staff of the United Nations, wrapped in its glass and steel cocoon, drugged by laudatory handouts, does not understand this.

Most of them, in consequence, fail to realize, and probably would not admit it if they did, that the United Nations is going downhill. For most this is still the U.N. of Trygve Lie or Dag Hammarskjöld. What good we are doing! How people listen to us! Oh, how lucky we are to be here and working in this best of all possible organizations!

My time at the U.N. covered three major crises, two of which arose from situations with which it had been dealing with bewildering ineffectiveness almost since its establishment. The conclusions I formed on these occasions may show why I value the organization so lightly.

The first crisis arose out of the brief war between India and Pakistan in the autumn of 1965. The lesson I drew from that crisis was that the United Nations, although eager to preserve peace and stop wars, almost invariably shies from attacking root causes. A resolution of the Security Council stopped the fighting, but the resolution itself stopped short of assessing the causes of the fighting. The conflict between the two states over Kashmir was left to simmer.

In my innocence I began to ask diplomats and permanent officials why this should be so. The great powers had an interest in halting the war: why could they not dig into the causes? The replies were illuminating but not particularly comforting. Such digging, I was told, would offend many people besides the Indians and Pakistanis. There were other countries besides India, whose rights to pieces of real estate were as questionable as India's is to Kashmir. In other words: don't rock the boat. This is Article I of the Unofficial Charter of the United Nations.

The second great crisis was the war in June 1967 between the Arabs and the Israelis. The Middle East had been a concern of the United Nations for years. Bureaucrats spoke about the area's explosiveness and thanked God, or Allah, that there was a United Nations force between the Egyptians and the Israelis. What did Secretary General U Thant do when President Gamal

Abdul Nasser of Egypt asked him to order out the U.N. forces? He ordered them out.

Anyone with a smidgen of understanding of power would have known that the retirement of the troops would exacerbate the situation. They were there to keep the peace. Did U Thant ask Nasser to think again? Did he temporize, find excuses for delay? Not at all. The troops left, and those in Cairo hesitant about war lost one important excuse for procrastination.

The war began and ended quickly in a decisive Israeli victory. The United Nations has been trying ever since to bring about a settlement. Despite resolutions and speeches nothing much happened for six years.

In 1967 and since then the Arab and pro-Arab delegations have far outnumbered those supporting Israel. We shall never know, I suppose, how much this preponderance influenced U Thant in his decision to order out the U.N. forces.

The invasion of Czechoslovakia by her friends and allies in the summer of 1968 was the third great crisis. No one expected the United Nations to do anything, but it was reasonable to expect that the shock felt around Europe would result in some slashing indictment of the Soviet action by the Security Council. Not at all. A resolution was passed, but it was pretty weak stuff. U Thant, as I recall, deplored the invasion in terms suitable for reproving a slovenly waiter, adding the gratuitous remark that at least the Russians had not used napalm against the Czechs. By which he meant to remind the world that the Americans were using napalm in Vietnam.

In theory the permanent officials of the United Nations, led by that august figure the Secretary General, do not take sides in international controversies. In practice, of course, they do. U Thant and his closest advisers never missed an opportunity to deplore and criticize United States actions in Vietnam. U Thant seldom raised his voice against the outrages committed by the Vietcong against the south Vietnamese civilians or American prisoners.

The attitude of the Secretary General and his staff toward American bombing of North Vietnam illustrated their bias against the United States and their ignorance of the realities of power.

They did not regard bombing as military tactics but as a

peculiar evil invented by the United States. They repeated incessantly that "the whole world" was bitterly critical. So it was,
if the world is what the Communists say it is. They whispered
that bombing would "bring the Chinese in," at the moment
when the Chinese Communists, happily destroying what stability
they had in pursuit of the Cultural Revolution, were in no
position to fight Nepal, let alone the United States.

U Thant and his colleagues believed that the United Nations
was destined to play a role in settling the Vietnam war. The
Secretary General visited Asia, talked to the North Vietnamese,
and returned to repeat their propaganda. When, finally, the two
sides moved toward a negotiation, the United Nations had nothing to do with it. In view of its past record, this is probably
just as well.

Why is the U.N. running down? The cause most favored by
the Secretariat is the duel between America and Russia. Certainly the failure of the two superpowers to work together to
solve the world's ills has been an important factor. This rivalry
has been compounded by the entry into the United Nations of
scores of small, newly independent nations.

The right of these nations to membership, once they have
achieved sovereignty, is seldom questioned within the organization. A larger question, however, is whether the presence of so
many small states does not make agreement between the two
superpowers on issues involving other states virtually impossible.

The new nations have all been affected by the superpowers'
struggle. As I learned on tours of Africa, Asia, and the Middle
East, many are countries in name only. Often there is a capital,
a government that sometimes has more than local authority, but
more often the country is a geographical area having no proper
qualifications for nationhood and deeply divided by tribal
rivalries.

For reasons of economic or military survival and, occasionally,
for ideological reasons these new nations have been forced to
choose one side or another. There is nothing particularly ig-
nominious about this. Small countries have been doing it for
centuries. But this plethora of client states impairs the ability
of the superpowers to reach an agreement. The prospects for
a Middle East settlement would be greatly enhanced if the

Soviets did not have to listen to Cairo and Damascus and if the Americans were able to treat Israel simply as an independent state and not as a ward.

The crush of new members, therefore, has played a role in reducing superpower agreement within the United Nations. But I believe the world organization has played and is playing an important role in bringing these new states to international maturity. This is one of the signal services performed by the organization.

Many of these countries, perhaps a majority, are unfitted for international life. Except where the British, French, or Dutch have left behind a civil service, they lack functioning bureaucracies. They are innocent of diplomats and ignorant of diplomatic practice. There is one school to which they can go and where their mistakes and occasional lapses of taste will be overlooked: the United Nations. Day by day it is possible to see them maturing. Under the aegis of the world organization this process does less damage than it might in conditions of uninhibited and isolated nationalism.

Obviously this is not much of an achievement when one recalls the extravagant hopes that attended the birth of the United Nations. But it is something. As the organization goes its weary, futile way, as the decibels mount in the council chamber and committee rooms, as the piles of paper grow ever more mountainous, United Nations' supporters can solace themselves with the thought that the great glass house on Turtle Bay provided the surroundings in which scores of new nations could learn the rules of the game.

This will not satisfy either the organization's supporters or its permanent officials. Talking to these supporters I have often been moved by the unworthy thought that they do the organization more harm than good. Very few of them—eager matrons in Santa Barbara or long-winded school teachers in Bombay—really know anything about the United Nations. Almost invariably they think of it as a world government, which it is not and which it was never intended to be. They always are certain that the U.N. is ordained to end poverty and misery in the world. They are shaken and often downright unhappy when they learn that the great advances in new, more productive wheat and rice strains are not the result of the United Nations but of individual organizations, usually American. In short, in one way or another, they expect too much from the U.N.

The job of Chief Correspondent at the United Nations is like no other on *The New York Times*. Although he is just across town from the head office, the correspondent is a member of the foreign news staff, and the bureau's copy is handled by the foreign news desk. I found it a job very much like war: long periods of almost unbearable boredom bedevilled by lunatic complaints from officials about the failure of *The Times* to give adequate space to tedious speeches in unimportant committees by fledgling orators from the "third world."

There were moments of high drama, when the United Nations assumed a temporary importance, as during the Kashmir war, the Arab-Israeli war, and the invasion of Czechoslovakia. But there was an underlying strain of unreality. What these earnest, well-intentioned men said, U Thant's occasional coherent thoughts, Premier Alexei Kosygin's dull reiteration of Communist propaganda, all meant nothing. The decisions were taken elsewhere, and the United Nations was, as it remains, only an unexampled platform for national propaganda.

CHAPTER 12

AFRICA AND ASIA— AND VIETNAM

1967-72

The World is a bundle of hay,
Mankind are the asses that pull,
Each tugs in a different way—

Lord Byron

I

At the sound of our motor thousands of birds, bright orange bellies and black wings sharp against the African sky, started out of their nests in the almost perpendicular banks of Chad's Chari river. A hippopotamus sounded on our right, settled, and regarded us with unwinking pigs' eyes. A Boukouma fisherman glanced up from his work on a net. A bend in the river hid Fort Lamy. The motor was the only sound.

I told Brewster Morris this was the Africa I had sought but that in six weeks of travel had eluded me. He said it wouldn't last long. In ten years or so the big elephant herds of the Chad would be gone, motels would rise along the Chari, and the Boukoumas would abandon their nomadic life for shanty towns.

But, if on my travels I had not found the old Africa, I had not found the widely advertised new one, either. The "emergent Africa," the new, eager, striving states so beloved of orators at the United Nations, had escaped me. I was slowly learning Africa's lesson, the lesson Russia had taught me twenty years earlier: one learns what not to believe.

I visited Chad, Ethiopia, Kenya, Tanzania, Nigeria, Ghana, and Zaire, then called the Congo, the Ivory Coast, and Zambia. Each was independent and sovereign and therefore to be equated, supposedly, with Norway or Spain or France. Yet the difference between these black African countries and organized, coherent states in Europe seemed as great as that between the France of the Middle Ages and the France of today. In a village in Tanzania fifty miles north of Dar-es-Salaam the only manufactured object I saw was a hatchet.

The pretenders, however, were busy in the capitals of the new states. In Nairobi or Abadan or Addis Ababa the visitor was steered to able and energetic young men, speaking in the accents of Harvard or Oxford or the Sorbonne. They would discourse at length on political trends and public opinion, gross national product and wage structure, the Organization for African Unity and black Africa's confrontation with its white south. Then you would lunch at a restaurant or hotel that imitated those of London or Paris or New York, and, over the gin and tonic and the steak, the real Africa would seem even farther away.

Encounters with the governing elite are necessary to the reporter, who must deal with those in power, often transients like himself. But in black Africa more than almost anywhere else talk at the top obscures realities.

Tribalism is one reality. Political parties exist, although in most black African states there is only one party, the one that governs. But the essential political organism is the tribe; the Kikuyu ruled Kenya not as a political unit but as a tribal one. The Ibo, short on numbers but long on energy, education, and enterprise, were the most important political and economic group in Nigeria—as a tribe—before the Biafran war.

A second reality was and is that, whatever the pretensions by black governments, many of the black states are not coherent political organizations. They are places, not states. The government's writ runs a few hundred miles from the capital, often less. Beyond that limit lies a political and administrative limbo where the government is only grudgingly recognized and where the great issues, on which, according to the orators at the United Nations, all black Africans are united, are unknown.

The third reality, as evident now as it was in 1966, is that black Africa is on its back. The land is poor, the people are poor, and economic progress moves at a snail's pace. By Asian standards there is no population pressure. But every African city has its ghetto swarming with people from the bush striving to catch on, and very rarely succeeding, in the outwardly prosperous city. Except in those areas where Africa has what the developed world needs—in Zambia and Zaire the copper, in Ghana the bauxite, on the Ivory Coast the manganese, in Nigeria the oil —the people struggle along, living on what they raise, occasionally accumulating enough surplus to buy manufactured objects.

With one exception no African state conveyed the sense of immense, untapped resources, a feeling I often had in Russia. The exception was Ethiopia.

Mussolini once said that, properly developed, Ethiopia could feed the Middle East. He was right. But thousands of square miles of rich, upland soil go untilled, the farming villages are unkempt, the rich, agricultural promise has never been fulfilled. The young intellectuals who provided a "cocktail-party opposition" to the rule of Haile Selassie blamed this on the Emperor's restrictive policies. Perhaps they were right: much of the untilled land belongs to the Crown or the Church. But the question in Ethiopia, as elsewhere in Africa, is whether the people would develop their country unaided if political and economic freedom existed. In time, perhaps. But there is no guarantee that the government that succeeds the Emperor will be any more liberal in its economic and social policies.

Independence in black Africa has not been accompanied by the spread of parliamentary democracy. What we have had instead is the development of one-party government in states where, it was assumed, the departing colonial masters had left the beginnings of democracy based on the party system.

This development worries those who entertain romantic views of Africa's political future. Yet in the existing circumstances, it is perfectly logical. Tom Mboya, the Kenyan who was one of the most astute African politicians, in the year before his assassination explained that the British had given his people adequate training in everything but politics.

"They left us a bureaucracy, a military structure, communications, an advanced agriculture by African standards," he said.

"What they couldn't give us was a working political system. Political parties, unless they followed the London line, were out. I don't mean Mau Mau. I mean any party that criticized the British administration. And, of course, any responsible party would criticize it.

"So we are not ready for a two-party or a multiparty system. We have had centuries of authoritarianism. Our chiefs, the British governors. People just don't understand the business of opposition. Of course, we in the government argue among ourselves when reaching a decision. Just as there are arguments when the elders of a tribe reach a decision. But when the decision is taken, then that is the rule of the government or the tribe and not to be attacked. To attack, as your 'out' party does your government, that seems dangerous to us. Strong countries, developed countries, can stand the pressures that partisan politics generate. We can't. Maybe, someday."

The extension of one-party government in Africa goes on. It involves a potential danger for world stability. One-party states usually are more vulnerable to subversion than multiparty states, largely because of the absence of an organized opposition. Communist infiltration of the ruling Kenya African National Union, for example, would be relatively easy, because under present conditions no vigorous, uninhibited, organized opposition exists to detect and expose the process.

This condition is an extension of another, widespread in the African world and like one-party government, harmful to political development. The committee rooms of the United Nations echo with references to "African public opinion," and editorial writers, too, are apt to consider this opinion a serious factor.

African public opinion represents so small a segment of the population that comparisons with public opinion in the West are laughable. In the more advanced black countries, in Nigeria or the Ivory Coast for example, perhaps two per cent of the population is capable of understanding national political issues; and this may be an overgenerous estimate.

Black Africa is still too close to her primitive past to have an informed public opinion. The demands of her situation ask her to achieve in twenty years the political maturity that the West has painfully evolved in two thousand. It is a disservice to Africa to equate her political institutions with those of the Western world, and it is dishonest to proclaim, as politicians do, that Africa wants this or wants that. No one knows what Africa wants, because the ideas of the masses are unformed.

Tension between black Africa and the white governments of South Africa, Rhodesia, and the Portuguese territories of Mozambique and Angola is the most important political fact on the continent. It is accurate to say that black African governments abhor the racial inequality of Rhodesia and South Africa and the economic domination of the Portuguese, but to believe that these governments express the views of large sections of their nations and that millions of black Africans are so aroused that they are ready to take up arms against the white, southern third of the continent is nonsense.

I listened in Dar-es-Salaam to a tirade against South Africa and Rhodesia from Julius Nyerere, the president of Tanzania. It was impossible to doubt his conviction that Pretoria must be made to abolish apartheid or risk a great black crusade from the north to free the Bantu from Boer domination.

A couple of days later I was in a village twenty or so miles from Dar. I told my interpreter to ask the village storekeeper how he felt about South Africa and apartheid. After a long dialogue, my interpreter, who had been furnished by the government, reported that the storekeeper had never heard of either. I suggested that he try the tribesmen who were gazing at the shoddy wares in the government shop. The interpreter, willing to humor this lunatic visitor, went through the process again. The result was the same except that, in this case, he had to explain to the tribesmen that there were other white men in the world in addition to those they saw occasionally on the road.

Confrontation with the white governments imposes burdens on the black governments in the north. Because black leaders rightly consider apartheid an affront to themselves, they feel that they must, in public at least, maintain a violent, oral opposition. I was struck in my talks with Nyerere, Kenneth Kaunda of Zambia, and Jomo Kenyatta of Kenya with the irrelevance of their primary concerns, which were Rhodesian independence and South African apartheid, to the grave economic and social problems in their countries. They and other black leaders spend time and energy on issues they cannot resolve, while other issues, more important to their peoples, beg for attention.

Occasionally they would admit that education, health, and better trade balances were important. But always they returned to, say, what Ian Smith had said in Salisbury or to an editorial in an Afrikaaner newspaper.

Perhaps it is because they have attained—or, to be realistic, been given—so much in their life that these and other leaders appear to believe that solely through talk and agitation they can alter the policies of South Africa and Rhodesia. I abhor those policies. But they cannot be changed by talk, and they are less important to black Africa than the development of agriculture and industry.

Are these courteous, earnest men the real Africa? Or is Africa the tribesmen of the Cameroon watching a herd of elephant, perhaps two hundred strong, move like a column of tanks across the plains?

On the plains in the harsh sun and seemingly limitless space I felt the tremendous attraction of Africa that has caught so many. One can understand Baker, Stanley, and the other explorers of the nineteenth century. Oddly, although I have often been in the desert in war and peace and have poked around the souks and kasbahs of the Middle East, I never have been touched by the Arab world's alleged magnetism. But Africa: huge, empty, fearsome—that attraction I can understand. This, I felt that day, was the way it must have been when the world was young.

The herd moved steadily across the plain. An old tusker marched in front exactly like the point man of a platoon marching through enemy country. Other old males served as flank guards on the sides of the column. The herd itself, half obscured by dust, was a gray mass broken by the flapping of huge ears, tossing trunks. Above the mass flew the white birds that live on the elephants, picking insects from their hides. There was a chorus of squeals, grunts, rumblings, and trumpetings. Powerful, inexorable, the herd moved on.

We were a little too close. A bull stopped. His ears flapped. His head turned. The game warden raised his hand. It was the signal to freeze. I froze. We had been regaled with the tale of two French soldiers on tour who had been killed by an elephant on this spot the previous year.

A day or two later I flew from Fort Lamy to Lake Chad where

the United Nations and other international agencies are reclaiming lake bottom and turning it into agricultural land.

A dam was being built out into the lake. Eventually the water behind it would be pumped out and the reclaimed land farmed. This concept was implemented by the most primitive means. Down the completed part of the dam walked thousands of Africans, each bearing a basket of earth. When the African got to the appointed spot, he dumped his burden and returned to get more. As they walked through the pitiless sun, they talked, sang, and laughed. It seemed ineffectual, too light-hearted to be serious. But the dam grew out into the lake. Somewhere, in cool, aseptic offices, engineers had planned this work. Now, thousands of miles away it was being done. The contrast between the detailed scope of the plan and the haphazard, merry means was enchanting.

Occasionally a horseman would pass along the sand hills. A small, close-coupled horse, well groomed. The rider wrapped in robes and topped by a conical, brightly colored straw hat. The horsemen were from the northern Moslem tribes who live in the desert wastes of Chad that extend northward to the borders of Libya. A current of apprehension ran through the workers on the dam whenever they saw a horseman.

We went to the house where the engineers lived. It was on the edge of a village built by the French. There was the *mairie,* the bandstand, the forlorn little hotel. Laboring under that terrible sun in this sandy waste, the French had tried to reproduce the villages of France.

No moment in the African day is as mysteriously arresting as the coming of night. The sun drops, the drooping spirit revives, smells and sounds defeated by day strike the nose and the ear. I approached the old Africa on those nights; the firelight in the camps across the Charri, the sound of laughter from the town. Once along the river bank I saw four boys dancing, solemnly, silently in the light of a fire. Beyond them lay the river, now black and silent, studded with the backs of hippos. In the night, an elephant trumpeted. Africa.

To meet His Excellency, the President of the Republic of Chad, or his Foreign Minister or any number of dignitaries was, in those circumstances, interesting but irrelevant. Beyond the neat and orderly town the French had built, beyond the French

Army's barracks, lay tens of thousands of square miles untouched, untamed. That was the reality. A government, a bureaucracy, solemn talk about economic planning, these were the unrealities. I felt the same thing in Lagos, Abadan, Addis Ababa, even Nairobi. But never was the contrast between the reality of undeveloped black Africa and the smudged finger marks of European civilization stronger than in Chad.

Twenty-four hours after leaving Fort Lamy I sat in the expensive, modern bar of a hotel in Johannesburg talking to a business man from Durban encountered on the plane. He was an "English" South African; that is, he had been born in Worcestershire, had come out in the late 'forties, and had made a prosperous life. He had a house by the sea, a swimming pool, three stout sons, and a handsome wife. Like most of his kind he spent a good deal of time and many drinks attempting to convince me that most of what was written and said about South Africa and apartheid was nonsense.

The "English" South Africans, I found, are much more anxious to assure foreigners on this point than are the Afrikaaners. The latter don't give a damn.

In some respects the South Africans are an admirable people. They work hard, fear their God, who ordained that blacks be hewers of wood and drawers of water, are hospitable, are brave and, within the limits of their understanding, compassionate.

Tolerant, civilized conversation stops when talk turns to apartheid. Then one encounters, first, a grotesque view of the rest of the world, particularly the United States and Britain, and such segments of their population that have protested against apartheid. Then one encounters, first, a grotesque view of the minorities at the fullness of power. They do not talk of "the Reich that will last a thousand years" or boast that "one 'Sothron' can whip ten Yankees." But the echoes are there.

Their arguments in defense of apartheid are a jumble of half-baked racial theories, fear, conviction that what is being done is, in the long run, best for the Africans, and a dogged dislike of the twentieth century. One position, more a patriotic, racialist sentiment than an argument, dominates: This is *our* land, we South Africans built it, we fought the Zulu and the English, we have kept it white because it is ours. You, in New York or

London, know nothing about the land and the people. We know it, it is ours.

It is difficult, but possible, to talk to blacks who see things differently. Some accept fire and sword, the latter supplied by Moscow or Peking, as the only recourse of their race. One man, met by chance in a park near a bus station, laughed at this. His people, he thought, did not need force, only time.

"How many of us are there now?" he asked. "How many by 1980? When our tide runs high, they will not be able to keep us apart."

From the outside and to some of its defenders in South Africa apartheid seems the stoutest of ramparts. But rapid economic expansion is undermining the policy. Every year more and more blacks, in defiance of the laws regulating their employment, are slipping into positions of minor responsibility in the Republic's growing industries.

"We wink at those damned laws every day," an industrialist told me. "Couldn't keep the plants open, if we didn't. We don't change the job titles. Some damned Old Testament farmer in Parliament might find out. But we give them more to do, a little quiet instruction, and more money. Some of the Zulus I've got are as good as some of these lay-abouts out from England, a damned sight better in some cases."

South Africa is white Africa. The blacks occupy a role much like that of the slaves in the ante-bellum South: figures in the background, numerous but powerless. Driving to Pretoria from Johannesburg the visitor sees little to indicate that he is in a country caught in a terrible racial problem. The chatty bus driver tells you this is "white man's country." The neat houses, the well-stocked shops, the stalwart, handsome children, and the cars support him. It is only when the visitor goes north, away from this citadel of white supremacy in a black continent, that the undeclared, unending conflict between the races becomes reality.

The whites stand to their liquor like men at noontime in the Salisbury Club in the pleasant copy of an English provincial town that is the capital of the Republic of Rhodesia. They line the bar in their suits of English cloth and cut and their old school ties. Their talk is peppered with old-fashioned Army and Royal Air Force slang, and it's all very jolly and friendly.

They will show you everything you want to see. "No secrets here, old chap. You'll see that the blacks get on very well. We respect them and they respect us. Why, I've an old black on my place, I'd trust . . ."

The Rhodesians, certainly the "English" Rhodesians, are less racist than the South Africans. The visitor is not bored, as he is in South Africa, by long discourses, based on the most dubious scholarship, about the inferiority of the black race. But he meets a rampant nationalism exacerbated by the embargo against the country and by the censure of the United Nations. This same middle class is fearful of anything, such as black equality, that will imperil its economic status.

The majority of middle-class whites are living better than they did in England and, in most cases, doing less work. There is something painfully bogus about the society. They are not, these jolly fellows at the bar, the counterparts of the Englishmen they believe themselves to be. They are genteel men, not gentlemen, and the visiting Englishman who summed up the whites in Kenya as "the officers' mess" and those in Rhodesia as "the sergeants' mess" was snobbish but perceptive.

Since Rhodesia's independence there has been a definite turning away from Britain toward South Africa. That Republic was Rhodesia's one close friend on the continent. Through it passed exports that kept Rhodesia alive. The Rhodesians were one with the South Africans in seeing Moscow behind every criticism of their policies.

Despite a trade embargo, the massed denunciations of the majority of the Afro-Asian group in the United Nations, and the unanimous hostility of Communist powers, the Rhodesians had survived. They had been able to trade with and through South Africa and with the Portuguese African territories of Mozambique and Angola. They had sold tobacco through dummy corporations established in Mediterranean capitals, and they imported what they needed in addition to products bought in South Africa from similar corporations.

When I returned to New York and my post at the United Nations, I was told a great deal about the embargo, the naval blockade that the British maintained off Mozambique, and the universal rejection of Rhodesia's independence and racist policies. I wondered then, as I have so often about the United Nations: Whom do they think they're kidding?

Stress between black and white is almost totally absent in the Portuguese territories. Racial equality is the law of the land, and if this means, to paraphrase Anatole France, that both black and white can sleep under bridges, it is nonetheless true that in both Mozambique and Angola there are far more Negroes, mulattoes and quadroons in positions of importance within local governments than in the two "white" nations to the south.

For all their religious, political, economic, and cultural ties with Portugal, the two territories are essentially African. This is not simply a matter of African participation, on a low level, in administration, but it is in the texture, the atmosphere of the countries.

I spent a day along the Limpopo with a Portuguese district officer. He had a wife and three fine sons in Lisbon, he talked of the ballet in Copenhagen and of London clubs. But he was African in all but the color of his skin. When we visited villages within his territory, there was a rapport between him and the villagers far deeper than the master-and-man relationship evident during similar visits in Rhodesia. There was a shared experience, a conviction of mutual contribution, that had built that dam, dug that well, cleared the way for that road. Oldtimers tell me that something of the same feeling existed between British and Indians before independence: they had worked together and done great things, this was their land, white or black or brown, they were proud of common achievements.

I said as much one night. We were sitting on the porch of a district officer's bungalow, smoking and drinking brandy. Around us was the solid blackness of the jungle, alive with the noises of the night.

"Do I understand the blacks?" he asked. "Rather, do they understand me? We are building villages along the Limpopo for white and black settlers alike. It is no trick to get settlers from Portugal. We are a poor people. But I explain to the blacks why this will be a better life for them in the villages. Food supplies will be certain. Education. Medical care. Decent houses. They say they understand. But do they? Are we not trying to give them, here and elsewhere in Africa, something they do not really want?"

He rose, opened the screen door, and flicked his cigar butt into the bushes. Something moved in the blackness. He laughed.

"They come and watch us, you know. The wild animals. Often, in Angola, it was a gorilla."

He sighed and stretched, a long, luxurious loosening of the muscles of a man who has been hard at work for many hours.

"I love this country. I've been bitten by snakes, I've had the fevers, I've spent a night in a tree with only my rifle, waiting for rebels to come and get me and castrate me. We, Africa and I, are friendly enemies. I am not a political man. All I ask is a little more time. We will not turn them into quiet, pliable people. They will not become Europeans. But they will be better off than they are now. But time; time, my friend, we need that. And not just from America and London and the United Nations. But from Lisbon as well."

The Portuguese territories are the northern limits of that one third of Africa that represents what the United Nations considers "white colonialist" Africa. The Portuguese guerrillas were fighting there when I visited Mozambique and Angola, and they are doing so today. It is a war of ambush, of demolition, of raids on isolated farmhouses, fought on both sides with ferocity. This is the active fringe of the confrontation between black and white Africa.

South African "police" help the Rhodesians guard their frontiers, and sizable Portuguese forces are in the field. But in a real sense there is no military confrontation. The states of black Africa are too weak to fight, even with major guerrilla warfare, the white countries to the south. They cannot do this without a far greater measure of help than they now receive from the Soviet Union and its European allies or from China.

The day may come when black Africa, disillusioned by promises of support from western governments and by empty resolutions passed by the Security Council, decides to go all the way in accepting military equipment and training from Communist states. Already the arms used against white Portuguese and Rhodesians are Russian and Chinese. And no matter what is said at mass meetings or preached from pulpits and editorial columns in America, Britain, and elsewhere, black Africa is wise enough to know that the industrial nations are unlikely to sever trade and financial ties with South Africa and Rhodesia.

The mineral resources of Zaire, Zambia, and Angola are rich enough to excite Communist cupidity. What is Egypt, what is Taiwan, to the untapped wealth of middle Africa? Assistance to black Africa in the form of modern arms and military training could bring important political gains for the Russians or the Chinese.

Even if there is no major Communist move into black Africa, there is a potential of danger. The great struggle of the next century may not be between Communism and capitalism but between the unnumbered millions of Africa, Asia, and Latin America and the great industrial states. Racial injustice and economic inequality, powerful elements in the emotions of the "third world," could ignite a conflagration that would sweep across the earth.

II

The Arakan Buddha sits in the great pagoda of Mandalay. I asked a priest why the Buddha was called "Arakan." "Because that is where he came from, all men know that," he said in unaccented English. Those who worship buy a few grains of gold dust on a small piece of paper and reverently paste the dust on the great figure. The pagoda's dimness, contrasting with the glaring May sun outside, gave an illusion of coolness. It was a merry place.

Shops lined the passages leading to the Buddha. They sold candy, toys, jewelry, and knick-nacks. As I stood looking at the huge, gold image, I could hear good-natured bargaining and occasional laughter. One walked carefully in the passages. There the old slept, and fat, gurgling babies staggered from shop to shop. There was no overpowering ceremonial. There was a feeling of reverence, but an equable, friendly reverence. St. Paul's in medieval times, before they cleared out the shops, must have been very like the Arakan pagoda. The worshippers came and went as though participating in a happy community action. Religion was not the solemn and stately business it is in the West.

I left the Irrawaddy and Mandalay's palaces and pagodas and drove north to Maymyo in the hills. Are there greater pleasures than entering unknown country and leaving behind the familiar patterns of life? I am ordinary enough in most ways. I can abide routine, I like the creature comforts, I cherish old friends. But always there is the impulse to be up and away. The news stories one finds at the end of the road are only part of the lure. There are always stories too insignificant for a great newspaper but of the very stuff of life.

I noticed small clay images outside houses along the road. The driver told me they were set there to propitiate a legion of spirits of wood and water and air. But were not the Burmese ardent Buddhists? They were, he agreed, but they also considered it wise to stay on the right side of ALL supernatural beings, from the great Teacher to the spirit who lived in the trees by the well.

The car began to climb. At the halfway mark I got out to look at the Irrawaddy plain stretched before me. There was Mandalay half hidden in the heat haze. The river's coils flashed in the sun. I thought of "The Taking of Lungpungten"; does anyone read Kipling now? Then we went on, the air cooler with each mile we climbed.

Maymyo is a ghost town. When the British ruled Burma, civil servants, soldiers, and police withdrew to Maymyo to escape the summer heat of the plains. It was a smaller, less exciting Simla, the British summer capital in India. When I saw Maymyo twenty years after the departure of the British, their stamp was still upon the town. The men who laid out the bridle paths and the botanical gardens and planned the Tudor cottages under the pines were long dead. But they had left a bit of Surrey behind.

Walking in the cool of the evening—to my amazement after Bangkok and Vientianne and Saigon it was really cool—I ran across other vestiges of that empire upon which the sun has finally set.

There was something in the look of the man marching along one of the paths in the Botanical Gardens, a certain drilled competence, the stamp of self-reliance. He did not look Burmese. Chinese, perhaps? No. I had it: Ghurka.

Yes, the sahib was observant. He had been a noncommissioned officer of the Ghurkas and after the war had moved his family here. He had a small holding and his pension; the government, he said darkly, had not stopped that nor had it thrown his and eight other Ghurka families out of the country. The lowland Burmese who ruled the country he found a poor lot. The Shans and others in the hills fighting successful guerrilla warfare against the government were different. He had fought against them, and he knew.

Where had he fought? We sat on one of the benches in the Gardens in the twilight and talked. His English stumbled, but he had the names, and in that quiet place they conjured up the memories of desperate battles and half-forgotten sights; Benghazi and Sollum, Tobruk and Medinine. Had the sahib seen the attack across the Medjerda? Did he know of the Major Bryce, much of a soldier, had he seen what "we" had done at Cassino? I wrote his address and the names of some of the officers he had served with in my notebook. I once tried to trace them when I was briefly in London. But they were gone to wherever it is that the gay and gallant go.

I was anxious to meet representatives of the guerrillas. The next morning in the market I talked with a little fellow whose skinny arms were tatooed with designs in a violent blue ink. He was dubious about making contact with the leaders, but he would like to talk. I came from the United Nations. Did I then think that the Independent Shan government should send a delegation to New York to plead its cause before the United Nations? I said I didn't think one more delegation would do any harm, but that it would cost a lot of money.

He grinned and said they had plenty of money. Seeing my surprise, he said, "Opium, much money from opium, money for guns, mebbe for New York."

Most travellers learn that many of the great sights of the world are disappointing. A few, the Rembrandts at the Hague, the Grand Canyon of the Colorado, rejoice the soul. So it is with the Taj Mahal.

I saw it first across the clutter and dust of an Indian road. It rose at a distance, white, pure and serene, unbearably lovely. And this loveliness it retains even when, coming closer, the visitor encounters the stinks, the beggars, the grafting guides. Nothing, no baseness, can mar its beauty. I could only thank God that wars and riots and time had not touched Shah Jehan's memorial to his wife. In its presence one could only fall back on the thought, trite enough in all truth, that this is the greatest tribute man has paid to human love.

But I am of the earth, earthy. The refreshment of my soul

offered by the Taj Mahal was no more welcome than the refreshment to my body later that day when I dove into the cold, clear water of the hotel swimming pool. How much do I lose because my enjoyment, no matter how concentrated for the moment, is transient? Is the sensual pleasure in a Shakespearean sonnet marred by the appreciation of a whiskey and soda at the end of a long day? Where does the mind's enjoyment end, the body's begin?

Toward the end of the Asian trip I found myself in Peshawar in West Pakistan. I felt very much as I had halfway through my African trip. I had spent weeks listening to politicians, civil servants, and diplomats talking about Asia and her problems. I had studied the tremendous possibilities for Asia of IR-8, the miracle rice. I had listened to Madame Ghandi, India's Prime Minister, assail American policy in Vietnam and then, not three hours later, heard one of India's senior diplomats assure me that "whatever the Prime Minister says in public, you must understand that we do not want you to lose in Vietnam. Your departure could bring great dangers to us and to all Asia."

In Rangoon, Bangkok, Calcutta, New Delhi, Bombay, Karachi, and Islamabad I had digested endless statistics. I had plodded through rice paddies and seen schools, factories, farms. This is, of course, the staple of a correspondent's diet: he learns what to look for, the man in the government department who understands what the reporter wants, the incident that will give life to the mass of statistics.

Now in May I was at Peshawar hard by the Khyber Pass and the last vestiges of the romantic, fierce, and vigorous world of the northwest frontier. To walk in Peshawar itself is to return to the old India, the small shops with their grave merchants, the thousand smells and sounds. Beyond the city lie the hills and the pass.

It was difficult, but not impossible, to hire a car and drive to Kabul. Or, if the sahib wanted, a driver would take him through the pass and bring him back before sundown. No one travelled the pass at night. Why not? "Still bad mens in the hills."

The black road through the Pass twists and turns, often back upon itself. A few feet to one side of the road the sheer rock rises to cliffs topped by silent Pathan watch towers. On the other side there is only space and a glimpse far below of the road you have covered a few minutes before. It is lonely, remote, and beautiful. In midafternoon it was shaded and cool in the gut of the pass. The watchtowers on the summits of the hills above were bright in the sunlight.

The radiator boiled over, and the driver fetched water from a stream. Almost at once a tribesman appeared, much as trick photography makes figures appear on the screen. There was a cartridge belt around his waist and another over his shoulder. One large hand clasped what I recognized as a Lee-Enfield rifle. Over one ear was a red flower, another was twined through the coils of his thick, glossy hair. He wore leather sandals, long, white, baggy pantaloons, and a dirty shirt with the tails hanging free. His turban was wound loosely. The stock of the Enfield shone with polishing, and its muzzle was decorated with bright red and green strips of what looked like tinsel.

His face was long-jawed. There was a fringe of beard and hard gray eyes.

Did the sahib need anything more than water? Was he on his way to Kabul? No, the sahib intended to visit the fort at Landi Kotal where his father-in-law and brother-in-law had served.

Ah, the "Beritish Armee" he said in pleasant recollection. They had fought the British, and when the British were unsporting enough to bring planes and artillery and Ghurkhas, who had a taste for ambush that matched that of the Pathans', the tribes would hand in a few old rifles and retire to their hilltop fortresses to plan the next campaign.

Things are dull now. When the Pathans pick up a Pakistani official or merchant for ransom, often sending along a finger with the ransom note to encourage early settlement, the Pakistanis send the money. The British would send troops, and a brisk little war would entertain the Pathans until the cost became too high.

Blood feuds still are a part of life. A village landowner, starting for Peshawar with eggs for market, was taunted by a youth. He was not a landowner, just a peddler, the youth said. The landowner shot him dead, and another feud began.

Violence lives side by side with poetry. In the villages atop the hills old men at evening recite epics dealing with the heroic deeds of tribal leaders. Daily the Peshawar newspapers publish poems contributed by Pathan bards.

The Pathans have a diabolical vitality. No one knows how old they are or whence they came. The armies of Darius, Alexander the Great, Genghis Khan, Tamerlane, and Baber the Great Moghul threaded down through their passes to loot and ravage India. The Pathans fought all the *ferrangi* from Alexander's spearmen to the kilted Scots of Victoria whose pipes awoke the echoes of the hills with "Hey, Johnny Cope" and "The Desperate Battle."

The wars are over now. The Pakistanis dig wells and push roads into the hills. Shy, fierce young Pathans come down to the plains to attend school. Buses and trucks, moving through the passes, bring strange new products. This, one must suppose, is good. But, remember, when bureaucrats parrot their figures about Pathan education and warriors hang their rifles above the door, that something wild and free that gave life and color to the world is dying up there in the hills.

III

People have been saying and writing for some time now that the Vietnam war was unique, there never was a war like it. In one respect they are wrong. All wars are the same at the sharp end: the battlefield. Chaotic and formless, battles are like no other human activity, yet all the same. In the essentials a battlefield situation in Vietnam was no different from one in the western desert or Normandy. The difference between Vietnam and all our other wars was that we lost it, not through the skill and valor of the enemy, which were great, but because of a combination of circumstances that were in themselves alarming and are even more so when considered in the light of the Republic's future.

These circumstances, not necessarily in the order of their importance, were: a president, Lyndon B. Johnson, who knew little or nothing about war, a high command in all three services that began the war with highly unsuitable tactical doctrine and with forces largely trained for another type of conflict, a public sharply divided over the war, and an amorphous but important collection of liberals, workers in the media, academics, left-wing politicians, and intellectuals who played on the frustrations and fears of the public and swung a significant section against the war.

I may as well have my say about the war. I think it should have been won. I think it could have been won without the use of nuclear weapons. I believe that our failure to win it and the effect of the war on public opinion will cost us more in the future than we would have spent in blood and treasure in winning. President Nixon made great play with the phrase "peace with honor," words perilously close to those used by Neville Chamberlain after Munich. (I recall Bill Stoneman's remark, "Whenever I hear about 'peace with honor' I know someone's going to get screwed.") The future will include no peace for Indo-China and, consequently, no honor for the United States.

I saw the Vietnam war from a number of angles: from the United Nations, where U Thant, nominally neutral, led the chorus condemning America, from foreign ministries in Asia, where the war was publicly assailed and privately supported, from the peace talks in Paris in 1968 and 1969 and, most importantly, from the field in Vietnam.

The media's coverage of the war was a curious business. The emphasis was largely political: the rise and fall of governments in Saigon, the attitudes of the Vietnamese toward these governments, the execution or nonexecution of policies by a succession of American ambassadors. There were a lot of good reporters there, good in the sense that they knew what was going on. But too many of them were subjective. They were against this politician or that policy or the war in general, and their opposition showed.

I've been a reporter too long to believe that anyone can attain complete objectivity. If he did, his editor would spike his copy. But in the Vietnam war subjectivity went too far. The reader, the listener, and the viewer in America were short-changed. There *was* another side.

It was a peculiarly difficult war to cover in its military aspects. There were no coherent fronts. Fighting flared and died all over the map of Vietnam. Battles had to compete with political developments that, in many cases, were treated with greater attention by editors. Some major battles were virtually ignored by great newspapers. But there weren't many major battles. Most engagements were short, sharp encounters coming after days of fumbling for the enemy in the jungle.

One steaming afternoon in May of 1967 a helicopter landed me at a battalion headquarters in a clearing hacked out of the jungle near the Cambodian frontier. Trees and brush had been leveled over a couple of acres. At one end of the rough rectangle were six 105-millimeter guns. Scattered across the clearing were dugouts, their roofs heavily sandbagged. The damp, oppressive heat of southeast Asia lay over the clearing like a blanket. There were piles of captured enemy weapons.

The battalion was commanded by a thickset, genial Hawaiian. His people, he explained, had been pushing a North Vietnamese regiment for five days, groping in the jungle, running over a picket here, "fixing" a company there, hitting hard with automatic weapons, artillery, fighter bombers, and heavy machine guns mounted in helicopters.

"We kill fifteen, twenty, twenty-five a day for sure," the Hawaiian said. "Those are the bodies we count ourselves. But each of these jokers carries a rope with a loop at one end. When they have the chance, they rope a corpse and haul him away. Don't want us to find them, you see. Sometimes we find a dead guy still holding a rope attached to another body. Funny war, eh?"

An enemy mortar began to lob shells into the jungle west of the clearing.

"Watch Charlie, now," said a black lieutenant, much amused. "He'll mortar the hell out of that one spot. Won't shift. You know, when you're out after them on patrol, they're right smart. But most times, on things like this—that's a big Russian mortar —they're not. They keep firing, and the choppers and the guns find them. You watch."

The outrageous clamor of the 105's broke out behind us. From somewhere in the jungle I heard the spatter of automatic fire. At the headquarters dugout the Hawaiian was listening on a field telephone.

"Same bunch," he said. "We got the mortar. They're moving toward the Cambodian frontier. Once they're over that, it's good-bye, Charlie. Maybe we can catch some of them before they cross the river."

The Negro lieutenant didn't think much of the river as a barrier.

"Hell," he said, "I could jump across it."

An insignificant incident in a war that was made up of thousands of such incidents. It contained a lesson, however. How would the war have developed if the battalion had been permitted to pursue the enemy across the river into Cambodia? What happened in this case happened hundreds of times. The enemy, badly hurt, escaped across the river where, immune from attack, he rested, picked up supplies and replacements and, when all things were ready, recrossed the river into Vietnam. By then, of course, the battalion was miles away; it couldn't waste time watching the frontier.

At Military Assistance Command, Vietnam, the generals would tell you, "We're not going to lose the war in Washington the way the French lost it in Paris." But we did lose it, at least partially, in Washington, which forbade pursuit into Cambodia. When the Nixon administration did permit an offensive across the frontier in May of 1970, it was too late.

The constants of the fighting in the jungle were heat, dust and, in the monsoon, an enervating heavy dampness. The Vietnamese jungle teaches what "impenetrable" means. Much of it is as dense as the rain forests of Africa. You have the impression of silence, but the jungle is alive with sound: creakings, scrapings, murmurs, the calls of birds, the rustling of small animals in the undergrowth. Patrol work is like fighting blindfolded.

"You gotta be God-damned fast getting in the first rounds," a sergeant said when we discussed jungle patrols. "Also, you gotta be sure it *is* Charlie."

I did not find that the fighting men, soldiers in the jungle, fliers aboard the carriers, held any great grudge against the politicians or the protesters at home. They did feel strongly that until a person had been in Vietnam, had undergone what they had undergone, and seen what they had seen, his judgment on the war was open to question.

"Of course, you've got to listen to these guys, Fulbright, Kennedy, the others. They're elected officials," said a thoughtful soldier of the 1st Division.

A marine lieutenant said the same thing. Then the soldier

added, "You find some nice old Joe, who's talked to you, with his throat cut by Charlie. Or a couple of village girls ripped up the middle. It makes you wonder whether you're fighting men or animals. You ever see one of these villages after Charlie has worked it over. Jesus!"

There were, of course, people in the line or at various head-quarters who saw the war as a crusade against Communism. Just as there were others who regarded it as an impossible conflict that could not be won by military means. But these were minor notes. The prevailing opinion in 1967 was that the war should be won and could be won, whatever the reasons for fighting and winning it might be.

Four years later, when I returned to Vietnam, there was a sad-ness compounded of frustration and lost hopes. There were fewer soldiers on the streets of Saigon. In the huge embassy building old friends talked of missed opportunities and deplorable de-cisions by the Johnson Administration. The only optimists I met were the soldiers and airmen training the Vietnamese forces, and even they bewailed our tardiness in beginning the Viet-namization program. They were making progress, they said, but the job of training and equipping the Vietnamese should have begun years earlier.

One morning a helicopter flew me northwest to the 1st Cavalry Division. I was traveling with a saturnine lieutenant-colonel who, like so many, had little use for the media. For the first ten minutes he stared gloomily down at the countryside below us. Then he roused himself.

"You see what's happening down there?" he asked.

I looked down over the checkerboard of fields and saw peas-ants working.

"Take a good look," he said. "A couple of years ago they didn't dare work here. Stayed cooped up in the villages because the Vietcong had told them to stay there. Well, we came along and drove the Vietcong out. Took lots of casualties doing it, too. But they're back working now. You're looking at the fruits of victory, mister. Why don't some of those lazy bastards in Saigon come out here and write about it?"

I had been prepared by newspaper and television reports to find an army in dissolution. "Hell," they said at headquarters, "that stuff, fragging and all that, belongs in the back areas. Our kids are okay. Go and talk to them."

The G.I.'s admitted they were a little tired. But they had been pushing one of the enemy's main-force regiments pretty hard, and they were making progress.

"We drove them right off one of their food dumps," a sergeant said.

He showed me the dump. Much of the food, including the sacked flour, was American. It could only have come from the black market in Saigon. I said as much.

"Sure," the sergeant said. "They run the stuff up the road and then haul it into the jungle. Some bastard's making money out of it in Saigon. We'll never touch him. But, brother, we're giving his buddies a hard time."

Stories of undisciplined, motiveless American troops filled the papers back home. I asked the sergeant how his people were. He scratched a day's growth of beard and stared at the sky.

"We had a fire fight here three days ago," he said. "One dead, four hit. Not bad, walking wounded. But enough to get them out of this. But we had to keep after the 'Cong. When they heard we were going to attack again, these four tore off their wounded tags and went back into the fight. Good kids, good as any you'll want."

When I left at sunset, a patrol was moving out. The soldiers were calmly confident. A captain said, "When I read about these protesters back home and then I see these kids . . . Jesus, the country doesn't deserve such people. God damn all politicians."

Well, it's all over now. We're out, and it takes more imagination than I have to envisage the return of American troops to southeast Asia. We lost in the sense that we failed to inflict a clear-cut defeat on the enemy. The enemy lost, despite prodigious expenditure of manpower, because he failed to drive the Thieu government from power and install a Communist government over all Vietnam. He may do so in the future, although it will be a more costly business as a result of the training and equipping of the South Vietnamese forces. But I wonder whether we haven't lost more than is visible in Vietnam.

Since 1968, primarily in Vietnam but also in Europe and the Middle East, the United States has pursued a policy of disengagement otherwise known as the Nixon Doctrine. Plenty of wise men, Democrats as well as Republicans, argue for the wisdom of this policy. Clearly, it accords with the sentiments of millions of Americans, weary of wars and international complications. They seek a return to a quieter past or, in the case of the young, to an uninhibited life untroubled by any large measure of labor and responsibility. They are "looking for that happy land, where everything is bright, where highballs grow on all the trees and we stay out every night." They won't find it any more than their elders will rediscover the tree-shaded villages and comfortable towns of their youth. That America has gone.

Once a people assumes international responsibilities, as the United States did from 1945 to 1965, it cannot go back. Responsibilities may be dropped. Pledges and treaties may be broken. Clever academics may explain all this in terms of changing times and new national priorities. The economist may prate of dwindling resources and altered trade patterns. But there is a slow erosion of principle. Appeasement didn't die in 1940. We simply call it by other names today.

CHAPTER 13

MOROCCO TO THE PERSIAN GULF: Israel and the Arab World

1965-72

I cannot help remembering that the Jews have outlived
Assyrian Kings, Egyptian Pharaohs, Roman Caesars,
and Arabian Caliphs.

Benjamin Disraeli

The Israeli officer beckoned from a corner of the communications trench. I scuttled over, cramped in the flak-vest, the too-large helmet loose on my head. He gestured to a pair of binoculars. The Suez Canal ran across our front. The glittering water was shallow. I could see sand eight or ten inches below the surface. Across the canal were the broken buildings and shattered trees of the Egyptian town of Kantara. South lay the Egyptian city of Suez, largely destroyed by Israeli bombs and shells. This was the battle line. Within the binoculars' range was the flash point of the most dangerous area in the world, the Middle East.

That was true on that summer day of 1971. It is just as true today with one significant difference. The area of potential conflict has widened. The oil of the Middle East will in this decade become a primary source of energy for the great industrial states of east and west. Oil can fuel great international rivalries as easily as it does jets and cars. The danger zone stretches from the Mediterranean coast of Israel to the Persian Gulf. Past generations saw their destinies depending on the control of the North Sea and the English Channel. Ours and the next generation's may lie with the future of these ancient lands at the cross-roads of the world.

Three journeys have taken me from Morocco across North Africa to Saudi Arabia and from the Sudan north to Syria. I have seen the conflict between Jew and Arab against a broader canvas than that afforded by my visits to Israel and Egypt and Jordan. Listening to the Shah in Teheran and King Faisal in Riyadh I sensed that these two very different men both understood that their countries increasingly would be the objects of international rivalry, that the future could hold more than oil and wealth; it could hold conflict and chaos.

Behind the familiar façade of sand and palm, slum and palace, there is deep and extensive change from Morocco to Aden, change that will affect all our calculations about the Middle East.

Americans have assumed in the past, often with reason, that the Arabs are incurably disunited, inefficient, and backward. The Arab performance in war and peace since 1948 is the basis of this assumption. It is dangerous, however, to assume that any situation is static. The establishment of the State of Israel, its success in war and peace, have provoked a response in the Arab world. The pace of Arab reaction varies from country to country. But it is there; the winds of change are blowing.

Education is the most important aspect of the Arab revival.

King Faisal was more interested in talking about educational progress in his country than about the involved politics of the Persian Gulf. The Shah discussed the schools being built in hundreds of hamlets. On a less exalted level a young Moroccan stressed the movement away from purely religious teaching based on the Koran to a wider education that will prepare Arabs to use the technology of the West.

"The European or the American is our technician today," the Moroccan said, "because we lack the skills for technical work. This we must change by education, and this we will change."

For him and for others like him in the Arab world the western monopoly of technological expertise is an irritant, one more meaningful to the ambitious and patriotic than charges of American "neocolonialism" by Moscow. If the Arabs are to be masters of their fate, they, too, must be able to maintain tractors, build dams, and refine oil.

Corrupt and inefficient government impedes Arab progress, but too much can be made of this fact. Despite venality and nepotism at the top and a dizzying succession of rulers in countries like Syria and Iraq one sees evidence of progress in agriculture and light industry. The Arab world will not become another Israel overnight, but it is moving steadily toward the development of its resources. Oil money is already helping. There will be more of it as energy need increases in industrial countries and the producing states raise the price of oil.

Much of the progress is due to foreign assistance. The Soviet Union and its allies have helped in Egypt, Syria, Iraq, Algeria, and elsewhere. Americans, British, and French have helped in countries where they are still tolerated. The spur is the challenge of Israel's success.

The Arabs have been talking about unity since the end of World War I. In terms of unified policy and the burying of national differences it remains distant. But the easy assumption of some Americans that the Arabs will never unite is dangerous. Arabs in Fez and Riyadh, cities separated by the breadth of Africa and Arabia, offer exactly the same arguments for a united effort against Israel in support of the Egyptians, Jordanians, and the Arab guerrillas.

"The Egyptians and the Jordanians got themselves into this mess," King Faisal said, when we discussed the aftermath of the 1967 war, "but I and my people cannot remain neutral. The Jews have taken Jerusalem for their own. There is much to do in this country and in every Arab country. But no believer can rest while they hold Jerusalem."

Faisal was an old, weather-beaten hawk and, unusual in this century, an absolute ruler. His talk shifted from his intensive efforts to find other minerals than oil in Saudi Arabia to his personal efforts ("I am like a teacher in this") at assuring Wahabi elders that education for young women is a necessity and does not infringe on Islamic law. This was the Arab world of the twentieth century. Outside was the Arab world of the tenth.

A score of Faisal's "old companions" chatted, drank coffee, and slept on the rich carpets of the anteroom. They were lavishly armed; bazookas, pistols, submachine guns, and rifles were strewn around the room. These members of Faisal's bodyguard were festooned with belts of cartridges. They gave the hot, smoky room a medieval air.

Inside in the air-conditioned office the King talked on about modernization. As he talked, the skirts of his robe rose: he was wearing the queer old-fashioned boots one sometimes sees in Paris shops, brown leather lowers and brown cloth uppers with laces.

He and other rulers, whether they are royal, dictatorial, or elected, face what, to the westerner, are almost insurmountable difficulties in their drive to modernize Arab societies. Some Arabs are awake to the need for progress. But others are convinced by the inflamed rhetoric—one of the curses of Arab public life—that what is sought, in fact, has been attained. Others are content to slumber in the past.

The past dies hard. At Al-Hariq, south of Riyadh, we halted to escape the heat, 120 degrees at noon, and listened to the gossip of a group under the trees.

"The old man," my interpreter said, "says that we must mourn for Al-Kuds (Jerusalem) and that the Jews' occupation is a punishment on Islam. But he says the Christians held the city long ago for many years but that in the end it was reconquered by the Arabs."

The old man was talking about Saladin and the Crusaders. A far cry from Nasser and Moise Dayan. But not so long to people whose infants are told to go to sleep lest *Malik Ric,* Richard Cœur de Lion, get them.

For the rulers the Arab love of colorful, inflamed, extravagant language is a problem influencing every level of society. The best explanation of its effects came from a British intelligence officer.

"In 1967 we knew the Egyptian Air Force wasn't ready for war," he said. "The Egyptians knew it as well. Why, then, did they go to war?

"Purely because of their intoxication with their damned language. Nasser asked the air commanders about the air force. They knew it wasn't ready. But they couldn't put that into words. Partly because they could not believe that they were inferior to the Israelis, but mostly because their luxuriant language led them to say what they wanted to believe, that they were ready.

"As the language became more extreme, more emotional, they themselves believed what they knew wasn't true. And Nasser, although he must have had his doubts, was caught up by the stream of words and believed them, too. And when they got whipped, they couldn't accept a result so contrary to their language. So, using lots of extravagant language, they invented the tale that the Americans and British had flown with the Israelis. They couldn't accept a truth so far from their own words, that they'd been outthought and outfought by the despised Jews."

In no area of the world that I have visited is the political situation more fluid than in the Middle East. Conclusions on long-term developments are hazardous. But there are three factors that influence the situation now and will influence it for many years to come.

The first is the comfortable assumption that the present politico-military relationship between Israel and her Arab enemies is immutable. The Arab world is changing. Ten years from now it will certainly be stronger economically. The rulers of oil states will have billions of dollars at their disposal. The training and equipment of Arab forces will have progressed. A period of comparative peace and even a temporary end of the present siege atmosphere will reduce Israel's psychological preparedness for war.

Israel's strength in relation to the Arab forces, and even against a Soviet-Arab combination, has been inflated out of all proportion by Zionists and other well-wishers in the West. This is a disservice to Israel.

Fortunately, the high command in Tel Aviv is more hard-headed. Its members see the changes in the Arab world. They anticipate better trained, more technically efficient Arab forces. They do not talk loudly about one Jew's being equal to fifty Arabs. They have a high respect for the Jordanian Army.

"If there were thirty million Jordanians and three million Egyptians instead of the other way around," a senior general said, "we wouldn't be talking here today."

The second factor is the steady political polarization of the Middle East. At one pole are the Arab extremists: Algerians, Egyptians, Libyans, Syrians, Iraqis, all influenced by Soviet policy, all beholden to the Soviet Union for military or economic assistance, all embracing authoritarian governments. The other extreme is Israel and its patron, the United States. In between are nations that still maintain amicable relations with

America despite their hostility to Israel: Morocco, Tunisia, Jordan, Saudi Arabia, Kuwait, and the tiny states of the Persian Gulf.

Polarization is not a static factor. Fifteen years ago Libya and Iraq could be counted in the third group. Today they have shifted to the extremist camp. Some of the third group are held there largely by the will of a small ruling group clustered around the monarch. Who can say how long Hussein will reign in Amman, Hassan in Rabat, Faisal in Riyadh? What will happen in Tunisia, sandwiched between Algeria and Libya, when Habib Bourguiba dies?

Forces hostile to the foreign policies of these countries are active inside and outside their frontiers. Palestinian guerrillas stalk the ministers of moderate governments. The basic political trend is toward extremism.

Polarization will continue as long as a sizable section of the Arab world believes that Israel is an outpost of American imperialism, a steadily growing belief encouraged by the Soviet Union. In 1971 a sensible, worldly Egyptian official assured me that the Israelis' entire campaign in 1967 had been planned by the Pentagon and approved by Lyndon B. Johnson. The power of Arabic affects such myths. So many people repeat this or similar tales in increasingly exaggerated language that myth becomes reality.

One of the problems for American administrations is that many Arabs, originally friendly or, at least, not hostile to the United States believe that an even-handed approach to the Middle East by any American government is out of the question. As evidence they offer the financial support provided Israel by American Jewry, the influence on policy, always wildly exaggerated, of Jewish-owned newspapers and television systems, the necessity of winning the Jewish vote. In these circumstances they cannot foresee any reduction in American support for Israel. They cannot understand that non-Jewish Americans can support Israel for reasons that have nothing to do with race or religion.

As the myth of the Washington-Jerusalem axis grows in Arab minds, the influence of American diplomats and the security of American economic interests in the Middle East wanes. Individual American diplomats or businessmen may be popular. American policy is not.

A Polish doctor encountered in Tunisia thought Americans were painting themselves into a corner.

"You're going to make exactly the same mistake in the Middle East that you made in China. Ten years from now you and the Israelis will be alone, just as you and the Chinese Nationalists were alone, facing an Arab world united by enmity of the Israelis and their protectors in Washington. You make things easy for the Russians."

The third factor in the situation is the Russian interest in the Arab world. The Soviet Union is the most active foreign power in the Middle East. Syria, once a French colony, is as much under the Russian thumb as is Egypt, once dominated by Britain. From Algeria east to Yemen the Russians are at work, either overtly or underground. The overthrow of the remaining moderate governments is one of their objectives.

Talk of maneuvering the Russians out of the Middle East is futile. They are there to stay. The question is how they will use the influence they have attained. Although this influence is strong, it does meet opposition.

Every Arab nation includes men and women educated in America or western Europe or in schools run by westerners. Their social and political attitudes are strongly affected by that education. These "westerners," although by no means as numerous or as powerful as they were twenty years ago, still are important in business and government.

Then there are the young nationalists to whom all foreign politics are anathema.

"We hate the lot of you," a young Iraqi officer said one night in Baghdad. "Americans, British, French, Germans, Yugoslavs, Russians. Yes, even the Russians, though at least they are not allied with the Jews.

"We, I and my group, we distrust the Russians who take our young people to Russia and turn them into Communists. But we need their arms and their experts to beat the Jews."

Baghdad at that time stank of unrest and revolt. We were sitting at a table away from the riverside restaurant's bright lights, and I ventured as much.

"Of course, of course. We are trying to find our way. We must find a compromise between the old, good things of Arab life, a dignity we have lost, and the new things technology can give us."

Then he said something that I had heard in Tunisia and Jordan as often as in Syria and Egypt.

"We must find the way, our way. We must be strong, but we must not lose ourselves. We ruled all Islam from this city once. When I was a boy at school in England no one knew or cared about Baghdad or Cairo or Damascus. We must learn to care about our past, and we must plan for a greater Arab future."

The Russians have many advantages in the Arab world. But they suffer from one grievous disadvantage I noted there and in Africa. They don't really like anyone but Russians. There may be exceptions, but generally the white man's burden is not for Ivan. More ignorant of the world than most Americans, they are appalled by the filth, dirt, and poverty of underdeveloped peoples. This has always struck me as an odd reaction because, since Soviet propaganda never ceases to paint the horrors of colonialism, the Russian diplomat or soldier abroad should be prepared for the conditions he finds.

A Ghanaian official once told me that during Kwame Nkrumah's cultivation by the Russians in the 'fifties and 'sixties "you seldom saw a Russian off duty. "They would go to their compounds after work, sit around in their underwear, and play Russian songs on their gramophones. The British were into everything when they were here, shooting, catching butterflies, studying tribal customs. The Russians weren't interested."

In the Middle East the Russians, a sober and conscientious lot, are continually affronted by the frivolity of their charges.

Flying to Khartoum, I sat next to a Soviet major. We pieced together a conversation from what remained of my Russian and his English. How, I asked, did he like training the Egyptian army?

He threw into the air the old copy of *Pravda* that had been spread on his lap.

"A nonsense!" he shouted, "They are playing polo every afternoon at the Gezira Club."

I said that the British had played polo at the Gezira Club, but they had whipped the Germans at Alamein.

He gave me a pitying look.

"Now you are talking about responsible, intelligent European peoples."

I have a certain sympathy with the Russians as they grapple with Middle East attitudes. In Cairo I dined at the home of a senior Egyptian diplomat. The company was drawn from the "westernized" upper middle class: one or two politicians, a senior foreign-ministry official, an ambassador from an important Asian country. Midway through dinner one of the politicians addressed the lady on my left.

"Did you hear about the conversation between the President [Nasser] and the Foreign Minister?" he asked. The lady said she had not.

"The Foreign Minister told the President he understood the Russians had been very generous to us," the politician continued, "and the President said, 'Yes, they've given us enough equipment for three more defeats.'"

There was a burst of unembarrassed laughter. Remember, this was 1968. Egypt had suffered a complete and humiliating defeat less than a year before. Yet the elite joked about it. People didn't act that way in London in 1940, and I am certain they didn't act that way in Berlin in 1944.

I am sure that most of the members of that congenial dinner party were delighted when, in 1972, the Soviets withdrew from Egypt. They never liked the Russians, considering them barbarians. Equally, I am sure that they do not understand the perilous situation in which Egypt now is.

The Russian withdrawal involved all their fighter and reconnaissance squadrons, approximately seventeen thousand military advisors and technicians, and most of the SA-6 surface-to-air missiles. The SA-2s and SA-3s were left behind, and after the initial withdrawal some advisors and technicians returned to Egypt to complete training programs for the army and air force.

Strategically the move was a boon to Israel. Without the Soviet fighters, the mobile surface-to-air missiles, and a command and control system Alexandria, Cairo, and the Nile Valley are vulnerable to Israeli air attack. The threat, which certainly existed between 1969 and 1972, of a joint Egyptian-Soviet attack on Israel across the Canal has ended.

On the other hand, the withdrawal has not appreciably eased

the strategic situation of the United States Sixth Fleet in the Mediterranean Sea. The Soviets continue to maintain their Mediterranean squadron at between thirty-five and seventy vessels, depending on the season. The great majority of these ships are much more modern than those of the Sixth Fleet, and they were designed and armed with surface-to-surface missiles with the object of destroying the Sixth Fleet, particularly its aircraft carriers. There are ten to twelve missile-firing submarines in the squadron. If the numbers seem small, it should be recalled that, when Germany went to war in 1939, there were fewer than ten ocean-going U-boats at sea!

The Soviet squadron suffered to some extent from the loss of Egyptian bases for its long-range reconnaissance aircraft. But new bases are being established in Syria and Iraq, both radical Arab states, and there will, perhaps, be more in Libya or Algeria. Meanwhile the Soviets maintain a naval base at Latakia in Syria and have the use of Alexandria and Mersa Matruh in Egypt. The squadron has moved into areas hitherto dominated by the Sixth Fleet and NATO navies. The eccentric silhouettes of the helicopter carriers *Moskva* and *Leningrad* are seen off Greek islands. Soviet submarines rock in the swell off Alboran Island close to the strait of Gibraltar and lurk in the Sicilian channel. Flotillas visit Morocco and Algeria and the ports of the Persian Gulf.

Ashore the Russians are making headway in Syria, Iraq, and Libya, sending surface-to-air missiles and technicians to these countries. They are not as thick on the ground in any one of these countries as they once were in Egypt, but their number and influence are growing. As they do, the polarization of the Middle East increases in pace.

The stakes are high in the naval rivalry between the Soviet Union and the NATO powers. Of the fourteen thousand ships at sea every day in the Mediterranean more than ten thousand fly the flags of NATO members. Across the Mediterranean flows the oil of Libya and Algeria for the industries of western Europe.

Tours of the Arab countries and visits to the Sixth Fleet combined to give me a sense of deep anxiety. This was not simply the result of the turbulence of the area, the passions that Arab revival will unleash, and the strength of Soviet forces. It seems to me that the Middle East offers Soviet policy the greatest gain in the form of control of oil for western Europe and the United States at the smallest risk. And the Russians regard their involvement in the Middle East and the Mediterranean not as a remote and marginal operation comparable to their aid to North Vietnam but as an element of their national security.

Such thoughts are less gloomy after contact with the Israeli forces. I have seen a good deal of armies and of war. Seldom have I met such an engaging blend of the skilled professional and the enthusiastic amateur. Everywhere, in 1967, 1968, 1970, and 1971, there was the strong, unspoken dedication last encountered in the R.A.F. in 1940.

One dawn I flew south from Jerusalem. Beneath was the heart of Israel. I thought of Blake's line "And we shall build Jerusalem in England's green and smiling land." Here Jerusalem has made this green and smiling miracle out of dirt and sand.

Spring and the nights were chill. Farmers had covered young plants with hoods of plastic, and the fields glittered in the rising sun like the lakes one sees in summer in northern Norway. An Israeli officer gestures at the panorama with a wide sweep of his hand. Lots of blood and sweat have gone into this land, he says. Tears, too, I suggest. Yes, he says, tears as well.

We land at an airstrip twenty-five miles or so from the line on the Suez Canal. A sedan parked near the strip has a Hertz sticker on its bumper. How on earth did it get there? No one knows.

Briefing at battalion headquarters; a young, handsome lieutenant-colonel, not unlike Paul Newman in looks, explains the position. He is very careful to avoid mentioning Israeli troop strength. A buxom woman corporal serves fruit juice and sandwiches. The headquarters is clean, roughly but adequately furnished. The colonel, his staff officers, the soldiers, male and female, appear casually competent.

(You muse on all the other headquarters in all the years: France, Belgium, North Africa, Sicily, Germany, Vietnam. And all the good men in them who talked on field telephones, wrote orders, studied maps, and went out and died.)

Up to the line by jeep. Fifteen miles from the canal we don helmets. A major of tanks explains that the Egyptians sometimes shell the road. Then, very fast, through the ruins of Kantara and, bumping horribly over a rough track, to the Israeli position on the Suez Canal.

A company of infantry is living under conditions that seem strikingly similar to those described in books about the First World War. The strongpoints and blockhouses are protected by steel rails, sandbags, and heaped-up sand. Communications trenches connect the positions.

"The Egyptians watch us from just across the canal and we watch them," an officer said, adding needlessly, "keep your head down."

A few shells come over. They burst somewhere to our rear. The shelling stops.

"They never keep it up for long," the officer says. "Afraid our planes will spot them."

The lieutenant colonel joins us in a bunker. Around us men are cleaning weapons, reading, sleeping. The colonel says his name is "Tosti," and what did I think of the position? I say it seems very lightly held. His English is halting but emphatic: "Perhaps we not have too many. But we fight Egyptians, can take chance. Americans, British, they cross the canal?"

I say I think that they'd have a damned good try. "Of course," I point out, "you have control of the air."

He grins.

"Very good our air force." A silence. Then, laboriously, "Egyptians better soldiers now than four years ago. Sometimes cross canal at night. No noise. Don't bunch. Young officers better. You think they learn from Russians?"

We drank coffee. Like every food or beverage served in Israel outside private homes, it was terrible. A sergeant broke in (it is a very informal army) to ask whether I thought Nixon would send the planes they needed.

The colonel listened to my answer and then resumed.

"Egyptians get across canal we have big party. Lots tanks, lots planes on our side. Maybe they try, get hurt, and everything be quiet. Not good for Army sit down like this."

Two soldiers, eager to use their English, showed me around: the obsolete tank converted into an ambulance, the kitchen and the cook (they said he was a terrible cook, and I believed them), the clever camouflage, the underground barracks where the men who had been on duty the previous night were dressing. There was efficiency and discipline but not much spit and polish. It was very unlike the Egyptian army I had seen a month earlier.

That morning we rode in a tourist bus, gaily painted blue and white, along the road that runs across the eastern desert from Cairo to the city of Suez, which lies where the southern end of the canal runs into the Gulf of Suez. Our hosts were very emphatic about the risks we would run from Israeli bombs and shells.

You didn't have to know much about war to know that we were passing through a large military concentration. This was at the high noon of Soviet military aid.

The eastern desert is rough country. No one prevented me from using field glasses. I could see many guns, trucks, and tanks on the tracks leading into the hills. Some guns were covered with camouflage nets. The tanks were Russian T-54/55 s. The jeeps and trucks were Russian, too. All were painted in desert camouflage. From the bus, but only from the bus, it looked like the old British Eighth Army.

Suez was like any city that has been under constant, accurate bombardment. The population had fallen from twenty-four thousand to about ten thousand. Some, not many, had been killed. The others had been evacuated.

The Egyptian officers took us through one of the two oil refineries on the edge of town. The installation had been smashed by bombs. The manager, a hard-faced young man, said he could have the plant running in a month, "given materials and workmen." He didn't look as though he expected either.

The shattered center of the town was silent. A breeze off the canal fluttered the shades in a ruined home. The shield of the Dutch consulate hung crazily from a single nail. In the chapel of the Catholic hospital the altar was in ruins, and the figure of Christ on the cross had been pierced by a bomb splinter. The Egyptians spent a long time in the chapel; they wanted us to be sure and see the damaged Christ. It was their *pièce de résistance*.

Over sandwiches and beer I asked an Egyptian major whether we could go nearer the front.

"This is the front," he said. "Over there"—he gestured toward the hills across the canal—"they are watching us. They could shell us at any moment." He did not look happy about it.

I wandered around the streets with an interpreter talking to passersby. They were unanimous that the war must go on, Egypt must recover her lost territory. As we left, I heard a gun slam to the north.

In the five years after the 1967 defeat the Russians poured thousands of tanks, guns, trucks, jeeps, missiles, and aircraft into Egypt. It wasn't second-rate stuff rejected by the east Europeans, either, but the most modern equipment available. But the quality of the Egyptian Army and Air Force wasn't up to the equipment.

"These chaps will improve," a western military attaché said in Cairo. Bound to. Russkis are working 'em hard. Get some breakdowns, some desertions, some defections. But shouldn't wonder if they're not a lot better than in 'sixty-seven. Lots of them, too. But the Russians will have to stay with them."

Which is exactly what the Russians didn't do.

At the general headquarters in Tel Aviv old friends in the high command also thought the Egyptians were coming on. One of them said he'd give a month's pay to shut up some of the politicians. I told him a member of the Knesset had assured me that the only road to a final peace lay through Cairo, Amman, and Damascus.

"That's the way they talk," he said in exasperation. "As though a campaign was just a field exercise. "Fools, fools."

In those days in Tel Aviv they were pondering the effect in the United States of a successful new Arab offensive, one supported by the Russians. They thought at headquarters that many of the Americans who had urged withdrawal from Vietnam would clamor for intervention to save Israel. This clamor, they expected, would be unpopular with those Americans who felt a minority had forced the United States to run out of southeast Asia. But they concluded that Soviet support of the Arabs in the end would win over the diehards on Vietnam to back intervention on behalf of Israel.

A major general said, "Of course, the Egyptians are improving. All our intelligence shows that. But we're still ahead. Especially in the air. Look, the Phantom [the American F-4] is good, but the MIG-21 isn't far behind. Our pilots are the difference. More experience, greater dedication. You remember 1940, don't you? You've seen the army on the canal. Good, eh?"

I said they looked fine, but they were very thin on the ground.

His reply was the same as Tosti's: against Egyptians you could take risks that would be out of the question against other troops.

When we left for dinner, a sentry saluted and my host returned it. I said he saluted like an Englishman.

"Why not? I was Major —— in the Eighth Army."

The Russian withdrawal from Egypt, the instability of the Egyptian government, and the rejection of further military adventures by King Hussein have not answered Israel's gut question: How long? How long can a nation remain mobilized, physically and psychologically, amid neighbors whose hostility will not end with a peace settlement?

The Israelis and Arabs may not be more than halfway through their long duel. A changing Arab world will exert new pressures. In 1968 and in 1970 and 1971 the Israelis underrated the rate of change in the Arab world and discounted the importance of the guerrillas. Except in the army and air force a rather dangerous overconfidence was evident.

Guerrilla activity today, spreading across the world from Bangkok to Germany, may be an abomination to non-Arabs. But to most Arabs it represents their only weapon against Israel. Everywhere I have gone in the Arab world I have seen the rich and the poor giving sons, money, and jewelry to the guerrilla cause. Even the guerrillas' record of inefficiency must be set beside their accomplishment of keeping the Palestinian cause before the world, to some extent redressing the ideological imbalance.

From 1948 on the Jews have had an immense advantage in a cause that elevated and animated national determination. The Arabs, politically and ideologically divided, had no common ideology except vague appeals to Islamic unity. The guerrillas' ideology or, rather, mythology may be shoddy stuff. But it is there, a cement that, no matter how thin, serves to bind the Arab world.

I have often thought that King Hussein's defeat of the guerrillas in 1971, which drove them out of Jordan, was to Israel's disadvantage. As long as the guerrillas were based in Jordan, they used military tactics, raids, shelling and mortaring, sabotage. Irritating but not particularly damaging to Israel. Now the guerrillas have spread over the Middle East and spilled into Europe. Assassination is their strategic doctrine. Israeli actions against them inevitably include civilian casualties. Force is never universally popular even when employed for the highest of motives.

I am pessimistic. A settlement may be worked out. But it will not endure, even if all the Arab territories are returned by the Israelis—a remote contingency. The changed Arab world, financially, industrially and militarily stronger, will not allow it to endure. For even in peace the Israeli challenge will be too strong to permit the Arab world to return to the sloth of the past. There is a new wind blowing in that world.

The Soviet interest must be reckoned with. Is a tranquil Middle East, in which Israel dwells in amity with her Arab neighbors, to Russia's interest? The Soviets have sustained with money and arms insurgent elements in North Africa and the Middle East. They play on Arab hatred of Israel and distrust of America. They know that the moderate leaders that are friendly toward the United States are vulnerable to nationalist insurgents. The insurgents may not be overfriendly toward the Soviet Union. Moscow can live with that, if radical elements rule in Rabat, Riyadh, Tunis, Kuwait, and other capitals.

Clever fellows in Washington say that the Saudis or the Tunisians will not cut off their nose to spite their face, will not abandon the economic advantage of friendship with America for a harsher life under radical régimes sworn to destroy Israel. I am unconvinced. A wise old man once told me that the Middle East is carpeted with noses cut off to spite faces. Finally, whatever the character of the governments in the Persian Gulf and the Middle East, the West and Japan *must* have the oil those governments control in the coming ten years.

As the importance of maintaining good relations with the oil-producing states, whatever their governments, increases, the United States may be forced to reconsider its present policy toward Israel. Would America abandon an Israel beset by a stronger, more united Arab world of radical régimes supported by Russia? This is the question at the heart of the Middle East situation. Twenty years ago I would have been certain of the answer. Today I am not.

CHAPTER 14
EUROPE, RUSSIA, AND AMERICA
1972

Better fifty years of Europe than a cycle of Cathay.

Tennyson

Early in 1969 I returned to Europe. I was European Affairs Correspondent (a title that excited ribald comment by old friends) and was to make my headquarters in Brussels. That city, the "capital" of the Common Market and the site of NATO headquarters, was the obvious choice.

Working "out of" Brussels, as newspapermen say, I traveled extensively in western Europe and saw the momentous change that is taking place there from Germany west to Ireland and from Norway south to Sicily. This is the erosion of national differences. The process is far from complete. It probably will not end when the members of the Common Market move from economic to political cooperation. But it has begun, and the beginning itself is a fact of tremendous importance to Europe, the United States, and the world.

When I was a cub, travelling from Berlin to London, I passed through recognizably different countries. German architecture, food, agricultural methods, clothes, and cars differed from those in France, and those of France were equally different from those in England; national tastes and characteristics were strongly defined. The question was not one of like and dislike. Often Germans and Englishmen or French and Italians got along very well. But only after they had overcome initial feelings of strangeness, even distaste.

Field Marshal Alexander, the most sophisticated soldier I ever encountered, told me once that, although he "got along" with the French, his liking for them was colored by his awareness that they combined an exaggerated emphasis on the niceties of social intercourse with a personal greed he found distressing.

Alexander was a gentleman, a species that continentals believe grows in profusion west of the English Channel but which, romanticists to the contrary, was always rare. The least snobbish of men, he was all his life the object of snobbery because he was the younger brother of the Irish Earl of Caledon.

There is a story about Alexander after his great victories in the desert and Tunis. He had come home to London for leave and was standing in his uniform and decorations, the greater part of them honest-to-God medals for fighting, in the lobby of White's Club reading a newspaper.

A young, recently commissioned officer asked a club servant the identity of the impressive figure across the lobby.

"That, sir," said the servant, "is the Earl of Caledon's younger brother."

That Europe of 1939, with its rigid national boundaries, the ignorance of peoples about other peoples, and the conviction that the way things were done in Lyons or Milan or Dresden or Manchester was the only way such things could be done, was a far more exciting place than the Europe of today. It was also the seedbed for two civil wars that came close to destroying western Europe.

Even today it is difficult for Americans to look at Europe as a whole. The average tourist does not visit northern France or northwestern Germany but the Côte d'Azur and the Bavarian Alps. Consequently, most Americans have failed to grasp the erosion of national differences.

In 1970, just before the twenty-fifth anniversary of the end of World War II, I drove north and east out of Paris. I wanted to compare the land and the people in France, Belgium, and Germany with my memories. A romantic could have described me as searching for my youth. What I had in mind was a story.

Every place and every person looked the same. They drove the same cars, they wore the same clothes, they ate the same sort of food, they saw the same movies, and they watched the same sort of television programs. Were it not for the frontier posts, it would have been impossible to tell where Belgium ended and Germany began. I drove, not through France, Belgium, and Germany, but through Europe.

My mind peopled the hills, ridges, and fields with divisions and regiments that had fought there. That war had been the end of the old Europe. What I saw was the start of the new.

National egotism prompts those Americans who observe these phenomena to ascribe it to "the Americanization of Europe." This is superficial. Great industrial civilizations tend to become alike because they are centers of mass production and mass consumption. Europe's postwar industrial development, which had accelerated the erosion of national differences, came later than America's. But it was not intentionally imitative. People who live the same sort of lives, monotonous, and unexciting no matter how many vacations they may have and how high the salaries, are likely to be alike. It is hard today to find a German *gasthaus* serving that wonderful farmer's soup of peas and sausage. But you can get all the pizza you want and, if it is tasteless, remember that thirty-five years ago, for every one who had *bauersuppe,* ten got by on a bit of bread and cheese.

It is sad but true that local customs and products are dying out, that the past as preserved by folklore societies is pretty thin stuff. I will never again see a Highland village like those of 1939 or eat trout fresh from the stream in a Black Forest hotel. But I saw the village, I ate the trout, and I am content. The more so because my brain defies my heart and tells me that, provocative and entertaining as that old Europe was, her very differences, nation from nation, were the emotional bases for the nationalism that led to two terrible wars. Pizza in Aachen, Manchester, and Lyons is better than another Somme or Dunkirk.

To understand the new Europe now developing we must recognize its components. Foremost among these is contemporary Germany. It is the foremost industrial power from America east to Russia. My last tour in Europe coincided with one of the most adventurous periods of the Federal Republic's history, during which Germany assumed the political stature to which her economic strength had long entitled her.

I studied modern history under a scholarly and pompous professor who concluded every discussion with the portentous statement "The end is not yet." This phrase—how he used to roll it out—applies to what is happening in Germany, and it would be rash to attempt to envisage the outcome of the process.

Germany's assumption of her true political stature, which is that of the foremost western European state, was long overdue. The paradox of Germany as a political pygmy was not good for the Germans, it was not good for Europe, and it distorted relations between the United States and the Federal Republic. West Germany is not going to dominate western Europe as did Wilhelmine and Hitlerian Germany. Moral scruples and bitter experience will have little to do with it. Germany, powerful as she is, cannot aspire to preeminence in Europe while the Soviet writ runs to the Elbe and western Europe's defense rests on a military contract (the North Atlantic Treaty) with the United States.

In their new situation the West Germans set out in 1970 to regularize their relations with eastern Europe, meaning primarily the Soviet Union and secondarily the nearest important satellites, the Democratic Republic in East Germany, and Poland. There is, naturally, no guarantee that the West Germans will be successful. Indeed, it is likely that the best they can expect is superficial agreements that will look well in the ruling party's record but will mean very little.

West Germany's approach to the east alarmed many Americans. The geopolitical concept behind the agreements that established Bonn's independence and brought the Germans into NATO was that, as a part of western Europe, the Federal Republic would face west, not east. The American founders of West Germany—Dean Acheson, John McCloy, and Lucius Clay—were reasonably sure in the late 'forties that a strong Germany in a strong western Europe would exercise an irresistible attraction upon the east Germans and the other satellite states. However, things happened differently.

I believe that no other German but Chancellor Willy Brandt could have begun the process toward rapprochement with the East. Nor could any European power but Germany have done it. The French, when de Gaulle was riding high, tried and got nowhere. The Russians are interested in strength, not fine words and lofty sentiments.

Brandt's position is very strong. In view of his anti-Nazi past he cannot be accused of being a German ultranationalist. His advocacy of a wider European Common Market embracing Britain testifies to his belief in the need for a stronger western Europe.

In conversations with Brandt I never had an impression of the rashness others sensed in him. In discussing the Soviet Union he was far more skeptical than people like Maurice Couve de Murville, that sports-model Talleyrand of the Fifth Republic. He also knew a great deal more about Russia and Communism.

Recently someone suggested that the age of giants in Europe had passed with de Gaulle and that the continent was ruled by dwarfs. The exception is Brandt. Given reasonably good luck in domestic politics, which means a stronger Social Democratic Party, he should be at or near the top of German governments for years to come. The future will enable him to demonstrate to Europe and the world those qualities of heart and head which have brought him this long way.

In Bonn I have been struck by the relative unimportance of France in the Brandt government's international calculations. Some lip service is paid to the agreement of 1963 between Adenauer and de Gaulle, but the cabinet ministers' minds are on big countries, such as the Soviet Union and the United States, and on large European combinations, such as would include Britain, rather than on national identities.

The elimination of this artificial relationship between the two governments is all to the good. France's role as Germany's sponsor into European political life had some merit twenty years ago. It is absurd today.

The French, since the retirement and death of de Gaulle, have been recovering from an expansive, emotional period in which the General's rendezvous with history turned out to be a blind date. France is becoming accustomed once again to being a country in Europe and not the continent's leader. This is undoubtedly painful for those politicians, publicists, and voters who took the old Wizard of the Elysée Palace at face value.

French anti-Americanism, which de Gaulle unceasingly encouraged, remains distressing, no matter how much claptrap is mouthed by President Pompidou about Lafayette and the American Revolution. In the sense of active opposition to American policy, anti-Americanism is stronger in Paris than in Bonn or London or Rome.

French anti-Americanism is deeper than the familiar belief that France is the only country and the French the only people in the world. There is an obsessive urge to criticize American policy and an eagerness to obstruct which are—I can find no other word—frightening. No one who lived in Europe between 1945 and 1970 can overlook the mistakes in policy, the occasional boorishness, and the air of insufferable superiority of American officials. No one with any experience in the world can doubt that the protected dislikes his protector, the needy his almoner. De Gaulle and his supporters carried the business too far. We must deal in the future with a generation of French who are willing, indeed eager, to see the worst in Americans and to discern anti-French objectives behind every act of United States policy. The United States will survive. But what will so lopsided a view of an ally do to France and the French?

Clement Attlee once told me that the British are always a little better than they seem to be, when they are down, and a little worse when they are on top. They have been down for a long time now and, *pace* Mr. Attlee, the experience does not seem to have improved them. I conceived a great admiration for the British during the war. I still admire the British of that era and the few today who carry on with courage, energy, and foresight. But I wonder whether that spasm of greatness between 1939 and 1945 was not the last effort of a degenerating people.

For example, politicians, economists, editors, and mandarins of the BBC tell the British day in and day out that the country cannot survive as a first-class power unless it makes the effort necessary to raise the Gross National Product.

"We might just as well be throwing stones at the moon," Iain Macleod said shortly before his death. "They may hear us, although even that is doubtful. They certainly show no disposition to do anything about it."

The problem is basically one of morale. Learned discussion of sterling balances, access to resources, the stimuli consequent on entering the Common Market, will prove just talk unless some-one or something awakens the British.

British society will move ahead only after the trade union movement and a depressingly large section of the Labor Party have joined the second half of the twentieth century. Since the middle of the 'fifties successive governments, Conservative and Labor, have attempted to restrain the power of the unions to obstruct the introduction of more modern industrial methods. Such obstruction has been supported by the political primitives on the left of the Labor Party.

Anyone who knows the British, as I do, understands that there are many, many trade-unionists, perhaps even a majority, who are out of sympathy with the extreme demands of the shop stewards, the activists of the union movement, and who would welcome a more modern approach to industrial problems. Until now, however, this group has been powerless to defeat the reactionaries in the labor movement, whose minds were made up in the years of depression and dole.

Of course there are faults on the other side. Industry has been slow to modernize, laggard in efforts to push exports by which the country lives. But my considered opinion, after watching Britain with affectionate concern since 1945, is that the greatest share of the blame rests with the radical left. Some blame lies, too, with what Iain called "this damned lethargy" that he saw infecting his countrymen whenever a problem threatened time that should be devoted to sport, liquor, or women.

It may well be, as many believe, that membership in the Common Market will be the catalyst leading to a revival of British energies. I would like to believe it. At present, however, the British are prepared to let the Germans pay for their soldiers, the Americans furnish them with weapons, and transatlantic companies provide the financing and modernization of their industry.

Too many of the British—and this applies to a considerable extent to the middle class—have been living off the moral credit of 1940. No one admired them more in that period than I. But the great days of solitary defiance of Hitler are long gone. Dunkirk and the Battle of Britain, bravery and endurance under bombing, will not solve tomorrow's problems, and it is sad to see a nation grasping at memories of past glories as excuses for inactivity today.

Materially life is better in Britain as, indeed, it is in every northern European country. Class differences, although still stronger than in America, are disappearing. A measure of prosperity has promoted conformity. England, in what twenty years ago was hailed as the New Elizabethan Age, has become one big suburb.

What will this new Europe add to the sum of human achievement? Wandering around Rome in a May sunset, I thought that these Italians, with their cars, their weekends at the beach, their apartments, would never sire another Leonardo. In Westminster Abbey it seemed improbable that these English, the "couldn't care less" English of today, would produce another Shakespeare. Will modern France give us another Molière, Germany another Goethe? Complacency, my friends, there's the enemy.

I left Europe in 1970 profoundly disturbed. The patterns, political and economic, drawn at the end of World War II were changing. But this was not at the bottom of my anxiety. Instead there was the growing conviction that this prosperous, conformist Europe might not be as secure as it seemed.

Beyond the Elbe river the Soviet Union deploys a military machine that, even when conventional forces alone are considered, is far more powerful, compared with the NATO forces facing it, than the one with which Hitlerian Germany ravaged Europe. This is disturbing enough. Almost equally disturbing is western Europe's indifference to this development, an indifference shared by many Americans. Naturally there are some civil servants at NATO and obscure officers in defense ministries who view Russia's military program with deep anxiety. But the temper of the times is against them. In America the psychological scars of Vietnam are deep; not least the distrust and suspicion of the military. In Europe the superficial success of Brandt's *Ost Politik,* the increase in trade with the Soviet Union and eastern Europe, have overcome fears.

I have never been comfortable with the idea that the Russians have altered, for a number of reasons (concern over China, economic difficulties at home, appreciation of the horrors and destruction of nuclear warfare), their fundamental views of the non-Communist world and their objectives in that world.

The Soviet government and the Russian people have changed less than any in Europe since 1945, because the factors that have brought about change in other European countries have been absent from the Soviet Union. The U.S.S.R. is still an authoritarian, police state. Policies can change with changes in leaders, and they do. But the fundamental enmity to the west and all it stands for, however imperfectly, does not change among those who direct the destinies of the Soviet Union. And they, and not the Russian people, are the ones who count.

Once my travels led me to a watchtower in the hills east of Fulda in West Germany. There the United States 14th Armored Cavalry guards the frontier. Across the barbed wire and the mine fields on the East German side lay a village huddled in the snow. A fox stole out of a stand of pines, and a dog in a farmyard, picking up the fox's scent, began to bark.

I shivered, not entirely from cold. To the west lay peaceful, busy nations ready to believe that a new era had dawned, that the antagonisms that made the cold war were forgotten. To the east beyond the swirling snow lay the vast Soviet military machine: tens of thousands of aircraft, tanks, and guns. New weapons and new equipment flowing in a steady stream to the forces of the Warsaw Pact. The brave, hardy, docile soldiery filling the ranks. The steady growth of cooperation between the Russians and their allies. The Soviets have raised and equipped forces far stronger than those necessary for defense against attack from the West.

Why this enormous effort? We have a surprisingly accurate picture of Warsaw Pact capabilities. But the East's intentions are obscure. I have spent much time in the last three years seeking reasons for the Soviet effort. In one respect I am no wiser; I have no clear view of Russian intent. Yet I am troubled by many elements in the situation.

Governments do not build a global navy, maintain a sizable proportion of their divisions at war strength, and spend millions in military research and development merely to satisfy national pride. The melancholy record of history is that, when states amass great armaments, they in time use them against feebler neighbors. These neighbors may be good trading partners like Britain and Germany in 1914, but the time comes when national ambitions weigh more than a thriving commerce.

There is a comfortable, and therefore popular, theory in the United States that this formidable military effort is in preparation for a war against Communist China. If this is so, then why does the majority of the Soviet Union's new weapons and new equipment go to the Soviet forces in the German Democratic Republic, Poland, Czechoslovakia, and Hungary? Why do the new attack submarines operate from Murmansk rather than Vladivostock? Why do the Soviet forces in Germany stress river crossings in their maneuvers?

I do not believe that the Russians, under present conditions in the West, contemplate a massive invasion of western Europe. I believe—and here I am in agreement with a large number of experienced western officers—that Soviet military expansion anticipates a change in the West's defense posture within the next ten years.

The Russians, surveying developments in the West, can reasonably expect reductions in the political and military strength of NATO, including American ground and air forces. Because these forces are considered by both NATO and the Warsaw Pact to be the link between United States strategic nuclear power and the defense of western Europe, the Soviets may think that an American withdrawal makes the employment of nuclear power by the United States less likely. On the other hand, should American forces be kept at their present strength, about three hundred thousand soldiers and airmen, the presence of these forces would ensure the linkage and, consequently, deter the Soviets.

The thinking at the Soviet General Headquarters must be concerned with long-term trends in western affairs. We are dealing with authoritarian, military thinking that has made grievous mistakes in the past, not only in Russia but in other totalitarian states. No one can say with authority exactly how Soviet planners view the West. But we can be reasonably sure that they take into account recent political and social developments in this country and Europe.

Expressions of war-weariness and of hostility toward the military, rampant in some sections of American society, may lead the Russians to conclude that even a hint of foreign military involvement would arouse massive resistance to the government.

On this basis the Soviets may reason that adventures that might have been risky in the pre-Vietnam days are now reasonably safe.

The Russians, probably because of their xenophobia, are not particularly bright about other peoples. They misjudged the Germans in 1941, they misjudged the Americans over Cuba. They might, on the basis of what they read and hear from the eastern media, conclude that the Vietnam trauma has immobilized American strategy. This, too, could be a misjudgment.

My contacts with Soviet diplomats convince me that Moscow believes that internal conditions in the United States, particularly congressional pressure, will lead inevitably to drastic reductions in American forces in Europe. Here Moscow and the American administration are at one: the American forces at their present strength insure a credible defense of western Europe. Reduce them sharply, and that defense falls apart.

The unpredictability, to them, of American policy is a powerful psychological weapon in our dealings with the Russians. They did not expect President Kennedy's reaction over Cuba. The bombing of North Vietnam and the mining of its waters shortly before President Nixon's visit to Moscow were as unexpected as they were unwelcome. Americans sometimes talk about "those crazy Russians." To the Russians it is the Americans who are wilful, errant, unpredictable.

Between them, Congress and the White House together have pretty well blurred the dimensions of the troop-withdrawal problem. Take the idea that American force cuts would frighten the Europeans into greater defense efforts. No one in European defense and foreign ministries takes this seriously. On the contrary, Europeans think that peoples and legislatures would consider withdrawals evidence that American intelligence considered it safe to reduce the garrison in Europe and that, if the United States felt that way, why shouldn't they reduce their forces, too?

Henry A. Kissinger and President Nixon stress the importance of the strategy of flexible response in defending western Europe. Congress does not challenge this strategy. It had better not, because the alternative is John Foster Dulles's massive nuclear retaliation. But Congress can't have a strategy of flexible response without sufficient American troops in Europe. For if the strategy is to have any deterrent effect, there must be enough military resources to meet, in kind, any Soviet offensive; conventional weapons with conventional weapons, a mixture of conventional and tactical nuclear weapons with a similar mixture.

If the Russians use good judgment, they have all the cards. Good judgment means maintaining friendly relations with western Europe, meanwhile continuing the massive arms build-up that has been going on since the middle 'sixties. Few in western Europe and America will mind very much what the Russians are doing militarily, as long as trade with eastern Europe expands and there is a patina of détente. The inevitable result will be the erosion of NATO's strength in conventional forces.

The strategic consequence would be the early use of tactical nuclear weapons in any encounter with the prospect of escalation to strategic nuclear war. In the present American mood it is difficult to conceive of a President's risking a strategic nuclear exchange. The American nuclear umbrella, on which Europe has depended, is being furled and stuck away in the closet.

In the future, I believe, the Russians will be able to use their massive conventional military power without a real risk of meeting either a credible conventional defense or American nuclear intervention. Where and how would they move?

The Soviet navy needs unrestricted access to the Atlantic and the Mediterranean. This is denied it as long as Denmark and Turkey, both NATO members, hold the mouths of the Baltic and the Dardanelles, supported by a united alliance that includes strong American forces. Even the most pessimistic must believe that while those forces are intact the alliance would coalesce behind the United States and offer a credible defense of a threatened member.

But if the Americans depart and the Europeans reduce their defense efforts, the picture will be very different. Five years from now Soviet pressure, diplomatic and military, should suffice to drive Denmark and Turkey out of NATO. The dissolution of the alliance will then begin, and America's allies will degenerate into a rabble of fearful governments, each intent on reaching the best possible terms with Moscow.

Outside the window, the sun throws long shadows across the Connecticut hills. This quiet landscape is very different from London in that distant summer of 1939. Yet I move toward the conclusion of this book with the same sense of foreboding I felt then. It would be pleasant to believe that the wars are done, that man has learned his lesson. Pleasant and impossible.

As a talisman I recall some words of Winston Churchill's, spoken long ago at a desperate moment of the Second World War. He had been brutally frank about the situation in the Far East and the Middle East. As I rose to go, he said, "Do not be downcast. My experience is that the spirit of free men can overcome all."

I will finish my working life a good deal less well off than my contemporaries who entered other fields. When I leave *The Times* I will continue to write. I hope that the world then will be as exciting and stimulating as I have found it in nearly forty years of reporting.

This is no appeal for sympathy. I consider that my time has been well spent. I am infinitely richer in experience than most of my contemporaries, and I am grateful. What I would have missed had I stayed at that bank!

The R.A.F.'s fighters in the sky over Shakespeare cliff near Dover when they, and only they, stood between Hitler and the mastery of Europe. The American infantry columns winding through the Tunisian hills toward their hour. Churchill, hands on lapels, admonishing an unruly and fearful House of Commons that this would be their finest hour. Eisenhower playing with a Scotch terrier and making it clear he knew just how much the war was costing the troops. De Gaulle rolling a cigar in his mouth and imitating the average Frenchman's idea of an American.

Dawn breaking over the roofs of London to show the scars of a night's bombing. The night we swam in the Mediterranean and some trick of atmospherics brought the sound of Germans singing as they bathed a few miles to the east. Baghdad in the evening sun. The mosques of Cairo under the desert moon. Paris on that spring day in 1940. The Kremlin with its gold domes bright against a blue, winter sky. The solitariness of the African bush. Elephants bathing in the streams of Ceylon. The dust and heat of a fire base in Vietnam.

So much remembered has had to be left out. There is no space to tell of the football game at four in the morning when Red Muller dropped a lateral pass—and our last bottle of Scotch whisky—on a village street in Algeria. There has been no room for John Lardner or Mike Burke or Charlie Wertenbaker or Bob Casey.

The job has given me much—excitement, risks, the joy of competition, and all those fringe benefits that come to any reporter working abroad.

The Derby field coming around the final turn, a river of shining coats and gleaming silks. Ulanova dancing at the Bolshoi and Fontaine at Covent Garden. Paul Scofield's *Lear* and Olivier in *The Entertainer*. A Sunday lunch with Scotty and Sally at Père Bis. Hours and hours of talk with wits and great men, heroes and rogues.

People say, "It seems like yesterday." It does for me, all of it. Moments of despair, moments of triumph. I've been more successful in my chosen field than I had expected, although I have failed to do as much as I set out to do. My regret is that it has all passed so quickly. Where, indeed, has last July gone? But that is a minor complaint. I've had a hell of a good life and I'm grateful.